Biculturalism and Management

Rabindra N. Kanungo
Faculty of Management
McGill University, Montreal

Butterworths
Toronto

© 1980 Butterworth and Company (Canada) Limited
2265 Midland Avenue
Scarborough, Ontario, Canada M1P 4S1
All Rights Reserved.
Printed and Bound in Canada.

The Butterworth Group of Companies:

Canada: Butterworth & Co. (Canada) Ltd., Toronto, Vancouver
United Kingdom: Butterworth & Co. (Publishers) Ltd., London, Borough Green
Australia: Butterworth Pty. Ltd., Sydney, Melbourne, Brisbane
New Zealand: Butterworths of New Zealand, Ltd., Wellington
South Africa: Butterworth & Co. (South Africa) Pty. Ltd., Durban
United States: Butterworth Inc., Boston
Butterworth (Legal) Inc., Seattle

Canadian Cataloguing in Publication Data

Kanungo, Rabindra N., 1935-
  Biculturalism and management
Includes index.
ISBN 0-409-84190-0
1. Personnel management—Canada. 2. Biculturalism—Canada. 3. Work—Psychological aspects. I. Title.

HF5549.2.C36K36   658.3'04   C80-094287-6

Foreword

CONSIDERABLE RESEARCH ABOUT cultural differences has been done in the last ten to fifteen years. That cultural differences are a major factor in the satisfaction and motivation of people is by now almost an axiom. However, it is still too often overlooked and, even if one is sensitive to these differences, to manage them remains a very difficult problem.

A great number of studies have been made concerning markets segmented along cultural and linguistic lines, but these dimensions were recognized only after costly mistakes had been made. Since markets are external to the organization, they involve only a small part of it and, with some flexibility, an organization can adjust to them. This is not the case, however, when the organization itself is made up of people from more than one culture.

Professor Kanungo underlines in his book the possible conflict between different value systems and the development of national or international managerial policies. Here the problem becomes much more complex and there are no easy and readily available solutions. But to say that there is no easy solution should not lead us to deny or even be insensitive to these differences. The cost of doing so could be very high indeed.

Experience indicates that organizations also have a culture of their own over and above, if not independent of, group and individual cultures. It has always struck me that some of the misunderstandings, and indeed conflict, between business and the public sector stems to a great extent from cultural differences. In this case, the different cultures of the private and public sector.

Professor Kanungo makes a number of useful recommendations in his last chapter. Any particular organization will have to consider these recommendations in the context of its *own* culture to find out which are more readily applicable. For instance, training and the development of feedback process should be easy to manage in any organization; change in or adaptation of mobility policies may be more difficult according to the organization.

The most important message of Professor Kanungo's research is the necessity to be sensitive to these differences. Specific solutions will have to be found and implemented on a case by case basis. With this research, Professor Kanungo has made an important contribution to the management of culturally diversified groups which has implications far larger than for the two cultural groups he has studied. Anyone interested in the field of national and international business will be well advised to read it.

Laurent Picard, DBA
Dean, Faculty of Management
McGill University
Montreal

Preface

THIS BOOK IS a modest attempt to systematically explore the psychological profiles of Anglophone and Francophone employees in Canadian organizations. The results of several controlled field studies presented in this book reveal interesting similarities and differences in work attitudes of two culturally distinct groups of workers in Canada. The findings presented in the book are intended to assist the reader in developing an understanding of the nature of the bicultural environment and its effects on these two groups. Understanding of cultural variables and their effects on worker characteristics will help management to develop policies and practices sensitive to the real needs and expectations of employees.

For the past ten years I have been engaged in research and consulting in the area of cross-cultural management, trying to better understand how cultural variables influence work motivation and performance, and how management can identify these variables and deal effectively with them. During this period, I have noticed different reactions in colleagues and clients with whom I have discussed the topic. First, there are those who found this area of cross-cultural research novel, exciting and of practical significance. To them, I owe my inspiration for writing this book. There are others for whom the results of cross-cultural research are only a reaffirmation of common sense. This book may appear to them to be a restatement of what they already know. Most management practice is based on practical common sense principles, and the role of academic theories and research has been to provide further refinement and modifications to such practice. We should not forget that a major role of social science research is to systematize and organize common sense. On many occasions results of social science research may appear as common sense only after the results are presented by a social scientist. For instance, many practicing managers may express a vague feeling that Anglophone employees react differently to job situations than do Francophone employees, and yet they may not be able to verbalize exactly how the two groups differ. After reading this book they might say "I knew it all the time." In such a case, the role of social science research is to place the managerial hunch on firmer footing and to make it more reliable and practical. The research findings presented in this book may serve a similar purpose for some readers.

Finally, some critics have argued that cultural variables play a relatively minor role in worker motivation, particularly in Canada; hence, the variables are not worth investigating. I have found this viewpoint difficult to understand. How can cultural variables be unimportant when we know that an individual's personality is largely a product of cultural environment? This book recognizes the existence in Canada of two distinct cultures and provides some explicit descriptions of how each of these cultures affects work attitudes of employees. In this respect, I hope, the sceptic may find the book convincing and challenging.

Completing a research project and writing a book on it involves the cooperation of many organizations and the contribution of effort and ideas of many people. Acknowledgement is due to the American Psychological Association and to the Canadian Psychological Association for permitting me to reproduce material published earlier in their journals. I am deeply indebted to many of my colleagues and clients who have helped me in completing this project. In particular, I would like to thank Mr. Manuel Mendonca, Mr. Y. M. Memon and Miss Susan Ruckenstein for their assistance in the preparation of the manuscript, and Miss Jean Hepworth, who provided the secretarial assistance with meticulous care. A special mention should be made of my wife Minati; I am grateful to her for the infinite patience and tolerance she exhibited during this project. Finally, I owe a special debt of gratitude to another group of individuals who of necessity must remain anonymous. They are the management personnel and employees of several organizations who so willingly participated in the studies reported in this book. I would like to express my appreciation of their help and involvement in this project by dedicating this book to them.

Rabindra N. Kanungo
Montreal
September 1979

Table of Contents

	Foreword	iii
	Preface	v
Chapter 1	*Introduction: Culture and Employee Behavior*	1
	Meaning of Culture	2
	Importance of Cultural Influences on Employee Behavior	3
	General Plan of the Book	7
Chapter 2	*The English and the French Canadians in Industry: A Brief Historical Perspective*	9
	Impact of rural-agricultural vs. urban-industrial traditions	10
	Impact of Catholic vs. Protestant Work Ethic	11
	Impact of Educational Systems	12
	Impact of the Working Language in Industry	13
	Contemporary Trends in Quebec Society	14
Chapter 3	*The Nature of the Inquiry: Some Basic Considerations*	17
Chapter 4	*Job Perceptions of English- and French-Canadian Employees*	21
	Importance of Job Outcomes	23
	Sense of Personal Responsibility and Commitment	30
	Perceived and Desired Levels of Participation	32
	Job Enrichment Potential	34
Chapter 5	*Job Satisfaction of English- and French-Canadian Employees*	37
	Satisfaction with Job Outcomes	37
	Turnover Potential	43
Chapter 6	*Job Involvement of English- and French-Canadian Employees*	45
	The Concepts of Job Involvement and Job Alienation	46

viii TABLE OF CONTENTS

	Toward a Motivational Theory of Job Involvement	59
	Job Involvement Attitudes of English- and French-Canadian Employees	64
Chapter 7	*Job Mobility and Transfer Potential of English- and French-Canadian Employees*	71
	Readiness to Accept Transfer	72
	Reasons for Reluctance to Accept transfer	73
	Importance of Inducements	74
	Location Preference	77
Chapter 8	*Attitudes Toward Communication*	81
	The Study: A Brief Description	83
	Attitudes Toward Downward Communication	87
	Attitudes Toward Upward Communication	91
	Attitudes Toward Communication Channels	91
	Attitudes Toward Organizational Outcomes and Overall Communication Effort	93
	Relationship Between Satisfaction and Importance	95
Chapter 9	*Attitudes Toward Supervision and In-House Training Program*	99
	Attitudes Toward Supervisory Practice	99
	Attitudes Toward In-House Training Programs	110
Chapter 10	*Summary and Conclusions: Implications for Management*	121
Appendix A		129
Appendix B		137
Appendix C		145
Appendix D		151
Appendix E		157
Appendix F		173
Appendix G		175
References		181

Biculturalism and Management

CHAPTER 1

Introduction: *Culture and Employee Behavior*

IN A RECENT MEETING with a Canadian executive from the head office of a national corporation, I was confronted with the following executive dilemma. "We know the golden rules of business," said the executive, "and yet, we find it quite disappointing that our management policies to train and motivate our employees do not work the same way in Québec as they do in the rest of Canada." The executive was obviously disturbed by the fact that the application of a set of uniform policies throughout Canada did not produce uniform results. Apparently the management policies of the corporation affected the employees in Québec differently from what was expected by the management. Should the Québec operations of the corporation be treated differently from the other operations in Canada? What makes Québec operation so different? What should management do to identify and solve the problems of employees in Québec? These are important questions for an executive responsible for managing organizations that operate in a bicultural context such as exists in Québec. In managing an organization whose members come from very different cultural backgrounds, the executive should understand that the perceptions and motivations of people belonging to different cultural backgrounds may differ. Consequently, applying "golden rules" of business uniformly to all people may not be the best way to solve management problems. The executive should take note of one of the famous sayings of George Bernard Shaw: "Do not do unto others as you would that they should do unto you. Their tastes may not be the same."

Very often, managers have considered organizations as purely economic and technical entities. They have directed most of their efforts to manage physical and monetary resources. By viewing organizations as technical systems and by following policies that emphasize only material resource management, managers have neglected their most important function—managing human resources. After all, an organization is a social as well as a technical system; as a technical system, it utilizes physical resources, such as money and machinery, while as a social system, it is composed of individuals and groups from different socio-cultural backgrounds. The people and the physical resources of an organization constitute its internal environment. The external environment of an organization may include such things as available technology (know-how) of business operations, the nature of its competitors, the type of government controls and legal framework that direct the operations and the economic and social milieu within which the organization operates. Effective management requires that managers understand and respond appropriately to both the external and internal environments. Thus, management policies need to be geared not only to government controls and legal restrictions, but also to the nature of the employees forming the organization.

The external environment and its effects on management policies has been studied by organization theorists of sociological, economic and legal persuasions, who are primarily interested in macroanalysis of organizational behavior (Khandwall, 1977, Thompson, 1967; Woodward, 1965). Exploring the nature of employees and its effect on management practice, however, has been the main task of organization theorists of social-psychological inclination, who are primarily interested in microanalysis of the individual's behavior within organizations (Likert, 1961, 1967). The theses presented in this volume clearly fall into the latter category. The major purpose of this book is to develop an understanding of the nature of the internal environment of Canadian organizations that operate in a bicultural context.

Within Canadian organizations, particularly those that operate in the province of Québec, one finds two culturally distinct groups of employees: English and French Canadians. Very often managing these two groups of employees poses unique problems, the solution of which requires an understanding of the distinct culture-based characteristics of the two groups. In order to find out what these characteristics are and how they can influence management operations, several controlled field studies were conducted in large Canadian organizations. The findings from these studies and their implications for effective management are the main subject matter of this book. In taking a psycho-cultural approach to the understanding of employee behavior, this book attempts to study the influence of cultural forces on the perceptions, motivations and attitudes of employees. An understanding of how cultural influences shape behavior will help management to increase organizational effectiveness by formulating appropriate policies and practices in line with employees' needs and expectations.

Meaning of Culture

The term "culture" has been used in so many different contexts that its exact meaning may often be unclear. Broadly speaking, the term has a popular meaning and a scientific meaning. In its popular form, the term "culture" is very similar in meaning to the terms "cultivated," "educated," "sophisticated," etc. In this sense a "cultured person" is perceived as having knowledge and interest in music, art, literature, and social manners. The scientific meaning of the term "culture" as used in the social sciences, however, refers to the total pattern of beliefs, norms and behavior of a given society. Tylor (1877) was the first to use the term in its present-day scientific sense. He described culture as "that complex whole which includes knowledge, belief, art, law, morals, customs, and any other capabilities and habits acquired by man as a member of society [p. 1]." A further elaboration of the term was suggested by Ralph Linton (1945). He defined culture as "the configuration of learned behavior and results of behavior whose component elements are shared and transmitted by the members of a particular society [p. 32]." Linton's definition emphasized the fact that every person is shaped by his or her own culture. The learned behavior patterns exhibited in everyday life are partly a reflection of the culture to which he or she belongs. Linton's views of culture also implied that cultural influences are transmitted from one generation to another, not through any hereditary mechanism, but through social learning and imitation processes. An individual is not born with a culture. Rather, he learns how to view his world and react to it appropriately by imitating and learning from other members of the society. In a sense, each culture has a continuity of its own as long as it is represented by a group of people. A more explicit definition of culture emphasizing such continuity was recently suggested by Barnouw (1963): "A culture is the way of life of a group of people, the configuration of all of the more or less stereotyped patterns of learned behavior which are handed down from one generation to the next through the means of language and imitation [p. 4]." In this book, the word "culture" is used in this sense. The culture of a group of people refers to their way of life. Each generation learns from the preceding one both the language and the common social norms defining acceptable behavior. Thus, every human group has a distinct culture and distinct behavior patterns. In this sense, French Canadians and English Canadians have developed two distinct cultures in Canada, and the behavior of employees belonging to the two groups in any given organization has to be understood in terms of their cultural backgrounds. It must be recognized, however, that we can only explore and compare the characteristics of the two groups; we should not legitimately consider one group as having more culture than the other (Whyte, 1961), or consider the cultural practices of one group as being superior to the cultural practices of the other in some evaluative sense.

Importance of Cultural Influences on Employee Behavior

In terms of management practice, does it make any difference whether an organization contains employees from the same cultural background, or from two or more different cultural backgrounds? The answer to this question is in the affirmative. The management policies and practices that work reasonably well in an organization where all the employees come from the same cultural background will not work equally well in an organization containing culturally heterogeneous groups of employees. For instance, consider the following case brought to my attention while I was acting as a consultant to a multi-national corporation in Canada. Management found that the French-Canadian employees showed greater reluctance than the English-Canadian employees to accept promotions and raises in salary when these entailed a transfer to branch offices outside Québec. Management considered its nationwide promotion and salary policy to be fair to all its employees, and yet to its amazement discovered that the policy was not working effectively for one major group. Because of their cultural background the French-Canadian employees may have learned to value the security of their own cultural environment in Québec more than the increased salary or promotion when it required them to move to a culturally unfamiliar environment.

A single set of management policies and practices should not be considered absolute and universally applicable to groups of people with heterogeneous cultural backgrounds. In fact, management policies and practices should be considered relative to the culture of the society in which they are applied, and should be molded to fit the cultural background of the employees. In order to achieve the organizational goals, management may find it much easier to change policies and practices in accordance with the culturally-determined behavioral characteristics of the employees than to change the behavior of the employees with a set of rigid and inflexible rules. The effectiveness of a policy depends on how the employees react to it. If it creates resistance among the employees, management must understand the basis for such resistance, and adapt policies that are clearly consistent with the behavioral inclinations of the employees. Thus, in order to achieve any degree of organizational effectiveness, the management needs a clearer understanding of the culturally-determined psychological profile (needs and expectations, attitudes and behavior tendencies, etc.) of its employees.

Individuals enter an organization with certain beliefs, expectations, attitudes and values regarding work, and these influence their behavior within the organization. These forces are considered by psychologists to be relatively stable, enduring predispositions within the individuals, and they are acquired through the influence of cultural institutions such as family, religion, and various other reference groups with which the individuals identify themselves. Once these predispositions are acquired, they tend to contribute to how the individuals will respond to various stimuli in the organizational environment. As Zaleznik (1964) points out in reference to managerial behavior, "By the time an individual joins an organization to embark on a managerial career, he has established internal sets that frame how he seeks to engage his organization." This remark is not only applicable to managers, but also to all other employees in an organization. For instance, early socialization experiences of an individual will determine in his later life whether or not he will value autonomy and personal achievement on the job. Someone raised in a family and school environment that encouraged independence of thought and action, personal achievement, and impulse control is more likely to seek greater autonomy and opportunity for personal success at work. He is more likely to seek greater personal control over his work, and less dependence on others, including his boss. On the other hand, if an individual is brought up in an environment that values strong family ties and extended family relationships, he is more likely to develop stronger affiliative tendencies or greater dependence on others. In his later work life, he would probably look for better interpersonal relations in his job. Most of the time his job-related decisions would be colored by interpersonal considerations rather than by task demands. If an individual is a product of authoritarian family and school systems, his dependence on his boss and the rules and regulations of the organization he works for will be much greater than that of someone who is a product of liberal family and school training. Cultural influences shape the employee's needs and expectations, his hopes and aspirations, and his perception of desirable forms of conduct. Since a manager's task is to work through the employees, it is vital that the manager try to gain a more complete understanding of the cultural influences of employees' behavior, and to adapt his managerial philosophy and practice accordingly. Some past research on employee behavior within organizations suggest a strong influence of culture on the nature of organizational processes. For example, Graves (1972, 1973) has shown that different cultural backgrounds of employees create the need for different kinds of management and supervisory styles.

The same authoritarian style of supervision that may be effective in handling a group of mechanics working in a factory in India may not be equally effective in handling mechanics working in factories in Canada or in the United States. Because of the influence of their culture, workers in the United States value autonomy and independence at work more than do workers in India; consequently, American workers and their Indian counterparts tend to view the authority role of supervisors very differently.

Besides the nature of supervision, culture influences another important facet of organizational activity—the nature and pattern of communication among the employees within an organization. If an employee disagrees with his boss on how to deal with a job-related problem, should he discuss it face-to-face with his boss, or should he keep it to himself and silently comply by following the boss's orders? Employees belonging to different cultural backgrounds tend to follow different courses of action. In

Canada and the United States, for example, differences of opinion between a supervisor and his subordinate are resolved through face-to-face contact. In such discussion, the status differences between the two parties are de-emphasized and the problem is usually handled in a participative way. In other cultures, such as in Latin America or in India, face-to-face discussion of differences of opinion is generally avoided. Employees from these cultures (and other highly stratified societies) tend to place a great premium upon keeping harmonious interpersonal relations with superiors, and hence do not want to contest their superiors' judgments. In many instances, differences of opinions are resolved through the use of more formal channels (memos, written documents, appeal to higher authority, etc.).

Several studies have shown that the cultural background of employees can influence the nature and varieties of motivation at work (Kanungo, Misra, and Dayal, 1975; McClelland, 1961, McClelland and Winter, 1969). For some employees, it is the desire to achieve success that motivates them to work hard on their jobs. For other employees, however, it is the desire to find satisfying relationships with co-workers that keeps them motivated. Such achievement orientations or affiliative desires are largely acquired through the influence of culture.

Culture also influences job-related attitudes and perceptions of employees. For instance, an employee's attitude of involvement in or alienation from work is partly learned as a result of cultural influences during the early socialization training period. Members of a culture that emphasizes the "Protestant work ethic" tend to consider work as more central to their lives than do members of other cultures who may consider work to be of only peripheral interest (Basu, 1977; Webber, 1969). William F. Whyte (1961) highlights this point in the following remark:

". . . there are more important differences between our culture and some others regarding the value of work.

All over the world most people must work for a living. But in some societies work is regarded as simply a means to an end. If one has enough money to live in the style of his own social group without working, then he doesn't work. He has others to do the work for him.

Not so in the United States. The millionaire playboy may be a familiar phenomenon in the newspaper, but he is also the butt of strong public censure. We wonder how he can justify his existence if he doesn't work. In fact, most millionaires keep right on working, piling up more money or giving it away—or both. Even when we criticize some of the causes to which the millionaire gives his money, we recognize that he is working hard at giving it away and we respect him for that." [p. 57]

The importance of cultural influences on organizational activities and employee behavior cannot be overemphasized. In Canada, the presence of the Anglophone and the Francophone cultures dictate that a manager, to be effective, should understand the impact of the two cultures on organizational activities and employee behavior. Several studies reported in this book aim at providing such an understanding. By presenting some valuable data on culture-based characteristics of French- and English-Canadian employees of Canadian organizations, this book provides some direction as to how an organization operating in a bicultural setting can best utilize its human resources.

General Plan of the Book

My general objective is to provide some empirical verification of how the psychological profiles of French- and the English-Canadian employees differ from one another. In order to achieve a greater appreciation of the culture-based differences in the psychological characteristics of the two groups, a brief historical perspective on the role of the two groups in the industrial domain is provided in Chapter 2. Chapter 3 describes the nature of field studies undertaken to gather data on job perceptions, job motivations, job involvement, job mobility, and attitude towards communication, supervision and training. The remaining chapters describe and discuss the results on each of these aspects of employee behavior. Chapter 4 deals with the value or the importance of various job outcomes for English- and French-Canadian employees. The chapter also includes an analysis of how the two groups view their jobs with respect to their enrichment potential, participation in decision-making, and the degree of commitment. Chapter 5 deals with the levels of satisfaction experienced by the two groups with respect to various job outcomes. An analysis of the turnover potential of the two groups is also presented. Chapter 6 deals with the issue of job involvement and alienation among French- and English-Canadian employees. The chapter also presents a motivational framework for the measurement and understanding of job involvement of employees. The nature of job mobility among French- and English-Canadians within the context of a national organization is analyzed in Chapter 7. Such analysis provides some interesting data on why employees want or do not want to move to a different location, and on their preferences for various locations in Canada and abroad. In Chapter 8, the attitudes of the two groups of employees toward the nature of communication and its various forms and channels are analyzed. Chapter 9 deals with the issues of supervision and training of employees. The kind of supervisory behavior resulting in greater compliance and satisfaction among the employees, and the training needs of employees are the questions probed in this chapter. In Chapter 10, several implications of the results presented in previous chapters are summarized, and their value to management of national corporations in a bicultural context is highlighted.

CHAPTER
2

The English and the French Canadians in Industry:
A Brief Historical Perspective

A UNIQUE ASPECT of Canadian society, particularly as it exists in the province of Québec, is its bicultural character. Two culturally distinct groups of people, Anglophones and Francophones, live in Canada, sharing and contributing to Canadian social and economic life. They are the founders of contemporary Canadian society. Our understanding of the existing social milieu and our planning for a better future will depend largely on a better understanding of the psychological nature of the two groups of people. The existence of these two groups in the province of Québec and the insistence of each on maintaining their own cultural identity and linguistic rights have recently produced stresses in the political, social, educational and industrial sectors of Québec society. In the first three areas, the two groups have remained more or less in their two solitudes, but in the industrial sector they are forced to interact with each other. This has caused management problems for industry, both in the marketplace and in the work place. Basically, the problem faced by management is how to deal with the perceptions, orientations, motivations and attitudes of the two groups. In order to throw some light on this problem, field studies were conducted in controlled organizational contexts. The studies are reported in this book. The purpose of the studies is to identify some significant psychological characteristics of French- and English-Canadian employees and to effect a comparison so that management planning for handling human resources within the organization may be more effective. However, the results of the studies and their implications for management practice can be fruitfully interpreted only when they are considered in the light of underlying social, religious, economic and political forces which have shaped the psychological characteristics of people living in Québec.

Francophone and Anglophone employees in industry today have undoubtedly been influenced by their respective cultural heritages. They have also been influenced by socio-political changes that have transpired from time to time. The nature of the socialization process (which includes the influence of family, religious, educational, and political institutions) has been responsible for shaping the attitudes, opinions, needs and expectations of these employees. To the extent that historical forces have influenced their psychological makeup, it is important to briefly review industrial beginnings in Québec.

Impact of Rural-Agricultural vs. Urban-Industrial Traditions

French-Canadian society in Québec has been basically rural and agricultural in nature, while English-Canadian society was based on an urban-industrial tradition. Anglophones lived in urban centers such as Montréal, Sherbrooke and Québec City and were generally engaged in some form of business activity, whereas most Francophones led an independent farm life and preferred to stay in a secure and familiar rural environment. The rural traditions of Francophones were controlled by the Roman Catholic Church, which allowed very little scope for change from the traditional norms governing behavior. A main concern of the Francophone inhabitants was providing for children who had to leave the family farm. The steady growth of the population led to a resulting shortage of good farm land. In their attempts to preserve Francophone culture, the Roman Catholic clergy encouraged Francophones to increase their birth rates (Scott and Oliver, 1964). Canadian census reports indicate that the increase in birth rates among Francophones remained higher than the national average every year until 1962. Henripin (1957) points out that while world population increased by a factor of three, and European population by a factor of four, Francophone population increased by a factor of eighty. Sauvy (1965), a French demographer, estimated that if the population of France had increased in the same proportion as that of Québec, it would today be larger than that of the entire world.

As arable farm land became scarce, Francophones were forced into urban areas of the province where they had to accept jobs in industry. The expansion of industry and the shift in population is illustrated by Everett C. Hughes (1938):

> "Drummondville was formerly a small town living off the trade of a surrounding farming district. By the nineties . . . the chief industries (sawmills, tannery, smelting furnaces) had disappeared . . . Its population was smaller in 1911 than in 1891 . . . Between 1911 and 1933, the population multiplied by 5.44 and the number of industrial employees by 30.4. This revolution was brought by two large dams, which brought six textile industries and a number of small auxiliary plants." [pp. 82-83]

In his description of the functional relationship of industry to the traditional system of rural life prevailing in Québec, Hughes (1938) maintained that the industry introduced into the province was of the native-labour, foreign-management type, as opposed to industry in the northeastern United States, where management was native and labour migrant.

"Every industry of any size (in Drummondville) was founded at the instance of some company operating elsewhere. Managers and technical staff were sent to Drummondville to build and operate plants. These people are immigrants to the town; a majority of them are not Canadian. None of them is a French Canadian. In addition, a number of English-speaking foremen, skilled operators, and clerical workers are imported. Such people, with their families, constitute about one-twentieth of the population—an alien and socially isolated element, mixing little with the native labouring population; the poorer of these alien people live among French people in the inner part of town. The dominating managers and technicians are becoming somewhat segregated in the more desirable outlying sections. The segregation is not complete, for there are many local French people of the upper business and professional classes who live in the same districts." [pp. 83-84]

Hughes maintained that this was the typical Quebec industrial centre. The impact of this industrial development among the Francophone population was also explained by Hughes:

"Insofar as [the new industrial workers] have come directly from the farm, they have never lived in communities where there was any considerable class of people above them. In their new home they experience for the first time the constant presence of a group far superior to them in both standards of living and authority . . . No wonder that they attribute the trials of the new life not only to the industrial system but to the fact that it was introduced and is controlled by aliens." [p. 84]

Thus, from the very beginning of industrialization in Quebec, Francophones were absorbed into the lower levels of the industrial hierarchy. Their rural background and Anglophone control of industry prevented them from attaining leadership roles in industry.

Impact of Catholic vs. Protestant Work Ethic

The strong hold of the Roman Catholic religion on the Francophone population was responsible for lack of Francophone interest in business and industry. The relatively low status accorded to business as a profession by the Francophone élite was an important determinant of the low level of Francophone participation and leadership in industry. The careers of Francophones were studied by Jamieson (1938). He found that the Francophone élite was made up of members primarily in the priesthood, medicine and law, and secondarily in engineering and accountancy. He also found that the role of Francophones at managerial levels was to act as intermediaries. They served as links between English-language management and a mixed, largely French-speaking customer group. They also acted as intermediaries between management and a mixed labour force which was overwhelmingly French at the assistant foreman level and below. The non-acceptance of industrialization by the Francophone élite is documented by Parenteau (1954). According to Parenteau, the Francophones regarded industrialization of their society as pernicious, and

> ". . . they were convinced that only rural life could assure the survival of the ethnic group and safeguard the traditional moral values on which French Canadians prided themselves." [p. 97]

An insight into these traditional moral values is provided by Parenteau when he quotes a speech made by Msgr. Paquet to the St. Jean-Baptiste Society of Quebec in 1902:

> "Our mission is not so concerned with the management of capital as the cultivation of ideas, not so much the lighting of factory furnaces as the illumination of the hearth of religion and ideas.
>
> "Let us not descend from the pedestal upon which God has placed us to march in the vulgar footsteps of generations thirsting for gold and pleasure. Let us leave to other, less civilized nations, this commercial fever and this crude nationalism which debases them to the level of material things.
>
> "While our rivals assert their leadership in industry and finance, albeit in a well-mannered contest, we shall aspire above all to the honour of upholding the tenets of our faith." [p. 97]

It is not difficult to see the attitudinal difference between Francophones, and Anglophones who, it is claimed, are influenced by the so-called Protestant work ethic. For Anglophones salvation is determined by the degree of one's dedication to and involvement in work, particularly in industry and commerce. According to the Protestant ethic, the penalty for nonadherence to the work ethic is eternal damnation. For Francophones, adherence to the work ethic was equated with vulgarity and a "thirsting for gold and pleasure."

Impact of Educational Systems

In Québec, two separate educational systems, one for Francophones (most of whom were Catholic), and the other for Anglophones (most of whom were Protestant) were established as early as 1841. The type of education available to Francophones was geared to the liberal arts rather than preparation for industrial and business careers, and was pursued by a relatively small number of persons. As Sandwell (1962) points out,

> "The system of education in Québec until recent years has adapted itself slowly to the needs of the industrial society. It has provided excellent

training for members of the well-established professions, but few experts in the fields of engineering, chemical industry, commerce or finance. The situation is being corrected, but these changes are taking place rather late." [pp. 315-316]

Education became a provincial priority in the 1950s, and the government reviewed the quality and quantity of education in the Francophone community. During the following two decades several changes were introduced into the educational system. For instance, the legal school age was raised, free tuition to the CEGEP level was provided and special committees to study education in the province were appointed. As late as 1951, Québec's retention rate for secondary school students was the lowest in Canada. The Parent Commission was appointed in 1961 to overhaul the system, and its recommendations included creation of the CEGEPs, consolidation of school boards, and the creation of a bureau to examine university budgets and assist in future planning. Graduate and undergraduate schools of commerce and administration were created or strengthened at Francophone universities. The output of these schools increased the availability of Francophones educated for responsible managerial positions in commerce and industry.

Impact of the Working Language in Industry

Although more and more educated Francophones are entering business and industry, they face some new problems arising from the working language of industry. Brazeau (1963) succinctly described the problems faced by Francophones:

"The fact is that these graduates will be French-speaking people and trained in French, while English so far is the working language of corporate administration in the province. This social arrangement will continue to place many of them under a serious handicap. If, nonetheless, these persons have to be incorporated en masse in industrial society, new work will have to be found rapidly and new attitudes developed in Québec's enterprises." [p. 40]

The existence of this difficulty was also confirmed by the Royal Commission on Bilingualism and Biculturalism (1969), which found, among other things, that the use of English in business was a handicap for Francophones.

In the past, Anglophone ownership of large monopolistic industry in Québec resulted in English being the preferred language of business. These large enterprises imported their own English-speaking managerial personnel and employed Francophones as workers. Those Francophones who spoke English were the ones who obtained the better jobs in industry—those with higher prestige, more responsibility and better salary

(Scott and Oliver, 1964). Their purpose was to facilitate communication between English-speaking managerial personnel and French-speaking workers. Since their employment opportunities were not diminished as a result of being English-unilingual, Anglophones' attempts to learn French were indeed slight. This certainly was not the case for French unilinguals. Many Francophones residing in urban and industrial centers learned English in order to cope with job market demands and the Anglophone cultural surroundings prevalent in those areas.

Contemporary Trends in Québec Society

A major historical turning point appears to have occurred in 1960 with the beginning of "La Révolution Tranquille," from which later followed the 1962 "Maître chez nous" slogan of the Lesage government. A radical break was being made with traditional Québec society, a break which was to affect virtually every facet of Francophone-Anglophone relations. Much of the tension resulting from this break involved the minority Anglophone population of the province and the various "rights" which they had acquired or had had relegated, directly or indirectly, to themselves. Language use, availability of other than blue-collar job opportunities for Francophones, control of the economic assets of the province and the perceived threat to Francophone culture, education and nationalism were all part of these tensions.

The conflict over the dominance of the English language has been particularly in evidence. On the one hand it is claimed that the Province of Québec (Montréal in particular) is in imminent danger of becoming completely anglicized. Political agitation to impose the French language on all business activities has become more pronounced. On the other hand, businessmen feel that it would be impossible to carry out top management functions in French, particularly in the case of corporate head offices located in Québec. Employees have to be brought in from various parts of the country for training in middle-management positions, and it is not reasonable to have them learn French for a short period of time and then send them back to an English-speaking environment. A survey (*Montreal Gazette*, November 22, 1972) indicated that having French as the language of work doesn't seem to bother businessmen, mostly because they don't believe such a requirement will ever be enforced at upper management levels. It is noted, however, that if it is, they would feel forced to move their companies out of the province.

With the coming to power of the Parti Quebecois in 1976, the perceptions of management personnel at the middle and upper levels regarding the use of French at their own levels has changed. The Parti Quebecois government has insisted on a policy of francization at all levels of management.

This has led to two effects. First, to avoid future problems due to francization policy, several head offices of national and international corporations have moved out of Montreal in the past four years. Second, many organizations have started to provide opportunities to their senior level executives to make them more proficient in the French language. This move toward having French as the language of work started with the Gendron Commission report (The Commission of Enquiry on the Position of the French Language and on Language Rights in Quebec, formed on December 9, 1968). The report recommended that French be made the only official language of Québec, and any groups dealing with the government be required to use the French language. It also recommended that industries adopt French as their language of internal communication, and that French become the official language for all written business transactions. Following these recommendations, the two successive provincial governments enacted legislation and pursued the policy of francization of business and industry (for instance Bill 22 in 1974 and Bill 101 in 1977). A recent ruling by the Supreme Court of Canada has made portions of this policy of francization unconstitutional. As a result, the provincial government has made necessary revisions of the francization policy, recognizing the use of both English and French as official languages in courts of law and the national assembly. However, such revisions have not substantially affected the policy of francization in business and industry.

The job market and perceived job opportunities in recent years still tend to divide along language lines, the large majority of Francophones working in small local French firms and the large majority of Anglophones working in big national firms. For this reason, Anglophone-dominated national companies have been criticized for not doing enough to attract Francophones to middle- and upper-management levels.

Addressing the Policy Formulation: Canada conference, a professor of economics at Laval University claimed that French-speaking persons are discriminated against by the English- (or United States-) controlled businesses in Montréal (*Montreal Gazette*, November 15, 1972). These comments highlight the underlying feeling of lack of job opportunities in management for Francophones. In fact, the Gendron report confirms that at least 70 percent of the key corporate positions in the province are filled by Anglophones. According to this report, it is necessary for more French-speaking people to have access to middle management and executive positions in business.

A survey by the *Montreal Star* (May 22, 1976) reports that well-qualified French-speaking bilinguals are the most sought-after candidates by big firms. Even unilingual French graduates who are prepared to learn English on the job are being preferred. From the Francophone perspective, however, the job market situation is not good. The Francophone graduates of today feel that big business offers them no real future. There is a tendency on the part of many French-Canadians to try out a large English firm when they graduate and then leave one or two years later. As the *Montreal Star* reports:

> "Every year about 40 percent of the graduates from the University of Montreal's Ecole des Hautes Etudes Commerciales (HEC) go off optimistically to work in Big Business. One or two years later, a surprising three-quarters of them have left to work for medium-sized French-Canadian firms or the Québec Civil Service."

The reason for the Francophone's unwillingness to make a career in big business may lie in the fact that the Anglophone environment feels alien to the Francophones. According to the survey by the *Montreal Star*:

> "Many speak good English but are still under the strain of speaking it all day. Their co-workers are mostly English-Canadians and they miss the French-Canadian ambience. While few feel antagonism from co-workers, their view of the world differs and as a result they feel alienated. The cumulative result is that many start feeling like "immigrants"—foreigners in their own work places. Many leave for French-Canadian firms or the Québec civil service where they feel accepted and "chez eux."

These descriptions of the Francophone and Anglophone backgrounds in the Québec milieu highlight the fact that although both the groups live together in the same geographical location, they do perceive their physical and social environment quite differently. As a consequence, any differences in their behavioral or psychological characteristics have to be interpreted in terms of the perceived environmental realities in which they operate.

CHAPTER
3

The Nature of the Inquiry:
Some Basic Considerations

THE EFFECTIVENESS OF AN ORGANIZATION depends on the motivation and productive efforts of its employees. In order to motivate employees to engage in productive job behavior, managers should first identify and understand the nature of significant psychological characteristics of employees such as the job attitudes and work values which influence their day-to-day work behavior. They should then develop appropriate management strategies to cope effectively with their employees. Keeping these considerations in mind, the results of several field studies and their implications for the practice of management in a bicultural context are discussed in subsequent chapters of this book. However, before introducing the reader to the results of these studies, it is desirable to present a few basic facts about the methodology used and the issues the studies dealt with.

The studies reported in this book compare the psychological profiles noting significant job beliefs and job attitudes of Anglophone and Francophone employees of Canadian organizations operating within Québec and Ontario. In choosing the respondents, the studies followed a very specific research strategy known as intra-organizational comparisons. Instead of comparing one group of employees belonging to Anglophone organizations with another group belonging to Francophone organizations (inter-organizational comparisons), the studies compare the psychological profiles of Anglophone and Francophone employees working for the same organization and holding similar jobs. Such intra-organizational comparisons are more meaningful for managers who encounter the two groups of employees within their organization. Furthermore, since both groups are drawn from the same organization, any differences in job attitudes and work values cannot be attributed to differences in organizational or job environment. Differences between the two groups may be expected, however, on the basis of differences in their cultural backgrounds. It is assumed that although the two groups of employees work in the same organizational environment, and are influenced by the same organizational policies and practices, their job perceptions and attitudes toward the organizational realities would be different because of the differences in their socio-cultural backgrounds.

What areas of employee behavior and what specific psychological characteristics of employees should a manager identify and understand in order to best utilize human resources? In this book I have tried to develop a list of concerns after several interviews with representatives of management and rank-and-file employees of organizations from which Francophone and Anglophone respondents were drawn. Through these interviews, the needs and concerns of both the managers and their subordinates were first assessed, and questionnaires were then prepared to elicit information through employee surveys. (The various questionnaires used in the studies are appended at the end of the book.) These questionnaires are in both English and French and may be used by managers of any organization who want to identify behavioral problems of the organization in major areas. More specifically, these questionnaires are designed to explore the differences among the Anglophone and Francophone employees with respect to the following major categories of psychological variables:

Job perceptions The importance attached by employees to various intrinsic and extrinsic job outcomes, the levels of their job and organizational commitment, the levels of their perceived and desired participation, and their perceptions of their own abilities in relation to job demands are assessed to reflect the cognitive orientations or belief system of employees regarding their work.

Job satisfaction The degree of satisfaction experienced by the employees with regard to various intrinsic and extrinsic job outcomes is measured to reflect how job outcomes meet their needs and expectations. In addition, their desire to quit the job is also assessed to provide an index of their turnover potential.

Job involvement The degree of psychological identification with the job is measured to see how strongly motivated the employees are in performing their job duties.

Mobility and transfer potential Readiness of employees to accept transfer to various locations, their reasons for such readiness, and their location preferences are studied in order to understand the motivation underlying transfer mobility.

Attitude toward organizational communication Levels of satisfaction experienced by the employees with respect to upward and downward communication, channels of communication, and communications about job outcomes are assessed to indicate the need for changes in the total organizational communication system.

Attitude toward supervision and training Employee need for different types of supervision, such as close, coercive, reward-based, etc., are studied to determine which forms of supervision are most effective in eliciting compliance from the employees. The attitudes of the employees toward various training practices are also assessed to determine which kind of training environment is most conducive to employee development.

As pointed out earlier, this set of psychological variables was chosen after a series of discussions with key management personnel and a small sample of employees of organizations operating in a bicultural context. Both groups agreed that these variables play significant roles in making the organization more effective. Both groups also suggested that they were facing many problems in these areas because of inadequate organizational policies, and that the solutions to these problems require a controlled comparison of Anglophone and Francophone employees. Variables represent three sets of psychological dimensions: the cognitions, the feelings, and the behavioral intentions of the employees. Significant cognitive dimensions of employees were studied through the measurement of job-related beliefs, such as the importance attached by the employees to various job outcomes. The study of affective dimensions of employees involved measuring an employee's feelings, such as his satisfaction or dissatisfaction with the various job outcomes. Finally, the measurement of behavioral intentions included assessment of such things as employee turnover and transfer potentials. We now turn our attention to specific comparisons of Anglophone and Francophone employees on each of the variables.

CHAPTER 4

Job Perceptions of English- and French-Canadian Employees

AN INDIVIDUAL'S DECISION to accept a job in an organization and to continue in it will depend upon his perception of the rewards he expects to receive from his job. If he perceives that the organization and the job will bring him rewards that he values, then he may stay in the organization and perform well. If he finds that the organization and the job do not offer him the rewards he values, he will then withdraw from the job situation, either by leaving the organization or by performing poorly on the job. From a managerial point of view, therefore, it is important to know what organizational rewards or job outcomes employees value. Such knowledge will help a manager to develop an appropriate reward system within the organization to match the needs of employees. One cannot overemphasize the fact that an employee need-based reward system will go a long way toward reducing employee turnover and increasing employee job motivation.

Assessing the needs of employees and designing appropriate reward systems to fit those needs are vital for those organizations that operate in bicultural or multicultural contexts. Since cultural influences determine what an individual may value in life, employees belonging to different cultures are likely to have different value systems and need structures. Insensitivity to such differences may result in what is often referred to as "mirror management."

"Mirror management" refers to the phenomenon of top level managers in head office thinking that what is good for them is good for every other employee in the organization. For instance, if more responsibility on the job is what they want, they will make a policy of providing more responsibility on the job to every employee. In this case, managers are assuming that every employee needs and values more responsibility, and providing added responsibility on the job will make the employees happy. "Mirror management" is often responsible for low morale and low productivity among employees. It is an error to assume that all employees think alike and want the same kinds of job outcomes. As Dr. Vincent Fowlers stated, "most employee-motivation programs go haywire when they are developed by management types who think everyone wants exactly the same as management wants. This is 'mirror management' and it simply isn't true to life. Not everyone wants authority, responsibility, a private office—or even a retirement plan." [Cuthill, 1977, p. 25]

Motivation to perform well on the job and job satisfaction among employees are largely determined by the interaction of job characteristics (what jobs provide to employees) and employee characteristics (what the employees want from their jobs). When employee characteristics such as their needs and expectations are matched by job outcomes, motivation and job satisfaction of employees tend to increase. When, however, what the job provides falls short of meeting employee needs and expectations, motivation to perform and job satisfaction tend to decline.

Job characteristics refer to several job factors or outcomes. These have been broadly divided into two categories, intrinsic and extrinsic (Lawler, 1973). Intrinsic job factors refer to certain "internally mediated rewards" that an employee experiences while doing his job, such as responsibility and independence, a sense of achievement, and the interesting nature of the work. Herzberg (1966) considers these outcomes as job-content factors. They tend to be more abstract in nature and mainly satisfy ego and growth needs as proposed by Alderfer (1972) and Maslow (1954). Extrinsic job factors, on the other hand, refer to more tangible externally-mediated job outcomes. These factors are characterized by Herzberg (1966) as environmental or job-context factors. Lawler (1973), however, distinguishes two groups of extrinsic factors: (a) those that are organizationally controlled, such as salary and fringe benefits, job security, job status, working conditions, etc.; and (b) those that are interpersonally mediated, such as nature of supervision and peer group relations. The organizationally controlled extrinsic factors are mainly responsible for satisfying existence needs and maintaining a materially comfortable life. Interpersonally mediated job factors tend to satisfy social or affiliative needs (Alderfer, 1972; Maslow, 1954).

Employee characteristics refer to employee orientations and values with respect to job factors. Two groups of employees holding the same job within an organization, or holding similar jobs in different organizations, may have very different orientations. One group may attach greater importance to extrinsic job factors, while another group may attach greater importance to intrinsic job factors. Because of such differences, the two groups may derive different levels of satisfaction from what the job offers them and thus may be motivated differently on the job. The assessment of employees' motivation not only requires finding out what the job offers to each employee, but also requires an assessment of employee orientation and values with respect to job outcomes (Rowe, 1973; Vroom, 1964). As suggested in Chapter 1, differences among employees with respect to their orientations toward job factors may stem primarily from their cultural backgrounds or the norms of the reference groups to which they belong (Korman, 1971). The studies reported in this chapter have explored such differences in the bicultural society of Québec.

In large corporations in Québec, one often finds the two culturally distinct groups of employees holding similar jobs. It is quite conceivable that Anglophone and Francophone employees, because of differences in their cultural backgrounds, may differ in their orientations or perceived importance of various job factors intended to satisfy employee needs. For similar reasons, it is also conceivable that the two groups may differ with respect to the levels of their job and organizational commitment, need participation, and perceptions of their abilities in relation to their job demands. These possibilities were explored in the studies described below; the major question answered was whether Francophone and Anglophone employees in large corporations differ with respect to their value orientation and job perceptions.

Importance of Job Outcomes

There are several lines of existing evidence that suggest the possibility of finding some interesting differences in the job orientation of Anglophone and Francophone employees. For instance, Tremblay (1953) characterizes the French-Canadian social environment as an environment that discourages the development of the work ethic. English Canadians, on the other hand, are very much influenced by the Protestant work ethic, and tend to promote it. Taylor (1964), in his study of the French-Canadian entrepreneur, found "family orientation" to be the focus of behavior. The Francophone entrepreneur comes from a familial society and most of his actions on the job are guided by considerations for his family security and happiness. Such evidence suggests that Francophone and Anglophone employees in Québec perhaps have different orientations to life goals because of the influence of different cultural environments (Lambert, Yackley and Hein, 1971; Yackley and Lambert, 1971). Within an industrial context, Francophone employees may be working primarily to live a materially and socially comfortable and secure life outside the organization. For them "living" is perhaps the primary goal and "working" is perceived as secondary and instrumental to their attainment of the primary goal. The opposite may be true for Anglophone employees. Thus, in the context of the job, Francophone employees may be expected to attach greater importance than do Anglophones to those extrinsic job factors that satisfy material, security and social needs, and lesser importance to intrinsic job factors that cater to needs stemming from the Protestant work ethic.

The Questionnaire on Importance of Job Outcomes   The questionnaire for the study was prepared after several interviews with various management personnel belonging to three major divisions of an international firm with operations in Canada. In the interviews the management personnel revealed their major concerns regarding handling of human resources in a bicultural organization. They felt that, in order to handle management problems, they needed certain relevant information on the two groups of employees. The questionnaire items were designed to elicit information through employee surveys to meet these needs. The questionnaire was prepared both in English and in French using a translation-retranslation procedure. (Both versions of the questionnaire are presented in Appendix A, p. 129.)

The first part of the questionnaire was designed to provide personal demographic data about respondents, such as their positions within the organization hierarchy, their language-group affiliations, sex, age, education, income, and years of experience both in the organization and in the present job. In the second part, respondents were asked to indicate the perceived characteristics of their job by ranking fifteen job factors according to their perceived importance. The fifteen factors were listed in each questionnaire in random order. These job factors represented both intrinsic and extrinsic rewards. There were seven organizationally-controlled extrinsic job factors: adequate earnings (to maintain a good standard of living), fair pay (to provide a sense of equity), promotion opportunity (to increase job status), fringe benefits, job security, sound company policy, comfortable working conditions. In addition, there were four interpersonally-mediated extrinsic job outcomes: technically competent supervision, considerate supervision, good peer group relations, and recognition (given by others for good work). The remaining four intrinsic job factors were: responsibility and independence (sense of autonomy), a sense of achievement, interesting nature of work, and opportunity to achieve higher level of job skills (need to grow).

The Sample   The survey plan called for administering the questionnaire to all employees of the Québec region (most of whom were Francophones). For comparison purposes the questionnaire was administered to equivalent groups from the Ontario region (most of whom were Anglophones). The questionnaire was distributed to 882 employees of whom 646 or 74 percent responded.

The Procedure   The questionnaire was administered at branch offices. Every department head distributed the questionnaire in his own department. A forwarding letter from the branch manager requesting the employees to participate in the survey was attached to the questionnaire. To assure confidentiality, the following instruction was given to each respondent.

Employee Survey Questionnaire

This questionnaire is designed to collect systematic data on how you feel toward various aspects of your job. Such data will provide knowledge about your opinions and attitudes that will help the management formulate more rational policies to suit the best interests of employees and the company.

You are requested to complete each part of the questionnairie and respond to each question in it. Your answers to the questions will be kept completely anonymous, and will be used only for the purpose of gaining a better understanding of the nature of the employee reactions in the company.

Thank you for your cooperation.

Each respondent was asked to seal the completed questionnaire in an enclosed envelope addressed to the researcher. The sealed envelopes were mailed to the researcher by the branch office.

Demographic Characteristics of Respondents   Of the 646 employees who responded to the questionnaire, fifty-seven revealed that their mother tongue was either both French and English or some other language. Since these respondents could not be classified as either Francophone or Anglophone, they were eliminated from the analysis. Of the remaining 589 employees, 379 were Francophone and 210 were Anglophone. The percentages of respondents falling into the various demographic classifications are presented in Table 1. Francophone and Anglophone respondents were matched on every demographic variable except salary. There was a trend showing a greater percentage of Anglophones in a higher income bracket relative to Francophones. Considering the fact that salary and socio-linguistic background of employees were related, care was taken in the analysis of results (through covariance analysis) to eliminate the possible confounding effects of salary.

How Did Employees Value Job Outcomes?   The mean rankings of perceived importance of each of the fifteen job factors were calculated for the two groups of employees, and the mean profiles are presented in Figure 1. Interesting similarities and differences in how the two groups of employees value various job outcomes can be seen. (Managerial implications of these observations are discussed in a later chapter.) The two linguistic groups are similar in that both Francophone and Anglophone employees consider "interesting nature of work" to be the most important job factor,

TABLE 1

Percentage of Respondents In Various Demographic Classifications

	FRENCH (N = 379)	ENGLISH (N = 210)	TOTAL (N = 589)
Management function	14.1	15.8	14.7
Supervisory function	17.6	21.9	19.2
Education			
Grade school	1.1	0.0	.7
High school	37.0	38.6	37.6
University	22.8	30.0	25.3
Graduate studies	9.8	9.0	9.5
Other	29.4	22.4	26.9
Sex			
Male	83.9	81.9	83.2
Female	16.1	18.1	16.8
Marital status			
Married	72.1	76.7	73.7
Single	27.7	23.3	26.1
Age			
Under 29	62.0	60.0	61.3
30-39	30.6	32.9	31.4
40-49	7.1	5.7	6.6
50 and over	0.3	1.4	0.7
*Salary in thousands of dollars**			
Between 5-10	29.0	20.1	25.9
Between 10-15	39.1	31.6	36.4
Between 15-20	12.4	16.7	13.9
Between 20-25	9.5	15.8	11.7
Over 25	10.5	15.3	11.9
Tenure with organization			
1 year or less	19.5	18.1	19.0
2-5 years	56.5	53.3	55.3
6-10 years	17.9	20.5	18.8
11-15 years	5.3	7.1	5.9
16-20 years	0.8	1.0	.8
Tenure with job			
1 year or less	37.7	32.9	36.0
2-5 years	51.7	52.9	52.0
6-10 years	8.7	11.0	9.5
11-15 years	.8	3.3	1.7
16-20 years	1.1	0.0	0.7

* Distribution of Francophone and Anglophone respondents was significantly different in this case.

followed by "adequate earning for a better standard of living." Both groups also attach little importance to "the nature of supervision" and "interpersonal peer relations at work." The two groups differ in that Francophone employees attach greater importance to security, benefits, working conditions, equitable pay, and opportunity for training or improving job skills. Anglophone employees attach greater importance to adequate earning, company policy, recognition, responsibility and independence, and achievement.

This pattern of the perceived importance of job factors is quite consistent with the results of two earlier studies conducted in very different organizations but using similar procedures (Kanungo, Gorn and Dauderis, 1976;

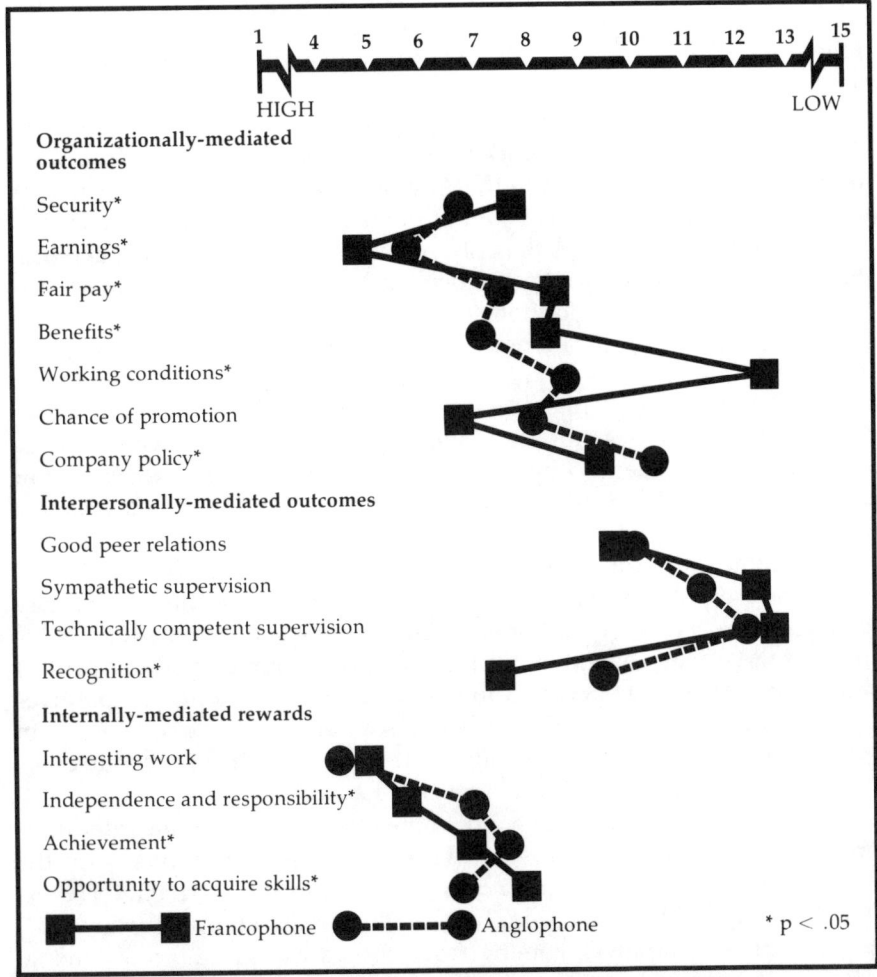

Figure 1: *Mean Perceived Importance Profile for Anglophone and Francophone Employees*

Jain, Normand, and Kanungo, 1979). The results are also consistent with the observations of Auclair and Read (1966) in their study of managers with a national sample drawn from different parts of Canada. They observed that "from a cultural standpoint, French-Canadian managers express much stronger needs for security and self-esteem at work than do English-Canadian managers. The self-actualization needs of the latter group, on the other hand, are greater than those of French-Canadian managers [p. 574]." If an employee's behavior is partly motivated by organizational rewards or job outcomes that are valued by the employee, then the present data suggest different motivational bases for Francophone and Anglophone employees. It seems that organizational reward systems catering to different needs and values would tend to motivate each group. Why is it that such value differences exist in the first place? In what ways can the socio-cultural differences between the two groups explain the differences in their cognitive value systems pertaining to job outcomes? Several explanations may be given.

First, Anglophones are more likely to be products of the Protestant ethic which places great value on work for its own sake. During their socialization in family, in school, and in the Anglophone-dominated organizations where they work, they are constantly trained to view work as the central core of their life and perhaps the only vehicle for realizing their capabilities. That is why autonomy, independence, and achievement are valued relatively more highly by Anglophone employees. The results of this study indicate that certain organizationally-controlled rewards such as soundness of company policy and earnings were also valued more by Anglophones than by Francophones. This may also stem from the Protestant ethic background that emphasizes individual ability and competition at work. Anglophones may be influenced by such notions as "a fair day's work for fair day's pay," or "what you earn is what you get," etc. They may have a stronger belief that individuals bring different inputs to their jobs and that their outcomes in terms of pay and other organizational rewards should match their inputs. A second explanation of the value differences may stem from family and school training. Anglophone family and school training tend to be more liberal in orientation and encourage development of traits or habits such as personal initiative and achievement, competitiveness, responsibility, and independence. An Anglophone employee from such a background will obviously value and seek those job outcomes which are compatible with these traits and habits.

Francophones, on the other hand, come largely from a more authoritarian family and educational system with a good deal of emphasis on the Catholic ethic. Such a background de-emphasizes the work ethic (Tremblay, 1953) and perhaps over-emphasizes the "family-ethic." (Taylor, 1964) A Francophone employee coming from such a background will tend to value his work not for its own sake, but for the sake of his family and friends. Thus, instead of emphasizing additional responsibility or achievement at work, he will emphasize working conditions, job security and status that will better his social image. These outcomes make his family and friends happy. Since these outcomes are valued highly by his reference groups, he feels more comfortable in placing value on them (Korman, 1971). In this regard, Auclair and Read (1966) pointed out that "the French Canadian much more than the English Canadian valued his role in life as being the 'breadwinner,' and being a good provider for his family constituted one of the most important motives for his aspirations to succeed in an industrial organization. Success in industry, in other words, was not something in itself as a means of self-fulfillment, but as a way of fulfilling his role as a good family man [p. 564]."

Studies in the area of child training and the development of "need achievement" can also partly explain Francophone and Anglophone differences. McClelland (1961) reports lower levels of need for achievement among Catholic French-Canadian children compared with Anglophone children. Such differences in need for achievement have been explained by several authors in terms of child training practices (Lambert, Yackley, and Hein, 1971; Rosen and D'Andrade, 1959; Yackley and Lambert, 1971). Children in French-Canadian families find their fathers playing a dominant role. Their experiences of authoritarian family atmosphere create in them a low need for achievement. Francophone employees coming from such families will have less achievement orientation and thus be less attracted to need-for-achieving situations in their jobs. Consequently, compared with Anglophones, they will not look for greater opportunity for "responsibility" or "achievement on the job."

There is another reason why Anglophones place relatively greater emphasis on autonomy and achievement in their jobs than do Francophones. Cultural differences in the socialization process, such as liberal or authoritarian family training, tend to create differences in the way the two groups perceive authority or power to influence others on the job. There is evidence to suggest that Anglophone employees perceive authority as vested in the person, presumably because of their liberal training. Francophone employees, on the other hand, perceive authority as vested in the organizational role. Graves (1972) has demonstrated that Anglophone managers in England, to be effective, tend to look for a maximum amount of autonomy for themselves because they think that the job gets done because of their personal qualities and not through their prescribed role in the organization. Francophone managers in France, on the other hand, tend not to assume additional personal responsibility and autonomy because of their belief that the job gets done only by virtue of the power of their position or prescribed role and not because of their own personal qualities. Similar processes may operate among Anglophone and Francophone employees in the present study. The latter may perceive their jobs in more formal ways and may accept responsibility only to the extent that it is inherent in their prescribed role.

Finally, it should be emphasized that the culture-based differences observed in the motivational orientations of Francophone and Anglophone employees must be understood within the larger context of the history of Québec. Industry in the province has been established and primarily controlled by Anglophones. Francophones are aware of Anglophone dominance in practically all aspects of their working lives. English is still used as the primary business language in almost all national and international organizations. This may have hindered Francophone employees from functioning effectively in their jobs. Whereas most Anglophones place a high priority on personal success in the business world, Francophones have tended to frown on this world (Parenteau, 1964), and they tended to be repelled by commercial life (Jamieson, 1938). Above all, the Francophone educational system, until recently, was not geared to business training. These orientations have existed for decades and are not easily modified. If Francophone employees put less emphasis on job outcomes such as achievement or recognition, the reasons may lie partly in the fact that they never perceived these outcomes as attainable goals. At the same time, the emphasis of Francophone employees on opportunity for training may reflect a new awareness on their part that success in the business world requires development of job skills.

Sense of Personal Responsibility and Commitment

In the same organization (using the respondents presented in Table 1), an attempt was made to assess the degree of personal responsibility and commitment of Anglophone and Francophone employees. Their sense of personal responsibility and commitment was assessed at three levels: in the job, in the department and in the organization as a whole. (The questionnaire used to measure these aspects of employee commitment is presented in Appendix A, p. 129.) For each level, the employees were asked to indicate the extent to which they felt really responsible and commited to achieving success. Their responses were measured on a four-point scale ranging from "feel no personal responsibility and commitment" (ordinal weight 1) to "feel responsible and committed to a great extent" (ordinal weight 4).

The results are shown in Figure 2. The mean scores of the two groups reveal that, in general, both linguistic groups show moderate to high levels of personal responsibility and commitment. Such results show a moderate to strongly committed work force in the organization. Two more interesting observations can also be made with respect to the employee commitment data.

```
                  Job              Departmental        Organizational
              commitment*          commitment*          commitment*
       4
              3.748
                                    3.611
                         3.601
                                              3.412
                                                          3.336
                                                                   3.066
       3
```

▓▓ Anglophone   ☐ Francophone

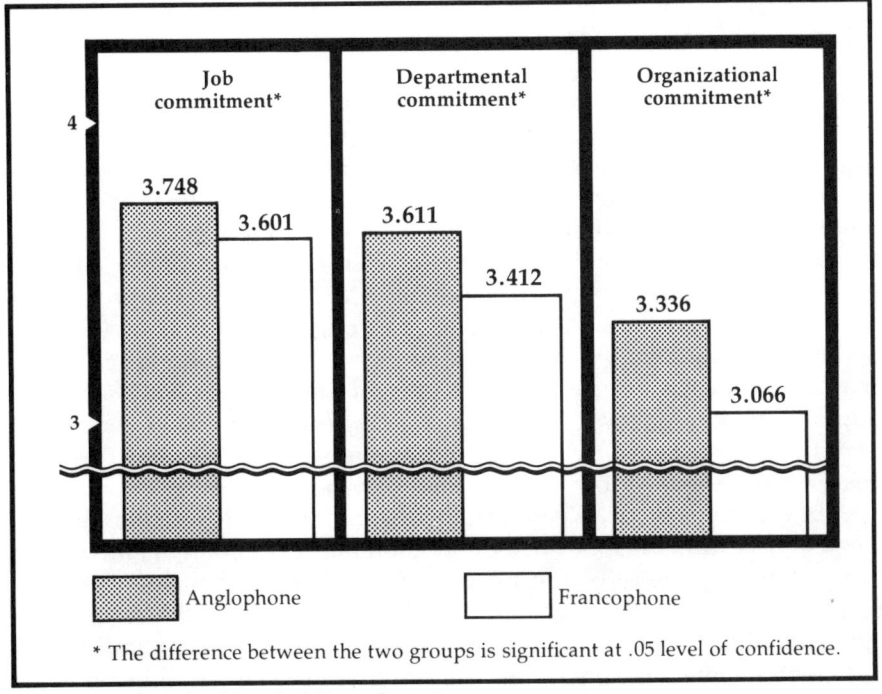

* The difference between the two groups is significant at .05 level of confidence.

Figure 2: *Perceived Level of Commitment*

First, the sense of personal responsibility and commitment of employees tends to decline as one moves from the job level to the department level, and from the department level to the total organizational level. Such a trend is expected. At the job level, the employees have greater control over their actions in meeting job demands, and they feel a greater degree of personal responsibility and commitment. At department and organizational levels, individual employees may not feel they have control over activities which achieve departmental or organizational goals. Because of the presence of other people at the departmental and organizational levels, individual employees may sense a tendency for diffusion of responsibility and commitment. Where a group is involved in achieving departmental or organizational goals, it is difficult for each individual to accurately perceive his personal responsibility. The larger the number of people in the group, the more difficult it becomes for individual group members to perceive clearly their own contribution. This may be why employees feel less committed to organizational success than to departmental success. Organizations trying to increase employee job commitment must create conditions whereby individual employees may clearly perceive that their job behavior (over which they have control) results in appropriate job performance. Moreover, if organizations want to increase employee commitment to departmental and organizational success, they must create conditions whereby individual employees feel that such success depends directly on each individual's job performance.

A second interesting observation from the data suggests that Anglophone employees tend to exhibit a greater degree of personal responsibility and commitment than do Francophone employees at each level. The greater commitment of Anglophone employees may stem from three sources. First, as was discussed in the section on perceived importance of job outcomes, Anglophone employees, relative to Francophone employees, emphasize responsibility and independence on the job (Figure 1). This tendency may create in Anglophones a stronger belief that they are responsible for their job success or failure. Second, Francophone employees may be somewhat unsure that their present job behavior will lead to job success, and hence they look for more training (Figure 1). Their uncertainty about job success is further reinforced by the fact that they must work in the English language, over which they may not have complete mastery. For these reasons Francophone employees may not like to assume a greater degree of personal responsibility and commitment. Finally, Francophone employees may perceive the organization as being English-owned and English-dominated; they may find it difficult to identify with the organization and call it their own. This perception may reduce their commitment at the departmental and organizational levels. (Suggestions to increase the level of commitment of Francophone employees are presented later in Chapter 10.)

Perceived and Desired Levels of Participation

How do employees view their levels of participation at work? Employees were asked to indicate how often their opinions and suggestions were *actually* solicited when job-related decisions that affect them and their jobs are being made. Responses to this question were measured on a four point scale ranging from "almost always" (ordinal weight 4) to "never" (ordinal weight 1). Responses to this question revealed the perceived level of participation of employees at work.

A second question was intended to measure the ideal level of participation that the employees desired. The employees were asked how often they *should* be asked to give their opinions and suggestions when decisions that affect them are being made. Here again the responses were measured on a four-point scale ranging from "should be asked always" (ordinal weight 4) to "should almost never be asked" (ordinal weight 1). (Both questions, worded in the way they were presented to employees, are presented in Appendix A, p. 129.)

Mean scores on the desired (ideal) and perceived levels of participation for the Anglophone and Francophone employees are presented in Figure 3. For both groups of employees, the desired levels of participation are higher than the perceived levels. The results clearly indicate that employees in this organization want more participation in the decision-making process. Generally, most jobs in modern organizations allow only very low levels of participation by employees. Such low levels are not a problem for organizations in which employees do not look for more participation in the decision-making process. However, if employees do want higher levels of participation, as in this study, it is of some concern to the organization. In such a situation, an organization may be better off restructuring the job in such a way as to provide greater opportunity for participation of employees in the decision-making process.

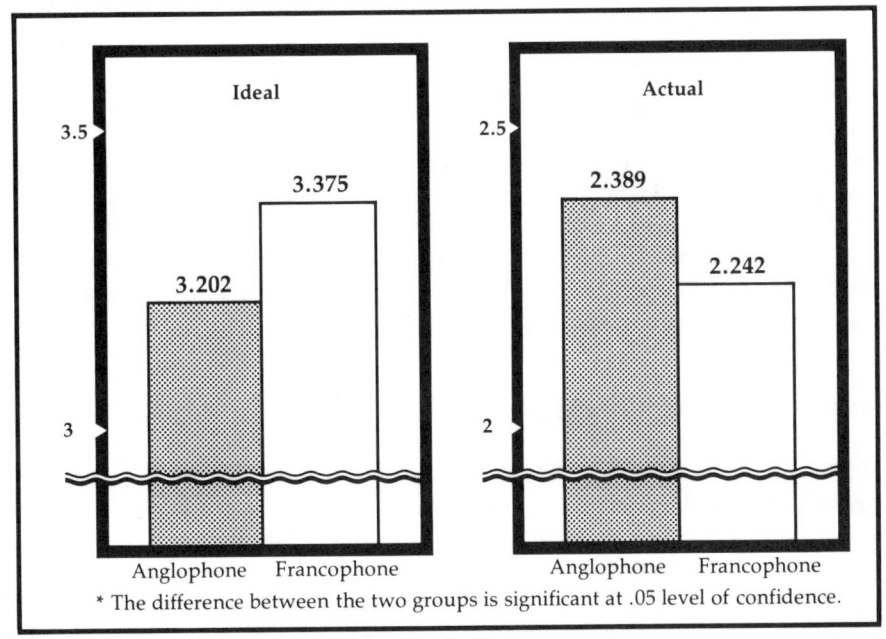

Ideal

Anglophone: 3.202
Francophone: 3.375

Actual

Anglophone: 2.389
Francophone: 2.242

* The difference between the two groups is significant at .05 level of confidence.

Figure 3: *Ideal Level of Participation Desired**
Actual Level of Participation*

The results in Figure 3 also suggest that Francophone employees perceive their level of participation to be significantly lower than the perceived level of participation among Anglophones. This is consistent with their lower level of perceived job commitment discussed earlier. At this point it is difficult to speculate whether greater job commitment on the part of employees leads to greater job participation, or initially finding a good deal of opportunity to participate on the job leads to greater job commitment. It seems that both job commitment and job participation variables interact in such a way that an increase in one leads to an increase in the other.

There may be two additional reasons for the lower level of perceived participation among Francophones (assuming that their perceived level of participation reflects how much they in fact participate in their jobs). The Francophone employees who were surveyed in this study actually worked under Francophone supervisors, and the Anglophone employees surveyed worked under Anglophone supervisors. It is quite possible that supervisory styles of Francophone and Anglophone managers differ. Francophone supervisors may be more authoritarian than their Anglophone counterparts. Such differences may in fact be culture-based in that Francophone supervisors also come from more authoritarian family backgrounds, and they may be showing a preference for an authoritarian supervisory role. For the same reasons, Francophone subordinates may show greater compliance with organizational rules and supervisory directives than do Anglophone subordinates.

The second reason for a lower level of perceived participation may stem from the role-bound characteristics of Francophone employees. As discussed earlier, Graves (1972) demonstrated that Anglophones tend to be more "person-bound" and to look for maximum personal autonomy on the job, whereas Francophones tend to be "role-bound" and to look for organizationally prescribed roles to guide their job behavior. If this is the case, Francophone employees will show greater compliance with rules, regulations and supervisory directives and perhaps take less personal initiative to participate in the decision-making process.

Job Enrichment Potential

If an employee's ability matches his job demands and he perceives that he is utilized to his limits, then there is no need for redesigning or upgrading his job. On the other hand, if an employee feels that he has ability that is not used in his job or if he perceives himself as being under-utilized, then there is a need for redesigning or upgrading his job; the job has enrichment potential and the employee can be given more responsibility, greater control, more variety, etc.

How do Francophones and Anglophones view their abilities in relation to their job demands? Employees were asked to what extent they thought their ability exceeded job demands. Responses ranged from "a great deal more ability than job demands" (ordinal weight 4) to "less ability than job demands" (ordinal weight 1). (The actual questions used to measure job enrichment potential are presented in Appendix A, p. 129.)

The mean scores of the Anglophone and Francophone employees are presented in Figure 4. The Anglophones perceive themselves as being more under-utilized. This tendency is consistent with the findings of the study on importance of job outcomes. Anglophone employees attach relatively greater value to responsibility, independence and personal achievement at work, and do not find enough opportunity in their jobs to meet their need for autonomy and achievement.

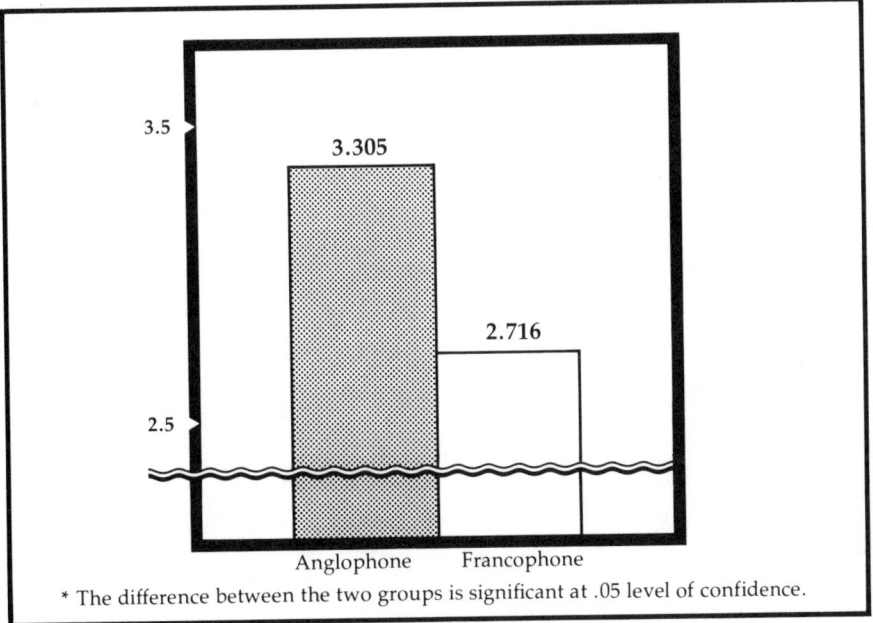

```
          3.5 ▸
                      3.305
                    ┌───────┐
                    │▓▓▓▓▓▓▓│
                    │▓▓▓▓▓▓▓│
                    │▓▓▓▓▓▓▓│       2.716
                    │▓▓▓▓▓▓▓│    ┌────────┐
                    │▓▓▓▓▓▓▓│    │        │
                    │▓▓▓▓▓▓▓│    │        │
          2.5 ▸     │▓▓▓▓▓▓▓│    │        │
        ~~~~~~~~~~~~│▓▓▓▓▓▓▓│~~~~│~~~~~~~~│~~~~
                    │▓▓▓▓▓▓▓│    │        │
                    └───────┘    └────────┘
                    Anglophone    Francophone
```
* The difference between the two groups is significant at .05 level of confidence.

Figure 4: *Perceived Ability in Relation to Job Demand (Job Enrichment Potential)**

Francophone employees, on the other hand, attach greater importance to job training. It is quite likely that Francophone employees see the possibility of accepting an upgraded job with additional job responsibility only where there is an opportunity of job training prior to such acceptance. A job with additional responsibility may pose a threat to their sense of security if they are to take charge of the job without appropriate prior training to develop their skills.

In summary, the study reveals some significant differences between Francophone and Anglophone employees working in organizations that operate in a bicultural environment. With regard to their motivational orientation, the Anglophone, in contrast to the Francophone employee, places more importance on job outcomes that satisfy salient personal autonomy and achievement needs. Francophone employees, on the other hand, put greater emphasis on job outcomes that satisfy salient security and affiliative needs. Such differences in the saliency of needs in these two culturally distinct groups also influence their sense of commitment, level of participation, and job enrichment potential.

CHAPTER 5

Job Satisfaction of English- and French-Canadian Employees

IN THE PREVIOUS CHAPTER it was emphasized that management must understand the salient needs of culturally different groups of employees in order to adopt the type of management practice that will satisfy needs of the various groups. Management practice, to be effective, should aim at increasing the satisfaction of employees' needs at work. When an employee experiences a high degree of satisfaction with job outcomes, he is less likely to remain absent from the job or look for other, more attractive jobs in other organizations. In other words, a high level of job satisfaction is a sign of organizational loyalty or of attraction of the job and the organization to the employee. Job dissatisfaction often leads to low productivity, grievances, strikes, absenteeism and turnover. Thus, it is important to measure job satisfaction of employees in the organization from time to time so that employee concerns that might cause future trouble can be detected early enough to take preventive action.

Satisfaction with Job Outcomes

Satisfaction with one's job depends on two factors: the quality and quantity of job outcomes, and one's expectations, values and perceptions of those outcomes. If an employee expects that he should not have a certain outcome, such as additional responsibility on the job, but finds that his job requires him to carry additional responsibility, he may experience less job satisfaction. On the other hand, if an employee feels that he should have additional responsibility and finds that his job provides him with such responsibility, then he may experience greater job satisfaction. Job satisfaction is determined by the difference between an employee's perception of his existing job outcomes and his beliefs or expectations about what those job outcomes should be (Lawler, 1971; Porter, 1961). When he feels satisfied, his job expectations are in line with his perceived job outcomes. However, a state of dissatisfaction with the job indicates that the perceived job outcomes do not match the employee's expectations. Since job satisfaction is partly a function of employee expectations or beliefs concerning job outcomes, it is quite conceivable that two employees holding the same job within an organization may have different job expectations and, consequently, will experience different levels of job satisfaction. The beliefs and expectations of employees regarding job outcomes and their feelings of job satisfaction are determined through a social comparison process (Festinger, 1954). Employees form opinions about what they should get from their jobs and how they should feel about their jobs by comparing themselves with members of the group to which they belong. Hence, differences among employees with respect to their job expectations and job satisfaction may primarily stem from the nature of their culture and reference groups (Korman, 1971).

This idea has been tested in the three different studies reported in this chapter. The studies deal with comparisons of levels of job satisfaction among Francophone and Anglophone employees. It is quite conceivable that Anglophone and Francophone employees, due to differences in their cultural background, may differ with respect to their need satisfactions on the job, given the same levels of job outcomes. The major question raised was what differences exist between the Francophone and Anglophone employees of a large corporation with respect to the satisfaction of various needs on the job.

The questionnaire to measure job satisfaction of employees used the same fifteen job outcomes as described earlier in connection with the perceived importance of job factors. There were seven organizationally-mediated outcomes (security, earning, fair pay, benefits, working conditions, chance of promotion, and company policy), four interpersonally-mediated outcomes (good peer relations, recognition, considerate supervision, and technical nature of supervision), and four internally-mediated outcomes (interesting work, responsibility and independence, achievement, and training opportunity). For each of these job outcomes, listed in random order, the employees were asked to indicate on a six-point scale their present level of satisfaction in their jobs.

The respondents were also asked to indicate their overall job satisfaction on a similar six-point scale. For the purpose of scoring the responses, ordinal weights 6 through 1 were assigned respectively to the six verbal levels on the scales: extremely satisfied, moderately satisfied, mildly satisfied, mildly dissatisfied, moderately dissatisfied, and extremely dissatisfied. (The questionnaire is presented in Appendix B, p. 137.)

The profiles of mean satisfaction scores for the Francophone and Anglophone employees are presented in Figure 5. The profiles reveal that both groups of employees show moderate levels of satisfaction with their job outcomes. This is to be expected in a healthy and thriving organization.

However, by looking at the profiles one can detect areas where relatively low levels of satisfaction are reported. Figure 5 reveals two such areas, promotion opportunities within the organization and salary (earnings and fair pay). It seems that management should attempt to improve employee satisfaction in these two areas by taking a closer look at existing policies.

Francophone employees, relative to Anglophones, seem to show a greater level of satisfaction with most of the job outcomes. The means for the Francophone employees are higher in the case of thirteen job outcomes. The mean differences are statistically significant in the case of nine

Organizationally-mediated outcomes

Security*

Earnings

Fair pay*

Benefits*

Working conditions

Chance of promotion*

Company policy*

Interpersonally-mediated outcomes

Good peer relations

Sympathetic supervision*

Technically competent supervision

Recognition*

Internally-mediated rewards

Interesting work*

Independence and responsibility*

Achievement

Opportunity to acquire skills*

Overall job satisfaction*

■——○ Anglophone   ●------● Francophone   * $p < .05$

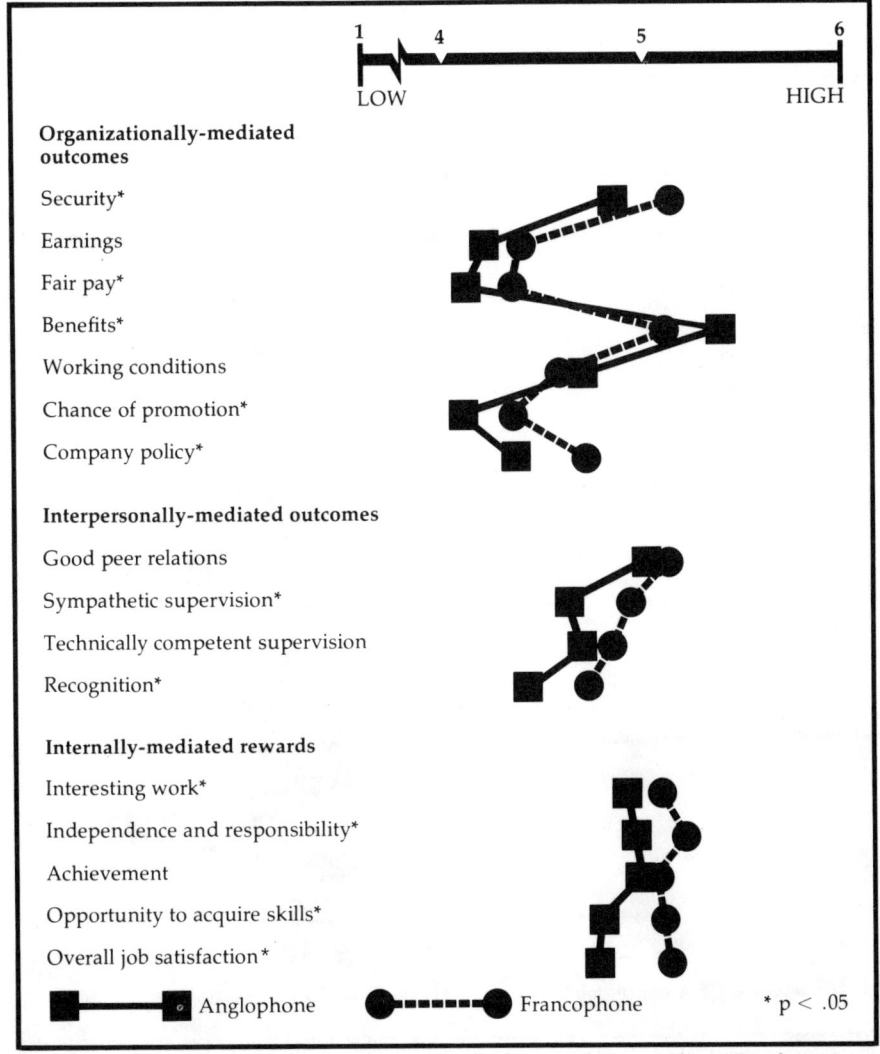

Figure 5: *Mean Satisfaction Profiles for Anglophone and Francophone Employees*

(security, company policy, promotion, fair pay, considerate supervision, recognition, interesting nature of work, autonomy, and training opportunity). The overall job satisfaction of Francophone employees is also significantly greater than that of Anglophone employees.

Very similar results were also obtained in two other studies. One of these studies dealt with the job satisfaction of 115 Anglophone and eighty-two Francophone managers of a large public service organization. Details of the study are reported elsewhere (Kanungo, 1975), but the results shown in Figure 6 indicate that Francophone managers reported a higher level of satisfaction with the various job outcomes, and also with the overall job, than did Anglophone managers. Another study that reported similar findings was conducted in Francophone and Anglophone hospital settings. Here again, the details of the study have been reported elsewhere (Jain, Normand and Kanungo, 1979), but the key results are presented in

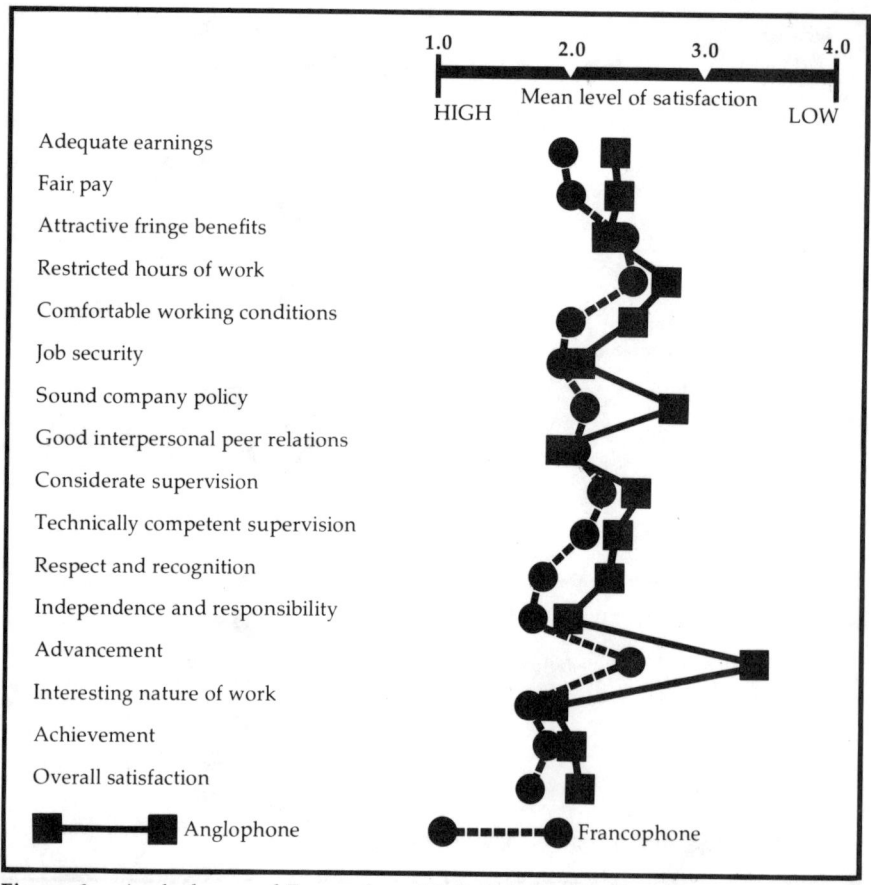

Figure 6: *Anglophone and Francophone Job Satisfaction Profile*

CHAPTER FIVE—JOB SATISFACTION 41

Figure 7. The mean scores of 108 Francophone employees again reveal higher levels of satisfaction with thirteen job outcomes and also with the overall job when compared to the mean scores of 102 Anglophone employees.

Thus, given similar job outcomes, whether in an industrial organization or a public-service organization, Francophone employees seem to experience greater satisfaction than do Anglophone employees. It seems that Francophone-Anglophone differences in job satisfaction can again be explained by cultural differences. Anglophones are more likely to be products of the Protestant ethic and the socialization process that places empha-

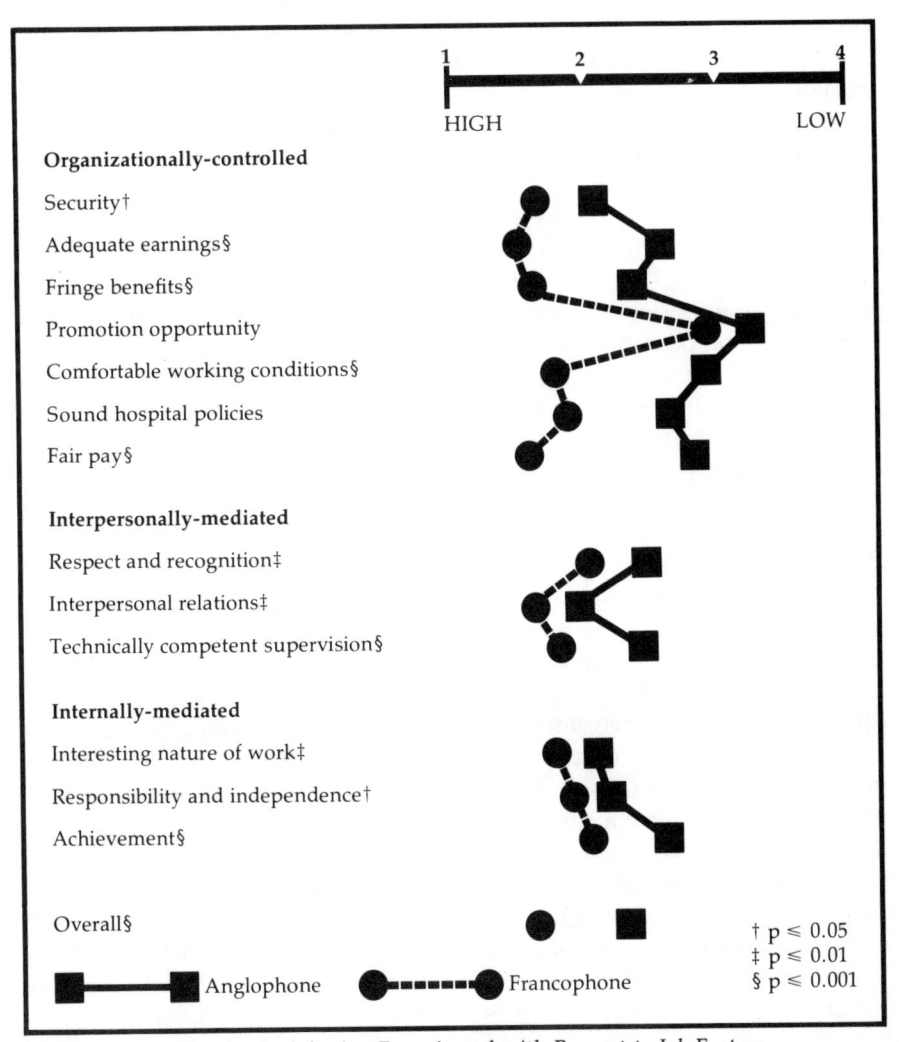

Organizationally-controlled

Security†
Adequate earnings§
Fringe benefits§
Promotion opportunity
Comfortable working conditions§
Sound hospital policies
Fair pay§

Interpersonally-mediated

Respect and recognition‡
Interpersonal relations‡
Technically competent supervision§

Internally-mediated

Interesting nature of work‡
Responsibility and independence†
Achievement§

Overall§

■————■ Anglophone   ●- - - -● Francophone

† $p \leq 0.05$
‡ $p \leq 0.01$
§ $p \leq 0.001$

Figure 7: *Profiles for Satisfaction Experienced with Respect to Job Factors*

sis on striving for more than one currently possesses. This may be reflected in less satisfaction with current job outcomes for Anglophone employees. The Catholic ethic and family-oriented training of Francophone employees, on the other hand, emphasize enjoyment of and contentment with whatever one has. This may be reflected in a higher level of job satisfaction.

The differences between the two groups in job satisfaction can also be explained in terms of different levels of expected job outcomes. Given the same levels of job outcomes offered by an organization, if one group of employees expects more of the outcomes than another group, then the former is bound to experience less job satisfaction than the latter. If satisfaction with job outcomes is a function of what one expects and what he actually gets (Spector, 1956), the present results suggest that Francophone employees perhaps expect lower job outcomes than Anglophone employees. There may be several reasons for these lower expectations. First, they may be a reflection of a lower level of need for achievement. Low-need achievers look for either very easy or very difficult goals for themselves, and the case of Francophone employees could be an instance of setting easy goals or low aspiration levels. In fact, McClelland (1961) has reported lower levels of need for achievement among Francophone children as compared to Anglophone children. Also, whereas the Anglophones place a high priority on personal success at work, the Francophones seem to frown on this idea. Their élite have tended to plead for collectivism rather than for individualism. Thus a Francophone employee may feel more satisfied with his job outcomes as long as he considers his outcomes equal to those of his coworkers. The Anglophone employee, on the other hand, seeks more or different job outcomes for himself, perhaps to distinguish himself from his coworkers and because he craves personal success. Such cravings may always keep Anglophone employees less satisfied with job outcomes.

Second, it must be emphasized that the differences in job satisfaction observed in these studies have to be understood within the larger context of the history of industrial development in Québec. Industry in the province has been established and controlled primarily by Anglophone-dominated organizations; the Francophones' experience with controlling their own organizations is recent. English is still used as the primary business language in most organizations and this has hindered Francophones in functioning more effectively in their jobs. Realizing that job success in Anglophone-dominated organizations is harder for them, Francophone employees may have developed lower expectations for job outcomes. Finally, perception of minority status in Canada may have caused lower expectations for job outcomes among Francophones. If Francophone employees have lower expectations for job outcomes, the reason may lie partly in the fact that they have never perceived these outcomes as attainable within the organization.

Turnover Potential

The turnover potential for employees is directly related to their job satisfaction. An employee who experiences satisfaction at work perceives his job and the organization as attractive, and therefore would prefer not to leave the job and the organization. Since Francophone employees show higher levels of job satisfaction than do Anglophones, it is expected that they will show lower turnover potential. In order to test this hypothesis, employees were asked to indicate on a four-point scale their chances of leaving the organization. The results are presented in Figure 8. The mean scores of the Francophone group suggest that their probability of staying in the organization is significantly greater than that of the Anglophone group. This finding can be explained in three ways. First, as suggested above, the lower turnover potential of Francophones may stem from their higher levels of job satisfaction. They are happier in their jobs than are the Anglophones, and hence do not look elsewhere. The second reason for their lower turnover potential may be due to the fact that Francophones find their choices of other jobs somewhat limited because of the language barrier. Anglophone employees do not face language problems, and thus find a wider job market in Canada and the United States. Francophone employees, on the other hand, may feel more secure staying in Québec, since they will less frequently find a language problem at work where they will have

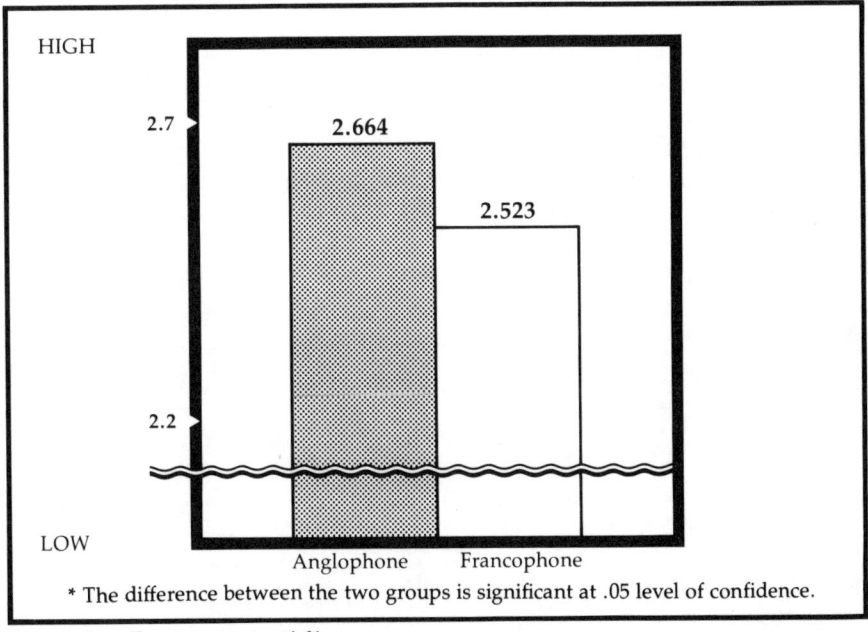

* The difference between the two groups is significant at .05 level of confidence.

Figure 8: *Turnover potential**

Francophone co-workers. In fact, Francophone employees may feel that due to their language barrier they would be less effective outside Québec, and such a feeling may discourage them from looking for work elsewhere.

Finally, higher turnover potential among Anglophone employees could stem from the personal achievement or success orientation of the Anglophones and the security and affiliative orientation of the Francophones. It is likely that an Anglophone employee would move from job to job or from one organization to another to seek his individual goals of autonomy and personal success. The more security conscious and affiliative Francophone employees, on the other hand, will be less inclined to engage in job-hopping. Instead, they will be more prone to seek and settle in work surroundings which are stable and socially pleasant.

CHAPTER 6

Job Involvement of English- and French-Canadian Employees

THE MAJOR TASK of every manager in an organization is to ensure that its employees put their best efforts into their jobs. It is not always easy to accomplish this task successfully. Very often a manager is faced with the problem of "alienation" among workers. This feeling of alienation seems to develop from two important characteristics of modern organizations. First, there is a trend towards an increase in the size of organizations, which demands greater coordination and supervision of workers. Managers tend to respond to these demands by establishing a formal bureaucratic structure with rigid rules and procedures. Such managerial actions often create in workers a feeling of impersonal control imposed from above, a feeling that their personal needs cannot be met by an entity which is perceived to be devoid of human qualities. Second, modern organizations have not only grown in size, but have also adopted mass-production techniques involving extensive mechanization of jobs. Management overemphasis on job specialization and job simplification has made work more monotonous and boring. Under these conditions, it is not surprising that workers are not only alienated from the organization, but also alienated from their own jobs.

Generally, alienated workers are less productive because they put in less effort on the job. In order to make them more productive, managers have to first identify the alienated workers and then create job conditions which will lead them to change their attitude. In a bicultural or multicultural context, an organization may have employees coming from different cultural backgrounds, which generate in the employees different need patterns and job attitudes. Thus it is possible that the job attitudes of culturally distinct groups of employees may show varying degrees of job alienation or involvement. It is the task of a manager to identify such attitudes and respond to them by developing appropriate personnel policies.

In this chapter, the attitudes of job alienation and involvement of Anglophone and Francophone employees are compared. However, before presenting the results and implications of the study, it may be helpful to understand the concepts of job alienation and involvement as they have been used in past research, and in this study.

The Concepts of Job Involvement and Job Alienation

The terms "job alienation" and "job involvement" have been used so often and in such widely differing contexts that they have acquired an aura of equivocality. As Seeman (1971) points out, the concept of alienation has been "popularly adopted as the signature of the present epoch. It has become routine to define our troubles in the language of alienation and to seek solutions in those terms. But signatures are sometimes hard to read, sometimes spurious, and sometimes too casually and promiscuously used. They ought to be examined with care." (p. 135) Similar concern has been expressed by Johnson (1973), who characterizes the concept of alienation as being capable of carrying a great deal of feeling "in an inexplicit, perplexing and deeply annoying way." (p. 28) Although in recent years many psychologists and sociologists have made several attempts to more clearly define the concept (Lawler and Hall, 1970; Lodahl and Kejner, 1965; Saleh and Hosek, 1976; Seeman, 1971; Vroom, 1962), none of them seems to offer a scientifically organized and meaningful view of the concept that could have broader cross-cultural generality. While most of the researchers try to explain the phenomena of alienation and involvement in social-psychological terms (Clark, 1959; Lawler and Hall, 1970; Seeman, 1959), the language they have used seems to have created more confusion than clarity. Sociological and psychological explanations seem to run parallel courses of their own without any serious attempt to develop an integral explanation. In fact, if one puts together the various explanations of the phenomena advanced by sociologists and psychologists, one ends up with greater conceptual fuzziness rather than understanding. If we take seriously Seeman's call for a careful and more rigorous examination of the concept, we ought to seek a clearer formulation of the issue.

Although work alienation as a psychological state of the individual (or as a collective social phenomenon) has been recognized for centuries, the scientific treatment of the concept with regard to its nature and its effect was attempted first by empirically-oriented sociologists and, more recently, by social psychologists. Thus the concept has lived through two distinct empirical traditions—the sociological and the psychological. In the following section, an overview of these two kinds of approaches is presented.

The Sociological Approach   The contributions of sociologists in explaining the nature of job alienation have been extensive and may be found in the writings of Marx, Weber, and Durkheim. Although Rousseau was the first to provide a sociological treatment of the concept, it was Marx, and later Weber, who put the concept on firmer analytical ground. The evidence of their powerful influence still persists in the works of contemporary sociologists (Seeman, 1959, 1971).

According to Marx (1844), labor is the "existential activity of man, his free conscious activity—not a means of maintaining his life but for developing his universal nature." Ideally, a state of work involvement results when the work situation elicits job behavior that is perceived to be (a) voluntary, (b) not instrumental in satisfying basic physical needs, (c) instrumental in satisfying the Maslow-type (1954) higher order needs, such as the need for self-realization or self-actualization, and (d) conducive to developing individuals' abilities to their fullest potential. In the absence of such perceptions, the individual worker is bound to experience alienation from work. According to Marx, most work set-ups provide conditions that alienate rather than involve workers. Marx identified two of these conditions: (a) separation of workers from the product of their labor, and (b) separation of workers from the means of production. The first implies that the product is perceived as not belonging to the worker. The worker also perceives that he cannot influence the disposition or quality of the product. Thus, he lacks a sense of ownership and control over the product and its quality. The second implies that the worker perceives a lack of control over the functioning of machines and other means of production. Finding that he has no control over his life, an individual's working life becomes separated from the rest of his existence (over which, Marx assumes, he has complete control).

It thus becomes obvious that it is the lack of autonomy and control of one's on-the-job behavior and its effects that defines the Marxian concept of job alienation. In motivational terms, it is clear that Marx intended to measure worker alienation in terms of the satisfaction of the ego needs for independence, achievement, and power. In the Marxian formulation, the role of other human needs (such as physical and social needs) has been completely disregarded, as if they exert almost no influence in causing states of alienation. This interpretation may appear oversimplified, but it is clearly reflected in the following quotation from Marx (1844): "What constitutes alienation of labor? First, that work is *external* to the worker, that it is not part of his nature; and that, consequently, he does not fulfill himself in his work but denies himself, has a feeling of misery rather than well-being, does not develop freely his mental and physical energies but is physically exhausted and mentally debased. The worker therefore feels himself at home only during his leisure time, whereas at work he feels homeless. His work is not voluntary but imposed, forced labor. It is not the satisfaction of a need, but only a means for satisfying other needs." Marx emphasizes the worker's experience of frustration of his needs for autonomy and control at work; whenever these needs are frustrated, work becomes external to the worker's self.

According to Marx, job behavior can be either instrumental activity which satisfies basic physical human needs (a means to an end), or it can be consummatory activity (an end in itself). Theories of human motivation suggest that human behavior is purposive; it has directionality, it is initiated by needs; and it is always instrumental in satisfying these needs. An individual's job behavior is also purposive; it is aimed at satisfying both extrinsic and intrinsic needs (Lawler, 1973). Marx sees job behavior as an end in itself (reflecting a state of involvement), but he does not recognize the fact that such behavior is also instrumental in satisfying a set of intrinsic human needs.

Weber's treatment of the concept of alienation is very similar to Marx's. As Gerth and Mills (1946) put it, "Marx's emphasis upon the wage worker as being 'separated' from the means of production becomes, in Weber's perspective, merely one special case of a universal trend. The modern soldier is equally 'separated' from the means of violence; the scientist from the means of enquiry, and the civil servant from the means of administration [p. 50]." Weber's exposure to the American way of life (political democracy and economic capitalism) and his study of the Protestant religion convinced him that the spirit of the Protestant work ethic is the key to the fullest realization of man's potential. He was impressed by the "grandiose efficiency of a type of man, bred by free associations in which the individual had to prove himself before his equals, where no authoritative commands, but autonomous decisions, good sense, and responsible conduct train for citizenship [p.18]." Like Marx, Weber also emphasized the freedom to make one's own decisions, assuming personal responsibility and proving one's worth through achievement at work. When translated into motivational terms, this would imply that if the work set-up cannot provide an environment for the satisfaction of the needs for individual autonomy, responsibility, and achievement, it will create a state of alienation in the worker.

Unlike Marx and Weber, who viewed alienation as resulting primarily from perceived lack of freedom and control at work, Emile Durkheim, the French sociologist, saw it as a consequence of a condition of *anomie* or the perceived breakdown or lack of socially approved means and norms to guide one's job behavior for the purpose of achieving organizationally prescribed goals (Blauner, 1964, Durkheim, 1893; Shephard, 1971). The condition of *anomie* is often considered to be a post-industrial phenomenon. As Blauner (1964) observes, industrialization and urbanization of modern society has "destroyed the normative structure of a more traditional society and uprooted people from the local groups and institutions which had provided stability and security [p. 24]." No longer able to feel a sense of security and belonging, we often find ourselves isolated from others. In its collective form this social alienation manifests itself in various kinds of urban and industrial unrest. In social-psychological terms, this variant of alienation seems to stem from the frustration of man's need to belong to groups for purposes of social approval and social comparison (Festinger, 1954; Maslow, 1954).

The strong impact of Marx, Weber and Durkheim is quite evident in contemporary sociological writings. For instance, Dubin (1956) defines involvement as "central life interest." According to him, a job-involved person is one who considers work to be the most important part of his life, and engages in it as an end in itself. A job-alienated person, on the other hand, engages in work in a purely instrumental fashion and perceives work as providing financial resources for more important off-the-job activities. Faunce (1959) also defines job involvement as a commitment to a job where successful performance is regarded as an end in itself rather than as a means to some other end. For both Dubin and Faunce, the concepts of involvement and alienation are intimately related to the Protestant work ethic, the moral value of work and personal responsibility as conceived by Weber.

In an attempt to clarify the concept of alienation, Seeman (1959, 1971) has proposed five variants on the concept: powerlessness, meaninglessness, normlessness, isolation, and self-estrangement. According to Seeman, each variant refers to a different subjectively-felt psychological state of the individual, caused by different environmental conditions. Several other researchers, particularly Blauner (1964) and Shepard (1971), have used Seeman's classifications and have tried to provide operational measures of the different categories of work alienation. They have also suggested antecedent physical and social conditions that produce each state of alienation.

Alienation in the form of powerlessness in the most general sense refers to a perceived lack of control over important events affecting one's life. Seeman (1959) has used this variant to explain and describe man's alienation from the larger social order. An individual's inability to control and influence political systems, industrial economies or international affairs may create a sense of powerlessness in him. This feeling of powerlessness also has been observed in job situations. For instance, Shepard (1971) describes powerlessness at work as "the perceived lack of freedom and control on the job [pp. 13-14]." Blauner (1964) also expresses similar views when he states that "the non-alienated pole of the powerlessness dimension is freedom and control [p. 16]." According to Blauner, this type of alienation at work results from the mechanization process that controls the pace of work and thus limits a worker's free movements. If one analyzes the sociological concept of powerlessness in motivational terms, it becomes obvious that if a situation constantly frustrates an individual's needs for autonomy and control, it will create in him a state of alienation based on powerlessness.

The second type of alienation is identified as a cognitive state of meaninglessness. In such a state, the individual is unable to predict social situations and the outcomes of his own and others' behavior. In the work situation, such a state results from increasing specialization and division of labour. When the work process is broken down into simple, minuscule tasks, and when such tasks involve no real responsibility or decision-making, the worker is robbed of any sense of purpose. The job becomes meaningless for him. Meaninglessness of work may also result when the worker is not able to see the relation of his work to the total system of goals of the organization (Blauner, 1964; Shepard, 1971). In motivational terms, this would imply that continued frustration of an individual's needs for personal responsibility and for gaining greater competence on the job (by being more knowledgable about the environment in order to influence it) causes this type of alienation. (It may be noted that both the "powerlessness" and the "meaninglessness" interpretations of alienation reflect the Marxian belief that lack of control and freedom over the work process is the main cause of alienation.)

The two other forms of alienation suggested by Seeman (1959) have their roots in Durkheim's description of *anomie*. Alienation based on feelings of "normlessness" and "isolation" result from such perceived conditions of one's social environment. An individual may develop a sense of normlessness when he finds that previously approved social norms are no longer effective in guiding his behavior for the attainment of personal goals; in order to achieve given goals he has to engage in socially unapproved behavior. Finding that he can no longer share the normative system because of its ineffectiveness, he may develop norms of his own to guide his behavior. Since his norms are different from those of others, he may eventually perceive himself as being separate from society and its normative system. The dissociation of oneself from others results in the perception of social isolation. The dissociation of oneself from social norms results in normlessness or cultural estrangement. Alienation in the sense of social isolation and cultural estrangement refers to the perceived state of "loneliness" and "rootlessness" respectively (Seeman, 1971). These two variants of alienation are related, since they stem from the same basic condition of *anomie*.

States of loneliness and rootlessness have also been identified in work situations. Blauner (1964) for instance, suggests that these forms of social alienation may be manifested on the job due to the lack of social integration of the worker. When an organization does not provide the worker with any opportunity for developing a sense of membership or of belonging in the social system, the worker is bound to show a sense of isolation from the system and its goals. From a motivational point of view, the two variants of isolation and normlessness seem to be based on two different social needs of the individual. Continuous frustration of the membership or belonging need for the individual may be the crucial determinant of "isolation" alienation. The "normlessness" form of alienation, however, is determined by continued frustration of the social need to evaluate oneself through social comparison (Festinger, 1954). In the context of social influence theories, social psychologists (Jones and Gerard, 1967) have postulated two major kinds of influences exerted by groups on the individual; these are the normative and the informational social influences. By being a member of the group and by adhering to group norms, the individual fulfills his need to belong, to love, and to be loved by others. However, when the group norms are perceived to be too restrictive and in conflict with the individual's personal goals, they cease to influence him. The individual becomes "isolated" in relation to the group. He perceives himself as one who no longer belongs to the group and is no longer loved by others in the group. Such a psychological state can be identified as "isolation" alienation. The individual also depends on the group norms for evaluating his abilities and opinions (Festinger, 1954). Group norms generally provide him with information on how to behave and what is right or wrong. When the individual finds that these norms do not provide useful information for self-evaluation, he may separate himself from these norms and experience a state of normlessness. Thus, in terms of social influence theory, these variants of social alienation result from the failure of the groups to exercise normative and informational social influence.

The final variant of alienation proposed by sociologists is "self-estrangement." The characterization of this category of alienation has posed some problems. Seeman (1971) admits that it is an "elusive idea [p. 136]" but then goes on to operationalize it. According to Seeman, a person is self-estranged when he is engaged in activity that is not rewarding in itself, but is instrumental (a means to an end) in satisfying extrinsic needs such as the needs for money, security, etc. Following Seeman (1959), Shepard (1971) considers instrumental work orientation or the degree to which one works for extrinsic need satisfaction as an index for the self-estrangement type of alienation. Blauner (1964) suggests that a job encourages self-estrangement if it does not provide opportunity for expressing "unique abilities, potentialities, or personality of the worker [p. 26]." In motivational terms, Blauner's observation means that whenever the individual finds his environment lacking in opportunities for the satisfaction of the self-actualizing needs (Maslow, 1954) he experiences a state of self-estrangement. Following Marx, many contemporary sociologists believe that self-estrangement is the eventual result of all forms of alienation. Blauner (1964) attests to this belief in the following remark: "When work activity does not permit control [powerlessness], evoke a sense of purpose [meaninglessness], or encourage larger identification [isolation], employment becomes simply a means to the end of making a living [p. 3]."

It may be helpful to identify some dominant considerations that have guided most sociological treatments of the concept of work alienation.

First, sociologists have been more concerned with states of alienation within organizations and consequent organizational unrest than they have with the identification of conditions for organizational involvement and personal growth on the job. Like Freudian psychologists who attempt to explain human nature through an analysis of pathological psychological states, sociologists, taking the lead from Marx, have emphasized the analysis of alienation and resulting pathological states to explain the nature of social systems. Just as Freudian influence in psychology delayed the formulation of growth theories of personality and motivation (Maslow 1954; Allport, 1961), the Marxian influence in sociology may have retarded the progress of sociological understanding of the nature of healthy and growing organizations. (As we will see later, current psychological approaches focus on the positive side through the study of involvement.)

Second, most sociological analysis of alienation has been at the social system level rather than at the individual level. This has created measurement problems. Although sociologists often talk of the growth of volatile activism, strikes, crime rates, etc., as indices of work alienation, they find it very hard to establish and theoretically justify the validity and the reliability of their figures. Very often incidents of activism, crime, and strikes go unreported. Even if the incidents are recorded accurately, it is often difficult to infer from these data states of alienation in individual members. For instance, an activist employee, in his desire to bring about changes in the organization, may be showing signs of greater involvement in the social system than does an apathetic conformist.

Third, sociological approaches generally describe the state of alienation not in specific behavioral terms, but in terms of "epiphenomenal categories." As Johnson (1973) points out, alienation is seen as *"an epiphenomenal abstraction,* collectively summarizing a series of specific behaviors and categorising them as 'loneliness,' 'normlessness,' 'isolation,' etc. [p. 40]." Such descriptions may have a flavor of intellectual romanticism, but they have very little scientific value, since they pose problems of empirical verification. The concept of alienation as an epiphenomenal abstraction tends to carry excess meaning and therefore eludes precise measurement. Such an abstraction describes but does not explain alienation.

Finally, most sociological approaches consider the presence of employee autonomy, control, and power over the work environment as basic preconditions for removing alienation.

The Psychological Approach   Interest in this area among psychologists is very recent, and they have essentially taken an empirical (and exploratory) approach to the study of the problem. Psychological theories to explain the phenomenon of alienation are simply absent from the literature. Furthermore, in contrast to the sociological approach, psychologists have attempted to analyze the nature of alienation only in the limited context of job situations. Unlike sociologists, psychologists have attempted to define and measure job involvement rather than alienation.

In trying to explain the nature of job involvement, psychologists have concentrated on the analysis of specific motivational states of the individual in work situations. Psychological explanations are based on motivation theories and therefore tend to emphasize the need-satisfying qualities of the job as basic determinants of job involvement. For instance, Vroom (1962) has proposed that when a person satisfies his needs for self-esteem through his job, it leads to job involvement. In his study, the degree of job involvement for a particular person was measured by "his choice of 'ego' rather than extrinsic factors in describing the sources of satisfaction and dissatisfaction on the job [p. 161]." Vroom seems to have emphasized intrinsic need satisfaction as the essential condition for higher job involvement. In his view, with higher autonomy extended to the individual, higher ego involvement results, which in turn leads to a higher level of job performance.

Lodahl and Kejner (1965) have proposed two definitions of job involvement. The first definition states that "job involvement is the degree to which a person is identified psychologically with his work, or the importance of work in his total self image [p. 24]." Such a psychological identification with a job may result partly from early socialization during which the individual may internalize the value of goodness of work. Lodahl and Kejner (1965) have recognized this possibility. They state that the concept of job involvement "operationalizes the 'Protestant ethic' and because it is a result of the introjection of certain values about work into the self, it is probably resistant to changes in the person due to the nature of a particular job [p. 25]." They also provide a second definition of job involvement: "the degree to which a person's work performance affects his self-esteem [p. 25]." These two definitions are quite distinct, and Lodahl and Kejner have made no attempt in their study to show how the two are related. In fact, the questionnaire measure of job involvement developed by Lodahl and Kejner includes items reflecting both definitions. Use of their questionnaire in job involvement research therefore provides data that are hard to interpret.

Recently Rabinowitz and Hall (1977) have critically reviewed the work of several researchers who have made use of the above-mentioned definitions of job involvement. Their review clearly suggests that there is a great deal of confusion and ambiguity in job involvement theory. Furthermore, as they point out, "the confusion does not stop at the theoretical level, but rather continues in the empirical studies of involvement [p. 267]."

Weisenberg and Gruenfeld (1962) have investigated the relationship between satisfaction with various job factors and job involvement. They conclude that increased job involvement is positively related to satisfaction with motivators or job-content factors (Herzberg, 1966) such as achievement, responsibility, independence etc. These motivators tend to satisfy the intrinsic needs of the individual. The extrinsic needs, however, are satisfied through the job-context factors such as company policies, nature of supervision, salary, benefits, and working conditions. According to these researchers, satisfaction with the job-context factors is unrelated to job involvement, but the latter can be predicted from the satisfaction with the motivators in the job.

Lawler and Hall (1970) distinguished for the first time the psychological state of job involvement from two psychological states of the worker, intrinsic motivation on the job and job satisfaction. A state of intrinsic motivation exists in a worker when his intrinsic needs (such as the need to achieve or the need to feel important at the work place) are satisfied through appropriate job behavior (succeeding in a job related task). A state of job satisfaction however can result when any need, intrinsic or extrinsic, of the worker can be met through the availability of job outcomes (such as a Christmas bonus) that may or may not depend on job behavior. Thus, intrinsic motivation in the worker results only when satisfaction of intrinsic needs are contingent upon appropriate job behavior, whereas, job satisfaction can result through the attainment of sought after job rewards that are not necessarily contingent on appropriate job behavior. Lawler and Hall argue in favor of the definition of job involvement suggested by Lodahl and Kejner (1965) based on psychological identification with work, or the importance of work to one's total self-image. In general Lawler and Hall suggest that job involvement refers to the "degree to which a person's total work situation is an important part of his life. The job-involved person is one who is affected very much personally by his whole job situation, presumably because he perceives his job as an important part of his self-concept and perhaps as a place to satisfy his important needs (e.g., his need for self-esteem) [p. 310-311]." It appears that in defining the concept of involvement, Lawler and Hall assume that intrinsic or growth needs (Alderfer, 1972) are central to the self-concept of the individual. To emphasize the centrality of intrinsic needs, they point out that "the more the job is seen to allow the holder to influence what goes on, to be creative, and to use his skills and abilities, the more involved he will be in the job [p. 310]." In the same article, Lawler and Hall reiterate their position: "other things being equal, more people will become involved in a job that allows them control and a chance to use their abilities than will become involved in jobs that are lacking these characteristics [p. 311]."

Patchen (1970) has identified three general conditions for job involvement. According to him, "where people are highly motivated, where they feel a sense of solidarity with the enterprise, and where they get a sense of pride for their work, we may speak of them as highly 'involved' in their job [p. 7]." When Patchen talks of workers being highly motivated, he refers to their high levels of achievement need or their wish to accomplish worthwhile things on the job. When he talks of workers' solidarity with the enterprise, he refers to their need for belonging to the organization. Finally, when he talks of workers' sense of pride, he refers to their feeling of high self-esteem. Thus, in Patchen's view, when a job provides opportunities for the satisfaction of one's achievement needs, belonging needs, and self-esteem needs, one experiences a greater degree of job involvement.

In a recent review of the psychological literature on job involvement, Rabinowitz and Hall (1977) have stressed the fact that among other things, a job-involved person believes strongly in the Protestant ethic, has strong growth needs and has a stimulating job that gives him a high degree of autonomy and opportunity for participation (p. 284).

In another review of the psychological literature on job involvement, Saleh and Hosek (1976) identified four different interpretations of the concept of involvement. "A person is involved (1) when work to him is a central life interest; (2) when he actively participates in his job; (3) when he perceives performance as central to his self-esteem; (4) when he perceives performance as consistent with his self-concept [p. 215]." The first interpretation of the concept of involvement in terms of "central life interest" (Dubin, 1956) is very similar to that offered by Lawler and Hall (1970). This interpretation holds that the psychological state of involvement with respect to an environmental entity (such as job, family, etc.) is a *cognitive* or perceived state of identification with that entity. The second interpretation of involvement in terms of participation suggests that the psychological state of involvement be viewed as *behavioral acts* of the individual directed toward the satisfaction of his needs for autonomy and control. Bass (1965), for instance, considers participative job behaviors such as making important job decisions, setting one's own work pace, etc., to be important indices of greater work involvement. The remaining two interpretations—providing a sense of personal worth (Siegel, 1969) and reinforcing one's self-concept (Vroom, 1964)—suggest that involvement may be viewed as the experience of satisfaction resulting from the fulfilment of an individual's self-esteem and self-actualizing needs. From the results of their own factor-analytic work, Saleh and Hosek have concluded that job involvement is "the degree to which the person identifies with the job, actively participates in it, and considers his performance important to his self-worth. It is, therefore, a complex concept based on cognition, action and feeling [p. 223]." (It is interesting to note that in order to achieve conceptual clarity Lawler and Hall (1970) tried to distinguish the state of involvement from intrinsic motivation and job satisfaction, but Saleh and Hosek have brought them together again.)

There is one common thread running through all the psychological formulations outlined above. All of them seem to emphasize the fact that job situations lacking in opportunity for the satisfaction of the intrinsic needs of the individual, such as self-esteem, achievement, autonomy, control, self-expression and self-actualization, will decrease the individual's involvement in the job. Even the recent studies on "central life interest" in work settings, organizational identification and organizational commitment (Dubin, Champoux and Porter, 1975; Hall and Schneider, 1972; Hall, Schneider and Nygren, 1970) reflect a similar bias. It seems as if lack of intrinsic need satisfaction is the basic condition for increasing work alienation. In this regard, the psychologists seem to have followed the sociological tradition of considering the lack of individual freedom, power, and control as necessary preconditions of the psychological state of alienation.

Sources of confusion surrounding the concepts The most common source of confusion in the literature on alienation and involvement is the application of the concepts to specific individuals and sometimes to groups of individuals. Particularly in sociological writings, one finds the concept of alienation sometimes used to describe the psychological state of the individual and at other times to describe pathological states of large groups, organizations, and other socio-political systems. As Johnson (1973) correctly points out, "there is a difference in meaning between these two applications that is not merely the difference between singular and plural categories. The phenomenology and the meaning connected with individual states of alienation are different both in quality and significance from those connected with the social, interactional, and collective applications of the term [p. 35]." For example, to say that a worker is alienated can suggest an instance of *collective experience* of workers' alienation as reflected in absenteeism, tardiness, goldbricking, sabotage etc., that results from the prevailing social and physical conditions (mechanization, impersonal control through rules and regulations, etc.) within the organization, or it can suggest an individual worker's personal view of his work that does not meet his salient needs (unique to the individual) regardless of how other workers view the situation. From a methodological standpoint, it is advisable to approach the study of alienation at the personal rather than the collective level of experience. Measurement and interpretation of the collective experience of alienation are often difficult and confusing.

A second source of confusion stems from the fact that the concept of alienation has been described and measured in two different ways. Sometimes the term alienation is used to imply *objective social conditions directly observed by others and later attributed to individuals and groups*. Blauner (1964), for instance, considers mechanization and division of labour to be the alienating conditions, and people working under these conditions are assumed to be experiencing alienation. At other times, alienation has been interpreted as *a subjective psychological state of the individual not detectable to outsiders but felt by the individual himself*. Such a difference in the usage of the term has obvious implications for the operationalization of the concept.

States of alienation measured through identification of objective conditions may not parallel the subjective measures of the concept. Mechanization and division of labour in an organization may be viewed by external observers as necessarily contributing to a state of alienation of the worker (powerlessness), but the worker may not perceive the situation in the same way. In fact, it is quite conceivable that for some workers (mentally or physically handicapped, unskilled, uneducated), mechanization and division of labour may actually increase their job involvement.

A third source of confusion results from a failure to maintain the conceptual distinction between the *antecedent conditions* of alienation and the *consequent states* of alienation. Here the confusion results from mistaking the cause as the effect. As Josephson and Josephson (1973) remark: "Durkheim's notion of anomie or normlessness can be regarded as an important *cause* of alienation but should not be confused with alienation as a state of mind . . . By the same token, alienation should not be confused with 'social disorganization,' since estrangement may be found in highly organized bureaucracies [p. 166]." In spite of such warnings, both the sociological and the psychological formulations bear the evidence of neglecting to maintain the distinction between alienating conditions and alienating states. In fact, most empirical researchers have attempted to measure the state of alienation through indices of alienating conditions, as if the two were equivalent. For instance, Seeman (1959) considered "normlessness" as the perception of a social situation where rules and norms which regulate behavior have broken down. Such perceptions may be the antecedent conditions of the alienated state, but they cannot be identified with the state itself. Similarly, "isolation," "meaninglessness" and "powerlessness" may describe different conditions or causes of alienation, but should not be equated with it. Even when self-estrangement is measured by Blauner (1964), he uses several indices of alienating job conditions, such as whether the job meets the worker's achievement needs. Shepard (1971) also measures different forms of alienation by measuring conditions such as whether the job provides opportunity for participation and control, information on how the job fits into the total operation of the organization, and the like. Clearly these kinds of questions probe into the assumed conditions or causes of alienation rather than the state of alienation itself. In the psychological literature similar confusion may be noted. For instance, Saleh and Hosek (1976) have proposed a measure of three distinct categories of job involvement. The first directly measures the state of alienation ("The most important things I do are involved with my job"). The second indexes the antecedent conditions or presumed causes of alienation ("How much chance do you get to do things your own way?"). Finally, a third category measures worker behavior and experiences that often (but not necessarily) result from the alienated state ("I avoid taking on extra duties and responsibilities in my work"). Thus, Saleh and Hosek (1976) combine indices of causal conditions and effects of alienating states into one single instrument. Such an instrument can not provide meaningful data on the state of alienation of the worker. Both for conceptual clarity and effective methodology in empirical studies, the state of alienation needs to be identified and measured separately from its causes and its effects.

Confusion also results from the description of the state of alienation as being a *cognitive* as well as an *affective* state. Most researchers have found it difficult to separate the concept of alienation from its negative affect. Traditionally, alienation is associated with negative emotional states such as anger, dissatisfaction, and unpleasantness, and involvement is associated with positive emotional states such as satisfaction and pleasantness. Many measures of alienation or involvement therefore contain items reflecting levels of satisfaction or dissatisfaction (for example, "The major satisfaction in my life comes from my job" in Lodahl and Kejner, 1965). Recent empirical studies (Lawler and Hall, 1970; Seeman, 1971) have clearly suggested that work involvement and job satisfaction are not the same, although they may be related to one another. It may be more useful to think of the states of involvement or alienation as cognitive or belief states of identity or dissociation (separateness) rather than psychological states necessarily associated with feelings of satisfaction or dissatisfaction. A cognitive state of dissociation may or may not accompany positive or negative affects under certain conditions. A highly involved worker may, under some conditions, feel a high level of satisfaction with his work while under other conditions he may experience deep dissatisfaction. In future, empirical research should identify conditions under which involvement and alienation are related to positive, negative and neutral affective states.

Finally, some ambiguity in the concept of alienation has resulted from confusing two kinds of causation: *contemporaneous* and *historical*. Sometimes a state of alienation in an individual is viewed as the result of the past history of the individual. For instance, Lodahl and Kejner (1965) have suggested that an individual's work involvement is determined by the early socialization process during which he internalizes the values of goodness of work or the Protestant ethic. In this sense, alienation from or involvement with work becomes a stable characteristic of the individual which he carries with him from one situation to another. Sociologists have viewed the historical causation of alienation in a slightly different way. Following Marx, many sociologists have considered job experience as being central to an individual's life. According to them, the long-standing social arrangements of technology, division of labour, and capitalist property institutions have created a state of alienation from work (Blauner, 1964). Since work is central to one's life, alienation from work necessarily leads to alienation from all other aspects of life. As Seeman (1971) puts it, "Perhaps the most important thesis concerns the centrality of work experience, the imputation being that alienation from work 'is the core of all alienation' and that the consequences of alienated labor color the life space of the individual in a profound and disturbing way [p. 135]." The state of alienation is also seen as being caused by contemporaneous events. For instance, Lawler and Hall (1970) have considered the job-involved person as one who is "affected very much by his whole job situation, presumably because he perceives his job as an important part of his self-concept and perhaps as a place to satisfy his important needs (e.g., his need for self-esteem) [p. 310-311]." These authors consider the worker's present perceptions of the need-satisfying potential of the job as a major determinant of the state of involvement. From the foregoing discussion, it is apparent that states of alienation from or involvement with family, religion or work may result from historical or contemporaneous events. Through the socialization process (cumulative learning and experience of the past) the individual may develop a set of relatively stable beliefs and values regarding work, family, etc., and later experiences may either reinforce or modify them.

Toward a Motivational Theory of Job Involvement

The following is a description of a conceptual motivational approach that can be used to study the pheonomena of job alienation and involvement. It uses existing motivational language to explain work alienation and involvement for two basic reasons. First, theories of human motivation (Maslow, 1954; Lawler, 1973) are generally advanced to explain all work behavior, including alienation or involvement. Second, while the existing motivational constructs can adequately explain work alienation, the explanation lies hidden in many of the sociologial and psychological formulations discussed earlier, and a clearer motivational formulation of the pheonomena is needed.

In defining the state of work alienation, this approach is limited to the analysis of the behavioral phenomenon at the individual level. The state of alienation is a cognitive belief state of the individual. As a cognitive state, work alienation becomes conceptually distinct from many associated covert feelings (affective states of the individual expressed in terms of satisfaction or dissatisfaction experienced on the job), and overt behavior (job participation, assuming responsibility, etc.). Emphasis is placed on clearly distinguishing the state of work alienation from its causes (antecedent conditions) and its effects (consequent conditions). Alienation is seen as being caused by historical and contemporaneous events. The fact that the cognitive state of work alienation has significant effects on subsequent job behavior and job attitudes is also stressed. This approach can integrate and adequately explain within its own framework the different types of work alienation suggested by sociologists.

It may be argued that the concepts of "alienation" and "involvement" should not be reduced to a single dimension, since they represent two distinct types of behavioral phenomena. Alienation has been described by sociologists at a collective level (alienation of labor, an alienated society etc.) while involvement has been identified by psychologists at the individual level (an involved worker). A closer scrutiny of the issue, however, reveals that even when sociologists describe the concept of "alienation" at a collective level, they try to explain it in terms of psychological states of individuals. A number of empirical sociological studies on alienation (Blauner, 1964; Seeman, 1971; Shepard, 1971) attest to this fact. If one considers both alienation and involvement as states of the individual, it would be helpful to consider both the concepts as representing a single dimension.

Definitions of the concepts In this approach, work involvement is viewed as a generalized cognitive (or belief) state of psychological identification with work, insofar as work is perceived to have the potential to satisfy one's salient needs and expectations. Similarly, work alienation can be viewed as a generalized cognitive (or belief) state of psychological separation from work, insofar as work is perceived to lack the potential for satisfying one's salient needs and expectations. Thus, the degree of involvement at work should be directly measured in terms of an individual's cognition of his identification with work. The individual's identification with his work depends on two things: the saliency or importance of his needs (both extrinsic and intrinsic) and the perceptions he has about the need-satisfying potential of his work.

Conditions of job involvement A schematic representation of this motivational approach to job involvement, its causes and its effects, is presented in Figure 9. An individual's on-the-job behavior and attitudes are a function of the saliency of the need states within him. At any given moment, the need saliency within the individual depends on the prior socialization process (historical causation) and the perceived potential of the job to satisfy the needs (contemporary causation). The cognitive state of involvement as a by-product of need saliency also depends on the nature of need saliency as historically determined through the socialization process, and the perceived potential of the job to satisfy the needs. Thus, an individual's belief that he is work-involved or job-alienated depends on whether he perceives work as having the potential for satisfying his salient needs. The importance of different needs for the individual is determined by his past experiences with groups of which he was a member (socialization process) and with jobs which he has held. Different groups of people are influenced by different cultural, group, and organizational norms, and tend to develop different need structures or set different goals and objectives for their lives. For example, the work motivation literature suggests that the sources of work involvement for white-collar workers within any organization may be very different from those of the blue-collar workers because of the differences in the need saliencies of the two groups. White-collar workers may value more autonomy and control in their jobs, whereas the blue-collar workers may attach greater importance to security and the sense of belonging. Such value differences essentially stem from the past socialization process and from the influence of group norms.

The studies reported in Chapter 4 have demonstrated that because of differences in the socialization process, Francophone and Anglophone employees exhibit different patterns of need saliency at work. The salient needs tend to determine the central life interests of the individuals. On the job, the saliency of need in an individual is reinforced when he finds that

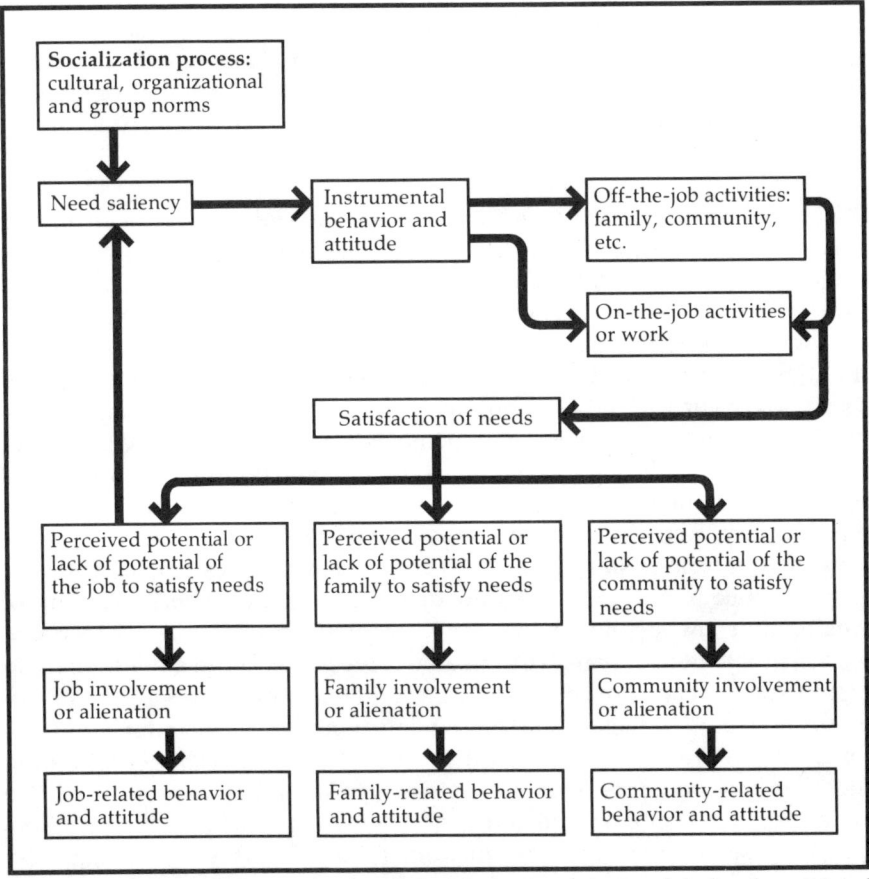

Figure 9: *Schematic Representation of the Motivational Approach to Involvement and Alienation*

through job behavior he is capable of meeting his needs. If he perceives that the job is capable of satisfying his important needs, he will devote most of his available energy to the job. He will immerse himself in the job and the feedback from his job behavior will lead him to believe that the job is an essential part of himself or that he is job-involved. If, however, the job is perceived by the individual as lacking in opportunities for the satisfaction of his salient needs, he will develop a tendency to withdraw his efforts from the job and will become alientated from it. For the satisfaction of his salient needs, he will redirect his energy by engaging in various off-the-job activities or in undesirable on-the-job activities.

Job involvement depends on both the past socialization process and the need-satisfying potential of the job environment. This seems to be supported by the work of several researchers (Rabinowitz and Hall, 1977). Some (Blood and Hulin, 1967; Hulin and Blood, 1968; Lodahl, 1964; Siegel, 1969) who have studied job involvement as an individual difference variable have proposed that job involvement has its roots in past socialization, while some (Argyris, 1964; Bass, 1965; McGregor, 1960) who have studied it as a function of the job situation have proposed that the root of involvement lies in the need-satisfying potential of the job environment.

Integration of sociological approach. The present approach can also be used to interpret the different types of work alienation suggested by sociologists (Blauner, 1964; Seeman, 1959). In terms of the present formulation, the "isolation" variant of alienation will be experienced by those individuals whose social and belonging needs are most salient and who find that their jobs do not have the potential to satisfy these needs. Blauner (1964) seems to concur with this position when he states that the state of isolation "implies the absence of a sense of membership in an industrial community [p. 24]." In Canada, the "isolation" type of alienation has been reported more often among French-Canadian workers than among English-Canadian workers, perhaps because, in the case of the former group, the necessary conditions for a state of isolation are present to a greater extent (salient affiliative needs of the French-Canadian workers and their perception of Anglophone ownership of industry). For very similar reasons, women workers may often experience a greater degree of isolation at work than do men workers. The "normlessness" and the "meaninglessness" variants of work alienation can be observed in persons who have a salient need for information to predict their physical and social work environment. Finding that their jobs do not provide the necessary information, they may begin to believe that their jobs are meaningless. Highly educated or skilled workers may have a strong need for information; if this information is lacking, they may have a stronger tendency to see their jobs as meaningless than do less educated or unskilled workers. Perhaps for similar reasons, the alienation of intellectuals tends to be of the "meaninglessness" type (Seeman, 1959; Mills, 1951). The "powerlessness" type of alienation may be experienced by individuals who have salient ego needs, such as the need for autonomy, control, and self-esteem, but who find the job environment incapable of satisfying them. Finally, the "self-estrangement" type of alienation may be experienced by people who have highly salient self-actualization needs, such as the need for achievement, and who find that their jobs limit the realization of their potential. Thus, from a motivational standpoint, the different types of alienation suggested by sociologists represent the same cognitive state of separation from an environmental entity; they are "different" only in the sense that they are caused by different needs in the individuals.

Some major differences between the present and the earlier approaches. Although the definitions of involvement and alienation as cognitive states of identification with work resemble the definitions of Lawler and Hall (1970), they differ in one important respect. As discussed earlier, Lawler and Hall put exclusive emphasis on the job opportunities that meet a worker's need for control and autonomy as necessary preconditions to the state of job involvement. In fact, all earlier formulations (both sociological and psychological) seem to follow this line of thinking. The present approach, however, suggests that job involvement does not necessarily depend on job characteristics that allow for control and autonomy need satisfaction. Workers have a variety of needs, some more salient than others. The saliency of the needs in any given individual is determined by his past socialization in a given culture (historical causes) and are constantly modified by present job conditions (contemporary causes). Different groups of individuals, because of their different socialization or different cultural background, may develop different need saliency patterns, and they may value extrinsic and intrinsic job outcomes (Lawler, 1973) very differently. This may result in different self-images in the two groups and, consequently, different job expectations among them. A group of workers that considers control and autonomy as the core of their self-image may get involved in jobs that are perceived as offering opportunity for exercising control and autonomy, while they may be alienated from jobs that are perceived as providing little freedom and control. Such job characteristics, however, may not be the crucial considerations for another group who may view security and social needs as the core of their self-concept. Citizens of the developed societies of the West may believe that all that counts in life is to have individual liberty, freedom and self-determination. Workers belonging to these societies may feel that work is of little worth without autonomy and control. In developing societies, however, economic and social security often are considered more important to life than are autonomy and control. Workers in these societies may find work very involving if it guarantees such security, but may not care very much for autonomy and control in their jobs. These people may value "equality" more than "liberty" as the guiding principle of working life. Rabinowitz and Hall (1977) have alluded to this possibility but could find no available research on "this lower-need-based form of job involvement [p. 280]."

In their attempts to increase job involvement among the workers, sociological (Blauner, 1964) and psychological (Lawler and Hall, 1970) approaches have analyzed the work situation from the standpoint of "job design" or the nature of the job. They have emphasized job characteristics such as the lack of variety in the job, mechanized and routine operations, strict supervision, etc., and their effects on the involvement of workers. There has been no attempt to understand the nature and the saliency of needs of workers. In presenting such a position, they have argued in favour of a universal prescription for increasing job involvement through designing jobs to provide greater autonomy and control to the workers, based on the assumption that these are salient needs in all workers. This position can be contrasted with the approach that Taylor (1911) advocated in his principles of scientific management. In his pig-iron loading experiment, he selected as his subject a physically strong individual who had a salient monetary need. In selecting the right man for the job, he looked into the past training and abilities, need saliency, and job perceptions of the worker. Obviously, Taylor thought that these characteristics have a significant influence on a worker's job involvement. The approach advocated in this chapter does not assume that the needs for control and autonomy are the most salient needs in all workers, but suggests that job involvement can be best understood if the nature and saliency of needs in workers as determined by prior socialization and present job conditions is ascertained. The design of jobs and the determination of their extrinsic and intrinsic outcomes for the sake of increasing job involvement should be based on an understanding of worker needs and perceptions. The findings of Lawler and Hackman (1971) seem to support this position: "There is no reason to expect job changes to affect the motivation and satisfaction of employees who do not value the rewards that their jobs have to offer [p. 52]."

Job involvement attitudes of English- and French-Canadian employees

In the previous chapters it was shown that Francophone and Anglophone employees exhibit different patterns of need saliency and different levels of need satisfaction. When two groups of employees with different salient needs and job expectations hold similar jobs in an organization, their perception of the potential of the job to satisfy salient needs—and their job involvement—will differ.

What is the nature of the difference in their job involvement attitudes? The question can be addressed from two theoretical stand-points. The sociological and psychological approaches to alienation that emphasize the importance of autonomy and control to the self-concept of workers, will suggest that, in the Canadian bicultural context, Anglophone employees, being products of a socialization process based on the Protestant ethic, will tend to value autonomy and achievement and show involvement on the job to a greater extent than do Francophone employees. On the other hand, the motivation approach to work involvement (as presented in Figure 9) will suggest that the two groups may or may not differ in their job involvement. When the two groups both perceive that their dominant needs are met by the job, they will be equally job-involved. Francophone employees would be expected to show greater job involvement when they perceive that the job leads to greater satisfaction of their salient needs for security and affiliation. Anglophone employees, on the other hand, would be expected to show greater job involvement when they find that the job meets their salient needs for autonomy and control. The results of the study described in Chapter 5 show that Francophone employees experience greater job satisfaction than do Anglophone employees, implying that Francophone employees perceive their job as having greater potential to satisfy their needs. On the basis of such results, it may be predicted that in the Canadian bicultural context, Francophone employees would experience greater job involvement than would Anglophone employees.

In order to test these predictions, a survey on job involvement was conducted in two large industrial organizations, both employing Anglophone and Francophone personnel. Data were collected through mailed questionnaires from a total of 325 Anglophone and 461 Francophone respondents belonging to the two organizations. In each organization, the response rate was above 72 percent. In administering the questionnaire, the employees were assured that their replies would be kept confidential and would be used only for research purposes. The general procedure used in the survey was quite similar to the procedure described in Chapter 4.

Job involvement of employees was measured by a questionnaire developed by Lodahl and Kejner (1965). The questionnaire, (in French and English) consisted of twenty items, each reflecting some aspects of an employee's involvement at work. For each item, the employees were asked to indicate their agreement or disagreement with it on a four-point "strongly agree" (ordinal weight 4) to "strongly disagree" (ordinal weight 1) scale. Higher scores reflected greater job involvement of employees. (The questionnaire is presented in Appendix C, p. 145.)

The validity of Lodahl and Kejner's twenty-item questionnaire as a measure of job involvement can be questioned on the grounds discussed earlier. However, the questionnaire is the most widely used and preferred measuring instrument currently available. It is considered quite reliable.

Reliability coefficients ranging from .72 to .89 have been reported by several researchers (see, for example, Saal, 1978). For the lack of a better measure of job involvement, the study used this instrument; in order to achieve a clear understanding of the respondents' scores on this questionnaire, scores on each item were analyzed separately.

The analysis of the demographic data revealed that the Anglophone and Francophone employees differed with respect to their tenure with the organization, salary and age. The Anglophone employees were older, had longer tenure, and received higher salaries. In view of the possibility that each of these demographic variables influenced job involvement, covariance analysis was employed to eliminate the effects of these variables while analyzing the differences in job involvement of the two groups.

The mean involvement scores of the two groups are presented in Figure 10. In the case of fifteen out of twenty items, the mean scores of Francophone employees are higher than those of Anglophone employees. Statistically significant differences between the two groups are revealed in the case of fourteen items. In ten of these, Francophone employees showed greater job involvement than did Anglophone employees. More Francophone employees say that their major satisfaction in life comes from work. This finding is consistent with the results discussed in Chapter 5 regarding job satisfaction. Furthermore, the Francophone employees consider work more important and more central to their life. They are personally more involved in their work than are Anglophone employees. They tend to judge people by their work and consider themselves as perfectionists at work. They also show stronger agreement with items such as "For me, mornings at work really fly by" and "I usually show up for work a little early to get things ready."

The Anglophone employees, on the other hand, show significantly stronger agreement on four of the items. They live, eat and breathe their jobs and are prepared to work even if they do not need more money. They seem to feel more responsible for their own mistakes and more depressed about their own failures.

Similar job involvement profiles on Francophone and Anglophone employees have been reported by Normand and Kanungo (1978). That study was conducted in two different hospitals and the sample consisted of 108 Francophone and 102 Anglophone employees. The mean job involvement scores of the two groups (controlling for other demographic differences between the groups) are presented in Figure 11. Here again, it may be observed that statistically significant differences are obtained for fifteen out of twenty items. The Francophone group shows higher levels of job involvement on ten of these items; the Anglophone group shows higher levels of job involvement on only five of these. On many of the items, the job involvement profiles of the two groups of hospital employees parallel those of the industrial employees sampled.

CHAPTER SIX—JOB INVOLVEMENT 67

| 1 | 1.85 | 1.95 | 2.15 | 2.35 | 2.55 | 2.75 | 2.95 | 3.15 | 4 |
LOW   HIGH

Greater Francophone involvement

The major satisfaction in my life comes from my job.

The most important things that happen to me involve my work.

Most things in life are less important than work.

Other activities are less important than my work.

To me, my work is a large part of who I am.

I am very much involved personally in my work.

You can measure a person pretty well by how good a job he does.

I'm really a perfectionist about my work.

For me, mornings at work really fly by.

I usually show up for work a little early, to get things ready.

Greater Anglophone involvement

I live, eat and breathe my job.

I would probably keep working even if I didn't need the money.

Sometimes I'd like to kick myself for the mistakes I make in my work.

I feel depressed when I fail at something connected with my job.

■———■ Anglophone   ●-------● Francophone

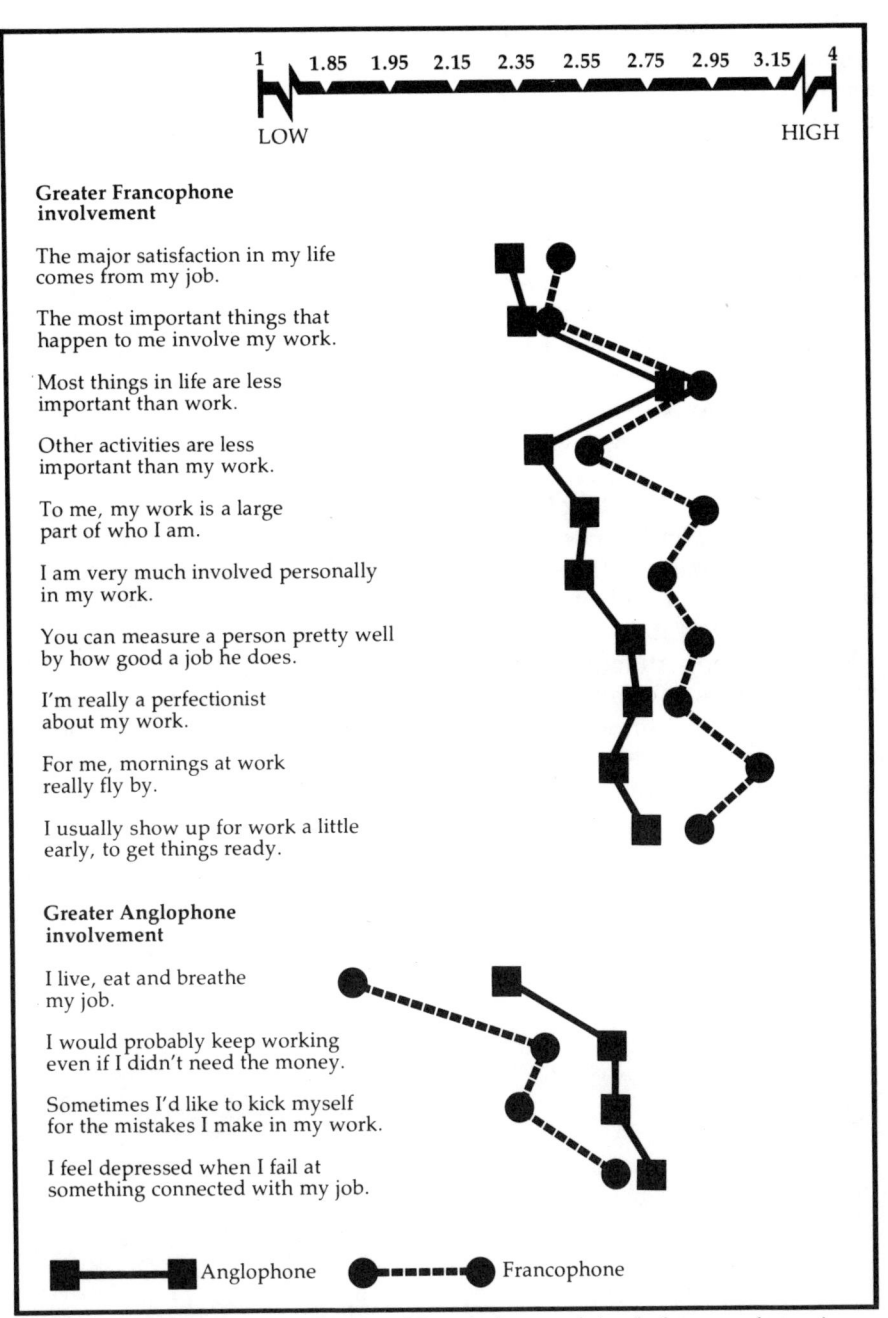

Figure 10: *Job Involvement Profiles of Francophone and Anglophone employees in an Industrial Setting*

Overall, it would appear that Francophone employees show a greater degree of job involvement than Anglophone employees. The reason for this may stem from the fact that they perceive their jobs to have greater potential for satisfying their salient social and security needs. Anglophone employees, on the other hand, may find that their jobs have less potential to satisfy their salient autonomy and achievement needs.

Greater job involvement of Anglophone employees can result only when the job provides for greater autonomy, responsibility and personal success. The Anglophone need for greater personal responsibility is reflected in their strong agreement with items such as "I feel depressed when I fail," or "I would like to kick myself for the mistakes I make." Their concern for achievement or personal success rather than for extrinsic monetary outcomes seems to be reflected in their response to items such as "I would probably keep working even if I did not need the money," or "I will stay overtime to finish a job, even if I am not paid for it." Thus, the motivational basis of job involvement for the Anglophones lies in their emphasis on personal autonomy and achievement at work. For Francophones, the basis for job involvement lies in their emphasis on social and security needs, which are easily met on the job; it is easier to provide security and comfortable social surroundings at work than it is to provide a job that has autonomy and achievement opportunities. This may explain why Francophones identify more with their jobs and derive greater satisfaction from them than do Anglophones. Because of their achievement orientation, Anglophones may find their jobs relatively less satisfying and consequently may regard other activities as more important and central to their lives than work.

CHAPTER SIX—JOB INVOLVEMENT   69

1   1.7   2.1   2.5   2.9   3.3   4
LOW   HIGH

Greater Francophone involvement

The major satisfaction in my life comes from my job.

The most important things that happen to me involve my work.

Most things in life are less important than work.

Other activities are less important than my work.

To me, my work is a large part of who I am.

I am very much involved personally in my work.

You can measure a person pretty well by how good a job he does.

For me, mornings at work really fly by.

I live, eat and breathe my job.

I used to care less about my work, but now it is more important to me than other things.

Greater Anglophone involvement

I'll stay overtime to finish a job, even if I'm not paid for it.

Sometimes I lie awake at night thinking ahead to the next day's work.

I never feel like staying home from work instead of coming in.

I never avoid taking on extra duties and responsibilities in my work.

I feel depressed when I fail at something connected with my job.

■——■ Anglophone   ●┈┈┈● Francophone

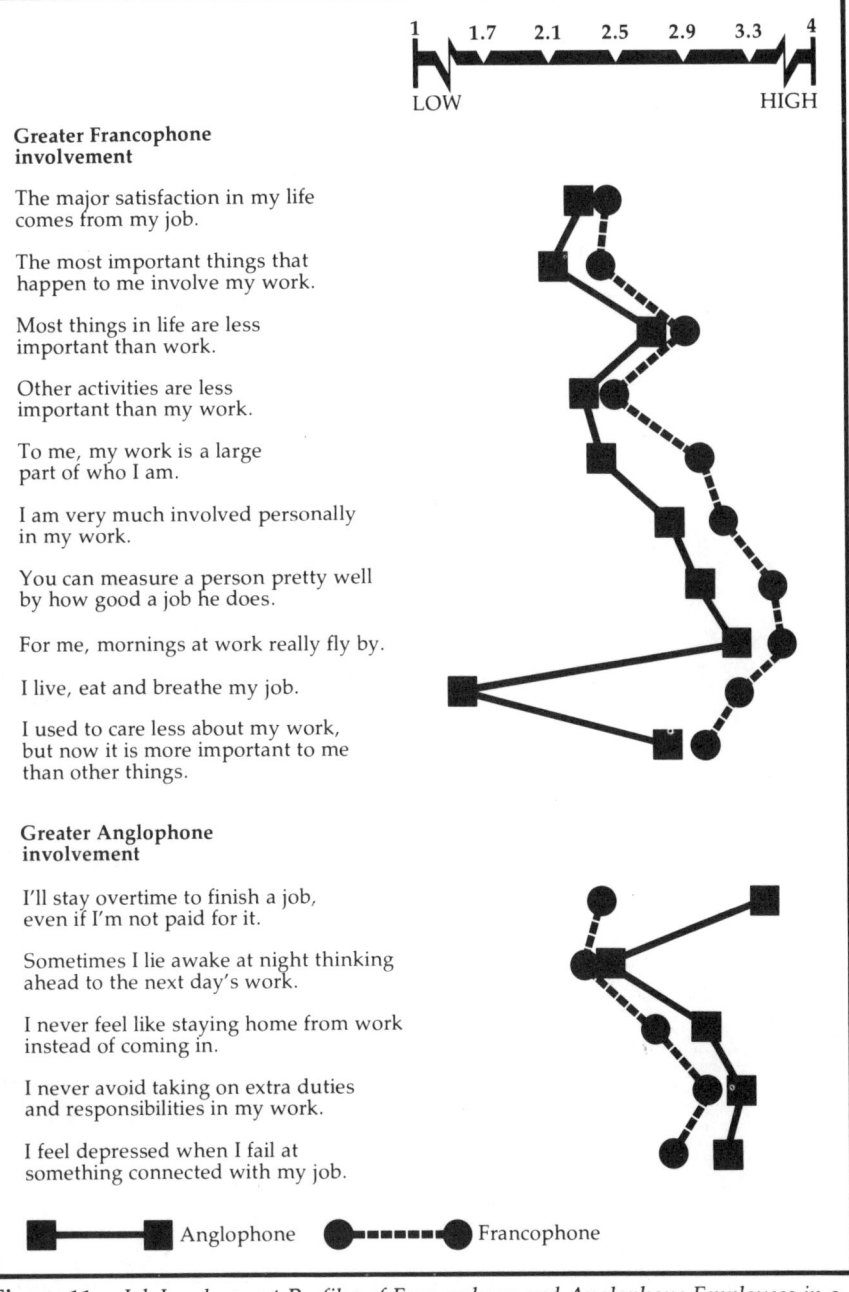

Figure 11: *Job Involvement Profiles of Francophone and Anglophone Employees in a Hospital Setting*

CHAPTER 7

Job Mobility and Transfer Potential of English- and French-Canadian Employees

EFFECTIVE UTILIZATION OF human resources within an organization requires effective planning and allocation of these resources to meet the manpower needs of the organization. Generally, manpower needs are determined by the changes that take place in the organization's external and internal environments. For example, the sociopolitical changes in Québec (the quiet revolution of the 1960s and the coming of the Parti Québecois to power) have forced most organizations in the province to adopt a policy of active recruitment of Francophones for managerial and professional positions. Similarly, in the United States affirmative action and equal opportunity legislation have forced organizations to hire more women and more people from minority groups. Expansions and mergers of organizations, elimination or modification of jobs, internal promotions, turnover and retirements—all necessitate personnel changes. To ensure the smooth and effective functioning of the organization, managers must anticipate such changes and plan for a proper allocation of human resources. Such a plan might include shifting employees from one job to another, from one position to another, and perhaps from one location to another.

Very often, managers face considerable difficulty in fulfilling this allocation function. A manager may feel that a small-town branch office employee could benefit from exposure to a corporate office environment, and decide to transfer him to the head office in a large city. But the employee may be reluctant to accept the transfer, either because he dislikes working in a large city, or he dislikes the new job, or simply because he is quite content with his present situation. From the manager's point of view, efficiency may require him to transfer the employee to the head office; but if the employee is unwilling, the transfer will result in dissatisfaction with the job, lower commitment to the organization and, consequently, lower productivity. The eventual effectiveness of any program of relocation or job design will depend upon the personal needs of the employee involved.

Therefore, every such decision should include an enquiry into the employee's views on transfer: Why does the employee want or not want a transfer? What are his preferences for the new location? Does he prefer a short-term or a long-term assignment in the new job? What are the reasons for his preference?

The problems of transfer and job mobility become more acute for organizations operating in a bicultural or a multicultural context, as is the case with Canadian organizations with Francophone and Anglophone personnel operating both inside and outside Québec. A manager of a Canadian organization needs to know how Anglophone and Francophone employees respond to transfers. Are the two groups equally willing to accept transfers? Do they differ with respect to their reasons for accepting or refusing transfers? Do they have different preferences for various job locations? Answers to these questions are of vital importance for managers concerned with manpower planning in a bicultural context.

The sample and the procedure used in this study are described in detail in Chapter 4. A total of 589 (379 Francophone and 210 Anglophone) employees responded to a questionnaire on job transfer. The questionnaire (in English and French) contained four sections: (a) readiness to accept transfer; (b) reasons for reluctance to accept transfer; (c) reasons for readiness to accept transfer; and (d) location preferences in accepting transfer. (The questionnaire is presented in Appendix D, p. 151.)

Readiness to Accept Transfer

Employees were asked whether they would be willing to accept a transfer to a different location for the sake of their own career progress. The degree of their readiness to accept a transfer was measured on a four-point scale ranging from "very much willing" (ordinal weight 4) to "unwilling" (ordinal weight 1).

The mean scores for employees' willingness to accept transfer are presented in Figure 12. The scores clearly indicate that the Anglophone employees express a greater willingness to accept job transfers and are more prepared to relocate to ensure advancement in their careers. The Francophone employees show more reluctance to accept transfers to other locations. The issue was explored by asking employees two sets of questions. One set probed the reasons for employees' reluctance to accept a transfer. The other set explored whether different kinds of inducements offered by the organization would increase the employees' readiness to accept a transfer. (An initial interview with several employees in a pilot study suggested that reluctance to accept transfers and organizational inducements to increase readiness to accept transfers should be considered as two distinct aspects of the issue. Reluctance of employees to accept transfers is a

CHAPTER SEVEN—JOB MOBILITY 73

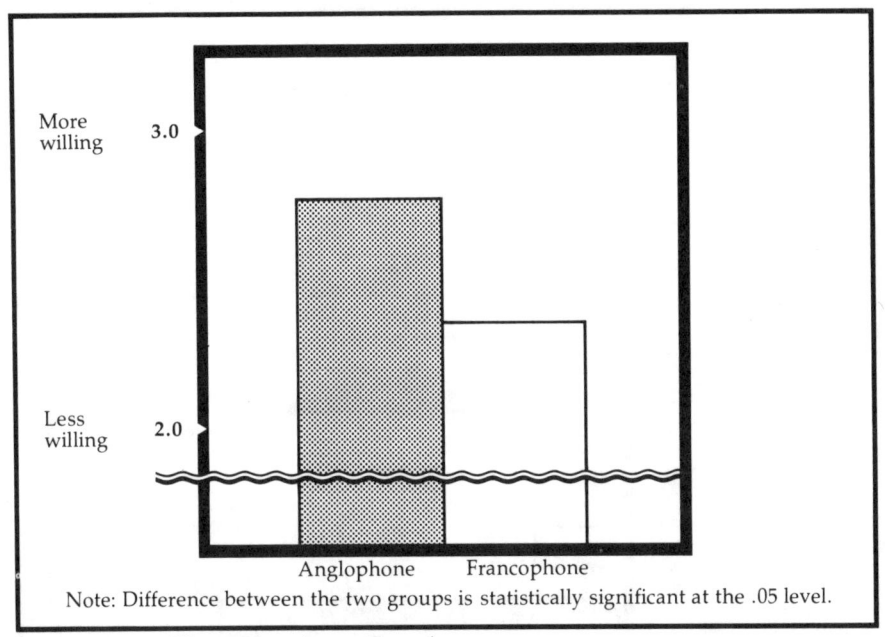

[Bar chart showing willingness to accept transfer, with Anglophone bar reaching approximately 3.0 (More willing) and Francophone bar at approximately 2.5, with 2.0 labeled as Less willing.]

Note: Difference between the two groups is statistically significant at the .05 level.

Figure 12:   *Willingness to Accept Transfer*

form of "avoidance" behavior; hence, the factors affecting such behavior should be distinguished from the organizational inducements directed at increasing employees' "approach" behavior, that is, their readiness to accept transfers.)

Reasons for Reluctance to Accept Transfer

Five major reasons for reluctance to accept transfers were identified in the pilot study and were included in the questionnaire. The items were: a sense of insecurity caused by the unfamiliar environment; social isolation because of language and cultural differences; financial loss caused by relocation; additional responsibility or different job assignments in the new job; and satisfaction with or liking for the present job. Each of the items was presented as a reason for reluctance to accept transfers, and the employees were asked to show their extent of agreement with each item on a five-point scale with ordinal weights of 5 (strongly agree) to 1 (strongly disagree).

The means scores of both Anglophone and Francophone employees on each item relating to reasons for reluctance to accept transfers are presented in Figure 13. Most of the employees belonging to both groups disagreed with the statement that additional responsibility or different activi-

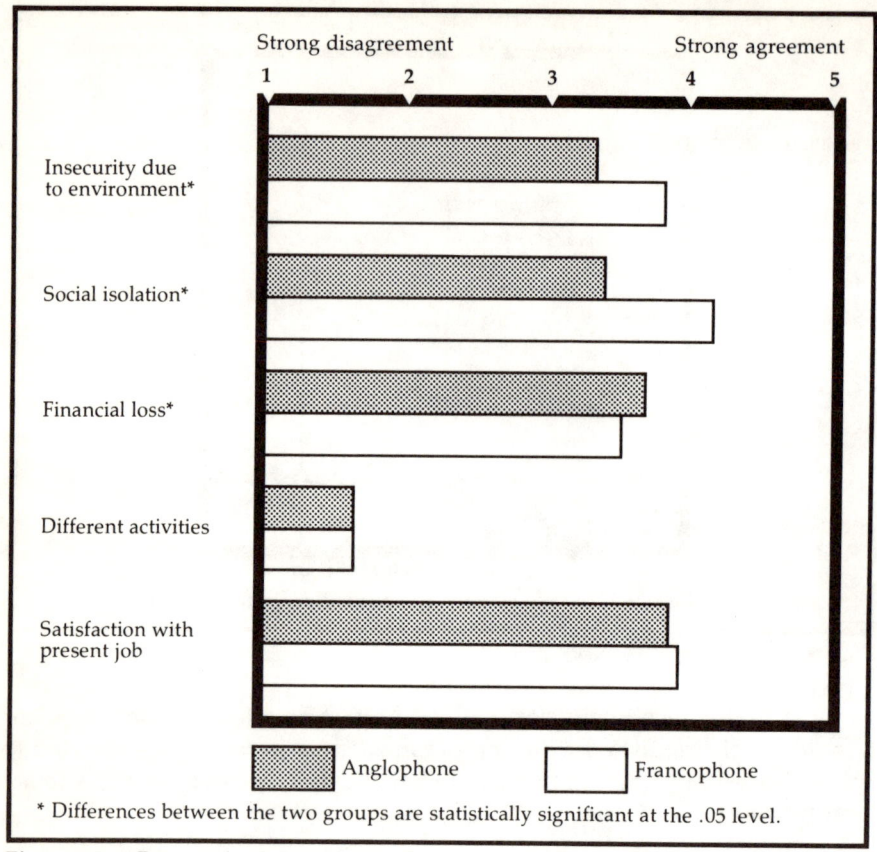

Figure 13: *Reasons for Reluctance to Accept Transfer*

ties involved in the new job assignment resulting from transfer was a reason for their reluctance to accept transfers. However, almost half of the employees in both groups considered "satisfaction with the present job" as a reason for not accepting transfers. The two groups of employees differed significantly with respect to the other three reasons. A greater proportion of Francophone employees were reluctant to accept a transfer because it would take them to an "unfamiliar environment" where they would feel insecure and culturally isolated. In fact, a majority of Francophone employees said that "social isolation" resulting from relocation was the reason for their reluctance to accept transfers. On the other hand, a greater number of Anglophones considered possible financial loss in relocation as a reason for their reluctance to accept transfers.

Importance of Inducements

What can an organization do to make transfers more attractive so that the employees will readily accept them? Obviously, the first step is to explore why employees show a reluctance to relocate and then to respond to employee needs in an appropriate fashion. In trying to meet these needs, the organization must not only alleviate problems anticipated by employees, but also provide some positive inducements to make transfers more attractive. In a pilot study, nine positive inducements were identified as possible facilitators in accepting a transfer. These were: an adequate raise in salary; a promotion to a higher-level job; a job that involves activities considerably different from the present job; a job that involves the same activities as in the present job; an opportunity to work with people of one's own linguistic and cultural background; an opportunity to work with people of different linguistic and cultural backgrounds; the environment of a big city; a smaller city environment; and the assurance of return to the home province after a specified period. These nine items were included in the questionnaire, and employees were asked to indicate on a five-point scale the degree of importance they attached to each item in deciding whether to accept a transfer. Ordinal weights of 1 (not at all important) to 5 (very important) were assigned to the five answer categories.

A comparison of the mean importance scores of both Anglophone and Francophone employees on each of the nine items is presented in Figure 14. Three inducements clearly stood out as being the most important for both Anglophone and Francophone groups. They are "raise in salary," "promotion" and "a job that involves different activities as compared to what is involved in the present job." It is clear that both groups of employees would accept transfers if such transfers can yield three positive outcomes for them: some financial gain, some gain in their status within the organization, and some broadening of their job skills. For both the Anglophone and the Francophone employees the cultural background of their peers at work (similar or different) and size of the city (large or small) were of relatively minor importance. Neither the city environment nor the opportunity to work with people of similar or different cultural backgrounds (the composition of the social environment inside the organization) seems to be an important positive inducement to accept transfers. Perhaps both groups are quite accustomed to working with people of similar and different cultural backgrounds and are quite familiar with large and small city environments. Hence, they do not consider such factors as posing unique problems or challenges in their transfer adjustment process.

Although Anglophone and Francophone employees did not differ in the importance they attached to the cultural background of their co-workers, they did differ with respect to the importance they attached to "an assurance to return to the home province." The Francophone employees considered "an assurance to return to the home province after a specified period" to be an important inducement for them to accept transfers; this was not the case with the Anglophone employees. The significant difference in the attitude of the two groups on this issue is quite consistent with the findings on the reasons for the employee's reluctance to accept transfer (Figure 13).

76 BICULTURALISM AND MANAGEMENT

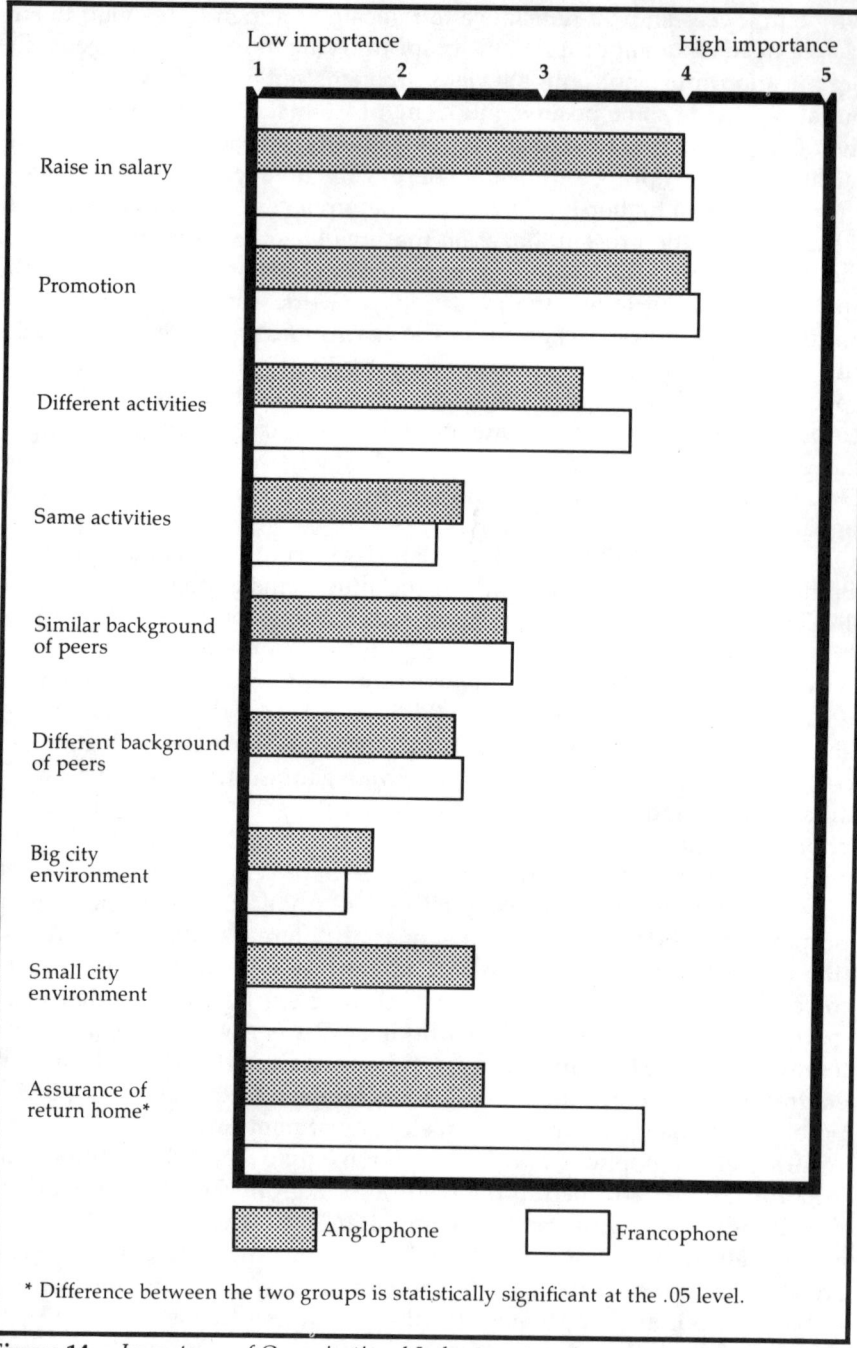

	Low importance			High importance
1	2	3	4	5

Raise in salary

Promotion

Different activities

Same activities

Similar background of peers

Different background of peers

Big city environment

Small city environment

Assurance of return home*

▨ Anglophone   ☐ Francophone

* Difference between the two groups is statistically significant at the .05 level.

Figure 14: *Importance of Organizational Inducements to Increase Acceptance of Transfers*

For Francophone employees, the job transfers that take them outside the province of Québec create social and cultural isolation. Such problems do not exist for Anglophone employees. The Francophone employees are apprehensive of the isolation which they fear they and their families will suffer. They would probably accept transfers if they knew that the transfer and the consequent cultural isolation are only temporary, and that during this temporary period of transfer, they could benefit from the opportunity of developing their skills and careers. The feeling of cultural isolation among Francophone employees transferred to places outside Québec is consistent with the view that for Francophone employees, Québec has a special status that no other place has. The province is the hub of French-Canadian culture and it is quite natural and understandable that the Francophone employees and their families feel most comfortable there; the province provides them with a strong sense of "belonging" that no other place can provide. The Anglophone employees, however, do not view Québec in the same way. For them it is just another province in Canada, and they do not experience any cultural isolation when transferred elsewhere. This difference in attitude was further explored in the study by probing the location preference of the two groups of employees.

Location preference

Location preferences were determined by asking employees to indicate their preferences for nine different areas to which they might be transferred in the interest of their career advancement. They ranked the nine locations in order of their preference by assigning 1 to the least-preferred location and 9 to the most-preferred.

The mean rankings of the Anglophone and Francophone employees for each of the nine locations are presented in Figure 15. For every location, there was a significant difference between the two groups with respect to the mean rankings. The Francophone employees showed a clear preference for locations in the province of Québec. The three most-preferred locations were Québec City, other smaller cities in Québec, and Montréal. The three least preferred places were England, Europe, (other than France), and the United States. Francophone preferences were clearly governed by the presence or absence of the French language and culture in these locations. A very similar trend was present in the Anglophone responses. The three most-preferred places for the Anglophone employees were large cities of Canada outside Québec, small cities of Canada outside Québec, and Montréal. (Although Montréal is in Québec, for Anglophones the city still represents a strong centre for English language and culture). The least-preferred locations for the Anglophones were cities in the province of Québec (except Montréal), and places in Europe (except England).

78 BICULTURALISM AND MANAGEMENT

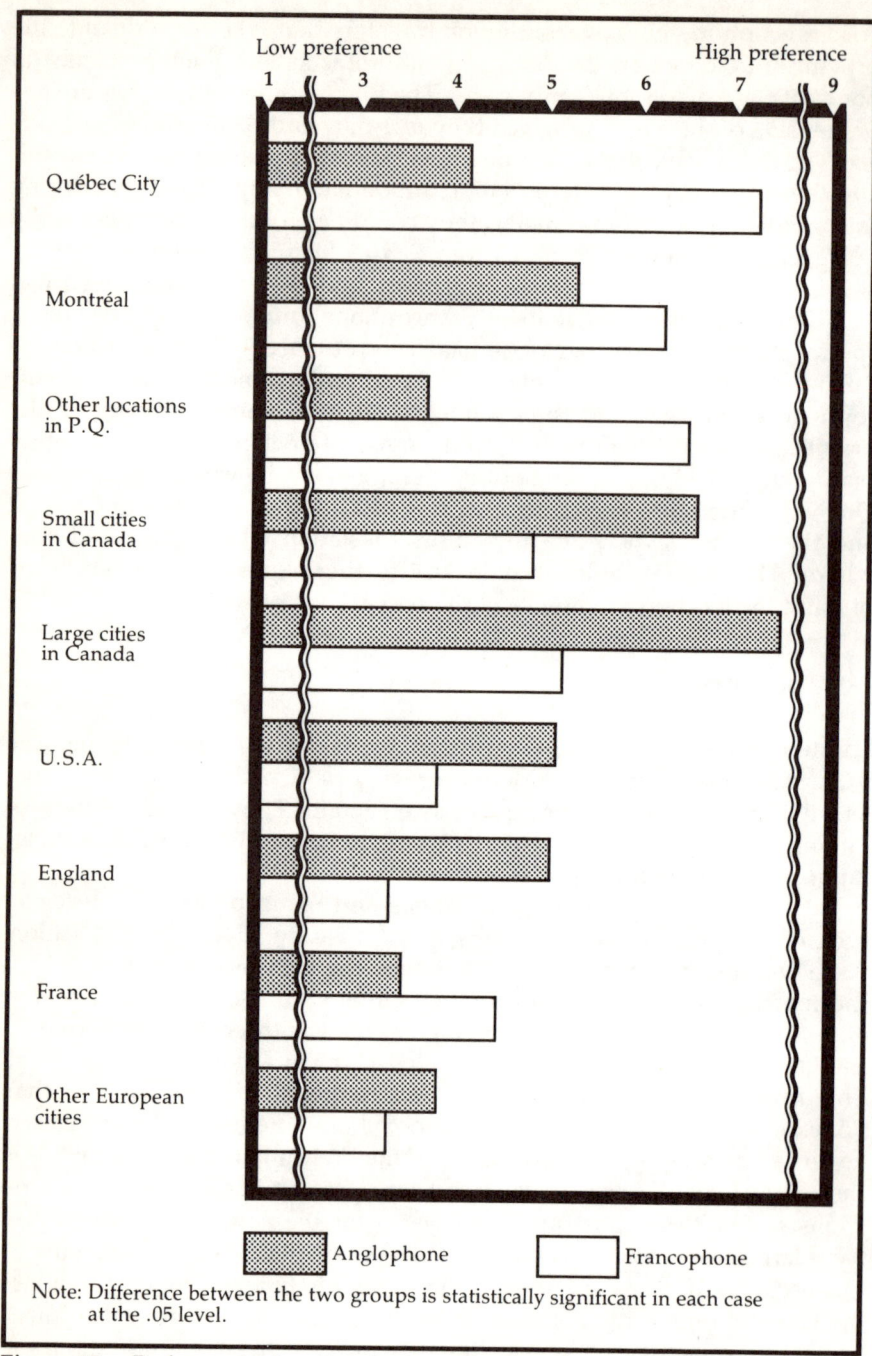

Figure 15: *Preference for Locations in Accepting Transfers*

Note: Difference between the two groups is statistically significant in each case at the .05 level.

The results shown in Figure 15 clearly suggest that employees, regardless of their socio-linguistic background, would prefer to be transferred to locations where the linguistic and cultural environments are similar to their own. Conversely, they would feel it to be a disincentive if they were transferred to locations with a socio-linguistic environment different from their own. Such an attitude places the Francophone employee in a position of relatively greater disadvantage than his Anglophone counterpart. This is particularly true in the North American context. Every industrialized city in Canada and the U.S., except those in the province of Québec, provides a socio-linguistic environment that is familiar to Anglophone employees but alien to Francophone employees. As a result, accepting transfers does not pose as much of a psychological hardship for Anglophones as it does for Francophones. Apprehensions about transfers leading to linguistic and cultural isolation and other psychological hardships for Francophone employees and their families may result in a greater resistance among them to accept transfers. They may tend to shy away from transfers that take them outside Québec, unless they are assured that such transfers are only temporary and that they would return to Québec after a specified period.

Francophone employees find themselves in a difficult predicament. To avoid cultural isolation, they may not accept transfers that take them out of the province of Québec. On the other hand, the staying-at-home attitude tends to block their future career progress within the organization. Thus, if they accept transfers, they suffer cultural isolation; if they do not accept transfers, their careers stagnate.

Although it is recognized at the corporate level that Francophones suffer greater hardships than do Anglophones whether they accept or reject transfers, corporations have done nothing to alleviate the problems faced by their Francophone employees. This corporate attitude has been best described by Dominique Clift in an article in the *Montreal Star* (May 22, 1976), "The prevailing corporate attitude is that French-speaking people should be making a greater effort to adapt themselves to the manner in which economic and work activities are organized in North America and in other industrialized parts of the world. The burden of adjustment therefore tends to fall on French-speaking people rather than on corporate structures and practices."

From a motivational standpoint, the reluctance of Francophone employees to accept transfers outside Québec stems from a threat to the satisfaction of their salient security and social needs. If a corporation wants to utilize the full potential of its Francophone employees, and assist their career development, it must establish appropriate transfer practices which meet their social and security needs.

CHAPTER 8

Attitudes Toward Communication

IT IS OBVIOUS that communication between superiors and subordinates is essential for the effective functioning of any organization. Most managers would agree that communication is the lifeblood of an organization and that without effective communication between them and their subordinates, the organization would not thrive for long.

The goal of every organization is to achieve a common set of objectives. For example, the major objective of a manufacturing organization is to produce more and better products for the market; and the objective of a service organization is to provide better service to its customers. In order to achieve these goals through employees' concerted efforts, a manager must see that the objectives and the methods for achieving them are shared by every member of the organization. This can only be accomplished by establishing a proper communication structure or network, and using appropriate channels to reach the members of the organization. A manager must understand that sound management practice involves effective communication of "what needs to be said" to "who needs to know." As Lynn Townsend, the former president of Chrysler Corporation, once said "Every member of management must understand that effective communication is an essential tool of good management; and part of his job is to relay and interpret appropriate information and news, whether good or bad, to his subordinates and superiors. . . . There is a need to inform employees about matters which affect them or their jobs, to interpret management's position on relevant issues, and to persuade employees to take actions best designed to serve the long-range mutual interests of themselves and the corporation [quoted in Sigband, 1969, p. 34]."

Most organizations have a pyramidal structure with a hierarchy: rank and file employees, lower management, middle management and top management. In this kind of structure, communication must flow both up and down. Employees at the lower level must have "upward communication" with their superiors; they need to provide information about themselves and their work, so that such information can be evaluated and analyzed in planning and decision-making. Every employee needs to express his concerns about the organizational life to managers at higher levels with greater authority and control. The employee also expects that with effective upward communication he can influence the decision-making process and change his work environment to better suit his personal needs and expectations. Managers at higher levels of authority also have a need to understand the concerns of their subordinates so that they can develop appropriate organizational plans and policies. Understanding the nature of subordinates' concerns can be accomplished by providing opportunities for subordinates to freely communicate their feelings and ideas on issues of vital concern to them.

Both managers and subordinates also need effective "downward communication." Employees in subordinate positions need to know exactly what is expected of them, and what their job duties and responsibilities are. They also want to know about organizational policies regarding reward and control systems (pay, security, promotion, etc.). In order to meet these needs, managers must communicate with their subordinates and must issue directives and policy statements from time to time to keep their subordinates informed. Through downward communication, a manager helps lower-level employees to satisfy their "need to know" in two broad areas. First, an employee is more fully informed about his job, the manner in which it is to be performed, the way it is related to other jobs within the organization and how it is related to the organizational objectives. Second, an employee is more fully informed about the organization and the way it affects his family and community life. This is an important area of employee concern. For instance, every employee wants to know in some detail the compensation schemes of the organization, its policies regarding unionization and collective bargaining, and its plans for future expansion, merger or relocation. The effectiveness of downward communication rests on supplying adequate and accurate information on these issues to employees.

How much information regarding the job or the organization should be passed on to employees? How much scope should employees have to provide information on their own job perceptions, needs and attitudes to higher levels of managements? Answers to these questions will be found only if an organization regularly engages in an audit of its own communication system. Such an audit provides an assessment of employees' needs "to know" and "influence" organizational decisions, and indicates whether the existing levels of upward and downward communication are adequate to satisfy employees' needs.

Previous chapters have analyzed the attitudinal, motivational, and behavioral characteristics of French- and English-Canadians, and have demonstrated that these two culturally distinct groups in Canada tend to react differently to the organizational environment in which they work. Since a communication system is a part of the organizational environment, the two groups may differ in their perceptions of and satisfaction with the nature of the organizational communication system under which they operate. The study reported in this chapter explores this possibility. Data reported in Chapters 4 and 5 suggest that Anglophone employees tend to experience lower levels of satisfaction with the organizational outcomes than do Francophone employees. Similar trends may exist with respect to organizational communications. Furthermore, Francophones are known to have stronger affiliative tendencies than Anglophones (Auclair and Read, 1966). Anglophone employees, on the other hand, tend to exhibit a stronger need for autonomy at work. Such tendencies may cause Anglophones to exhibit relatively less dependence on organizational communications than do Francophones.

Research on communication (Redding, 1972) has shown that the attitudes, feelings, and perceptions of members of organizations about the prevailing communication system within the organization (upward and downward flow of information, content and channels of communications, etc.) have significant influence on the work motivation of employees, and consequently on total organizational effectiveness. The design of communication systems for Canadian organizations operating in a bicultural environment requires an adequate understanding of how the various aspects of organizational communication are viewed by Anglophone and Francophone employees.

In this study, two groups of employees in a large Canadian hospital were compared. The aspects of the communication system that were studied were as follows: (a) the nature of downward communication, or the kinds of information employees received from higher levels of management; (b) the nature of upward communication, or the kinds of information sent by employees to the management; and (c) the communication channels used for receiving or sending information within the organization. In addition, the study compared the two groups with respect to their levels of satisfaction with communication regarding several major organizational outcomes such as pay, promotion etc., and with overall communication efforts in the organization.

The Study: A Brief Description

The Questionnaire on Communication   The survey instrument used in the study was the Communication Audit Survey questionnaire developed by the International Communication Association (ICA). This instrument was designed to measure employee satisfaction with and perceived importance of several sets of items related to downward and upward communication, communication channels, and organizational outcomes. Each of the questionnaire items in the instrument used five-point Likert-type scales for coding the responses. Complete information about the development, reliability, and validity of the instrument has appeared in a report by Goldhaber (1976). The report indicates that the reliability of the scales have ranges from a low of .74 to a high of .93. The validity of the scales has been based upon their self-evident relationship to organizational communication, their ability to predict employee behavior, and their consistency with previously validated measures of organizational communication.

Each questionnaire was written in both English and French. The French version was prepared by a team of bilingual academic experts and hospital staff familiar with the content of the questionnaire. Face validity was ensured by using bilingual translators, trained in the content of the organizational communication audit. In addition, prior to administering the questionnaire to the entire hospital staff, a pilot test was conducted by administering the questionnaire to a small sample of twenty hospital members as a check on the accuracy and readability of the translation. Bilingual assistants were present during the administration of the questionnaire to help any respondent in need of assistance.

Responses to the items in the questionnaire were elicited on the two dimensions of perceived importance and level of satisfaction, using five-point scales. The scale for perceived importance ranged from "extremely important" ("extrement important") to "not at all important" ("aucune importance"). The satisfaction scale ranged from "very satisfied" ("tres satisfait(e)") to "very dissatisfied" ("tres insatisfait(e)"). Both scales were presented side by side against each item of the questionnaire. (The questionnaire is shown in Appendix E, p. 157.)

The Sample and the Research Site   The study was conducted in a large community general hospital located in a Canadian city. The choice of a hospital organization for the study of employee reactions to a communication system has some inherent merits. Hospitals as service organizations call for much greater coordination through communication than do industrial manufacturing organizations (Georgopolous and Mann, 1962; Jain, 1973, 1977). Hospitals have little tolerance for ambiguity or errors since human life is at stake. They are human rather than machine systems, where communication plays a crucial role in making the system effective (Georgopolous & Mann, 1962; Revans, 1964; Jain, 1973, 1977). The hospital chosen for the study was committed to the use of bilingual communications, especially with its transmission of written memoranda, letters and reports. While English was primarily spoken at most staff meetings,

French was often spoken by most staff members during informal communications. There were no special communication systems in the hospital for either English-speaking or French-speaking employees.

The hospitals had 610 beds and 1700 employees. A total of 1,483 employees, belonging to the four major sectors of nursing, administration, paramedical and medical services, were asked to fill in the questionnaire. A total of 977 (65.9 percent) employees responded and returned the questionnaire.[1]

The Procedure Used in the Study   All 1,483 employees were requested by their supervisors to participate in the study. Several survey centres were established to allow the employees to come in and answer the questionnaire with little interference from their day-to-day job activities. These centres continued to operate for six working days during both the day and the evening shifts. For the night shift employees, special teams of investigators were appointed to contact the employees individually. In all survey centres, a team of Anglophone and Francophone investigators was present to explain and administer the questionnaire to the employees. The employees responded to the questionnaire on machine-readable answer sheets. Although no time limit was placed upon the employees for completion of the questionnaire, most of them completed it within forty-five minutes.

Demographic Characteristics of the Employees   From a total of 977 employees, 623 indicated that they were either unilingual English Canadians (n=224), or unilingual French Canadians (n=399). The analyses of the data presented in this section are based on this sample of 623 respondents. The demographic characteristics of the Anglophone and the Francophone respondents are presented in Table 2. Both groups were matched on demographic variables such as sex, age, shift work, supervisory duty, and tenure in the organization and the present job. However, on two demographic variables, job sector and education, the two groups had different distributions. There were more Anglophone than Francophone respondents in nursing and paramedical jobs, while the opposite was the case in administrative services ($\chi^2=40.15$, df 4, $p < .001$). Since the nursing and paramedical jobs required higher levels of education than did the administrative services, the Anglophone respondents revealed higher levels of schooling than did the Francophone respondents (xs^2 for the two items on education variable were 56.01 and 81.94, $df=4$, $p/.001$ in both cases). Within each job

---

[1] The field work for the study was conducted by Gerald Goldhaber, Hilary Haron, Harish Jain, Tom Porter, Don Rogers, Michael Ryan and numerous other students from several Ontario universities and from the State University of New York at Buffalo.

sector, however, there was no difference with respect to the education levels between the two groups. Such differences in the distribution of the two groups for the job sector variable necessitated separate analyses of the results for each job sector. Within each job sector, no significant difference in demographic variables was observed between the two groups.

In order to see how the socio-linguistic affiliation of the employees within each job sector was related to the dependent variables of the study, the mean scores of the two groups on the dependent measures were compared and tested for significance. The separate mean comparisons for medical, nursing, paramedical, and administrative services yielded very similar results. Since the job sector variable did not affect the two groups of respondents differentially, the data from all sectors were combined for further analysis.

TABLE 2

Demographic Characteristics of Francophone and Anglophone Respondents Expressed in Percentages

	Anglophone N = 224	Francophone N = 399	Total N = 623
*Job sector**			
Nursing	42.0	28.3	33.2
Administration	8.0	27.3	20.4
Paramedical	34.4	27.8	30.2
Medical	10.7	8.5	9.3
Unknown	4.9	8.0	6.9
Sex			
Male	14.0	23.1	19.7
Female	83.0	74.4	77.5
Unknown	3.0	2.6	2.6
Tenure in organization			
Less than one year	23.2	18.8	20.4
One to five years	48.7	43.4	45.3
Six to ten years	12.5	20.3	17.5
11 to 15 years	8.0	7.3	7.5
More than 15 years	7.6	10.3	9.3
Tenure in present job			
Less than one year	26.8	24.1	25.0
One to five years	50.9	50.9	50.9
Six to ten years	13.4	17.0	15.7
11 to 15 years	4.5	2.0	2.9
More than 15 years	2.7	5.5	4.5
Unknown	1.8	0.5	1.0

TABLE 2—Continued

	Anglophone N = 224	Francophone N = 399	Total N = 623
Supervisory duty			
Supervision involved	47.8	37.1	40.9
No supervision involved	49.6	57.4	54.6
Unknown	2.6	5.6	4.4
Shift work			
Day shift	56.3	65.9	62.4
Night shift	4.5	3.5	3.9
Evening shift	5.8	6.0	5.9
On rotation	29.5	22.6	25.0
On call	2.7	1.0	1.6
Unknown	1.3	1.0	1.1
Age			
Under 20	0.9	5.8	4.1
21 to 30	51.4	51.0	51.1
31 to 40	23.6	21.1	22.0
41 to 50	16.8	13.5	15.0
51 to 60	7.2	8.5	8.1
Education (a)*			
Grade School	3.6	8.5	6.7
Some high school	5.8	24.6	17.8
Completed high school	29.9	31.8	31.1
Some college or CEGEP	42.0	23.8	30.3
None of the above	18.7	11.3	13.9
Education (b)*			
Completed college	22.8	11.3	15.4
Completed nursing school	36.6	20.8	26.5
Some graduate school	13.4	13.3	13.3
Completed graduate school	11.2	4.0	6.6
None of the above	16.1	50.6	38.2

* χ^2 tests revealed statistically significant differences between Anglophone and Francophone samples ($p < .001$) in the case of these demographic variables.

Attitudes Toward Downward Communication

The kinds of information received by employees from management (downward communication items) were grouped under two broad categories: information about the job and information about the organization. Employees were asked how satisfied they were with the information they received with respect to each of these. The mean levels of satisfaction are presented in Figure 16. The degrees of importance attached to these items are presented in Figure 17.

88 BICULTURALISM AND MANAGEMENT

Information about your job

Information on job requirements*
Reasons for specific job assignments
Relation of job to the total operation
Feedback on progress in your work*
Feedback on results of your work*
Feedback on how you are being judged*
Feedback on what is done to protect job security*
Feedback on pay and benefits*
Feedback on promotion opportunity
Information about changes affecting work
How technological changes affect your job
How decisions that affect your job are made*
How your job-related problems are handled*

Information about your organization

What your organization is doing
Mistakes and failures of the organization
Policies of the organization*
Decisions of the Board of Trustees
Reasons for important management decisions
Problems management faces in the organization
Important new developments in hospital services
Plans for expansion
Quality of patient care*
Government policies affecting hospital
Interdepartmental information
Safety information

■——■ Anglophone   ●------● Francophone   * $p < .05$

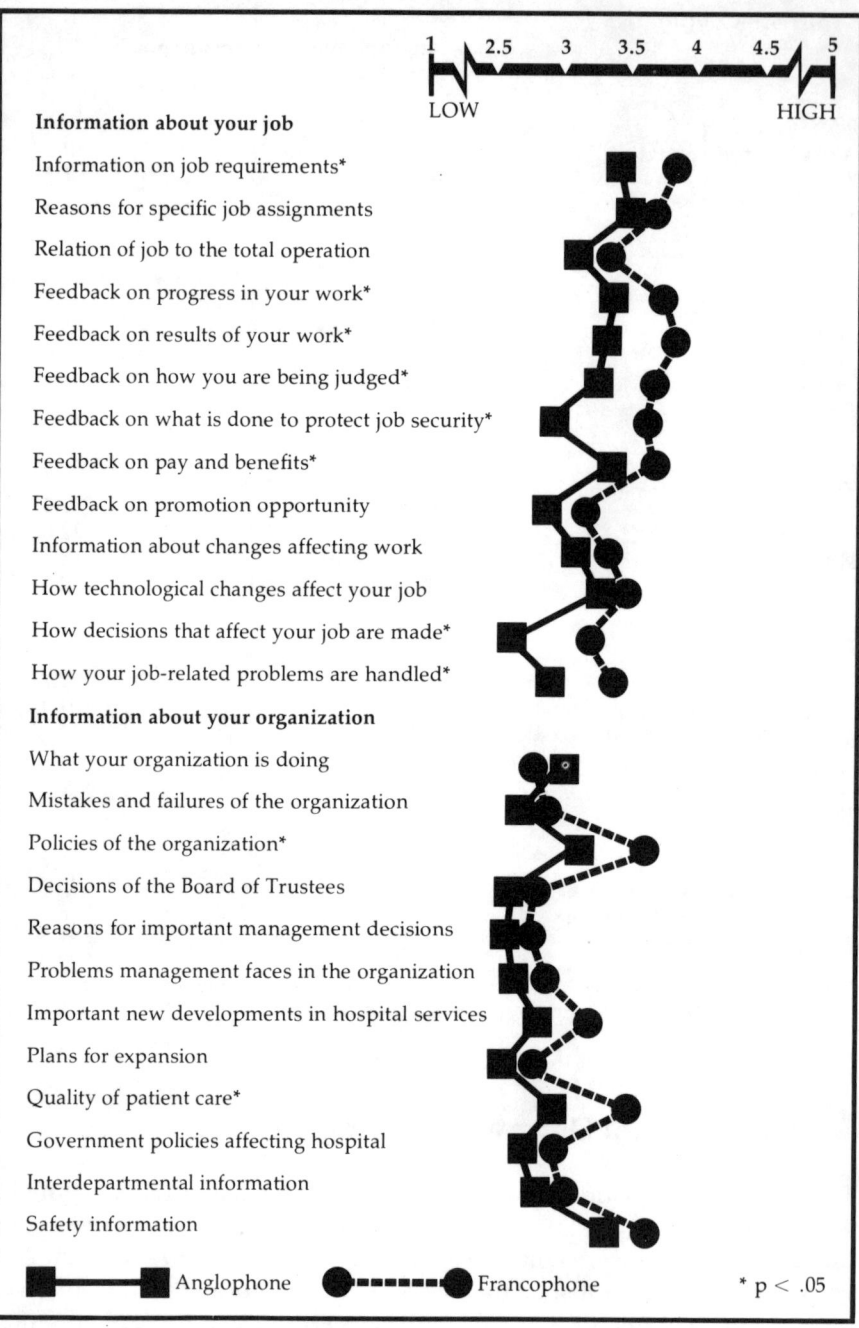

Figure 16: *Mean Satisfaction with Information Received*

CHAPTER EIGHT—ATTITUDES TOWARD COMMUNICATION   89

Information about your job

Information on job requirements
Reasons for specific job assignments*
Relation of job to the total operation
Feedback on progress in your work*
Feedback on results of your work
Feedback on how you are being judged
Feedback on what is done to protect job security*
Feedback on pay and benefits
Feedback on promotion opportunity*
Information about changes affecting work
How technological changes affect your job
How decisions that affect your job are made
How your job-related problems are handled*

Information about your organization

What your organization is doing*
Mistakes and failures of the organization*
Policies of the organization*
Decisions of the Board of Trustees*
Reasons for important management decisions
Problems management faces in the organization
Important new developments in hospital services*
Plans for expansion*
Quality of patient care*
Government policies affecting hospital
Interdepartmental information
Safety information

■━━━■ Anglophone   ●┅┅┅● Francophone   * p < .05

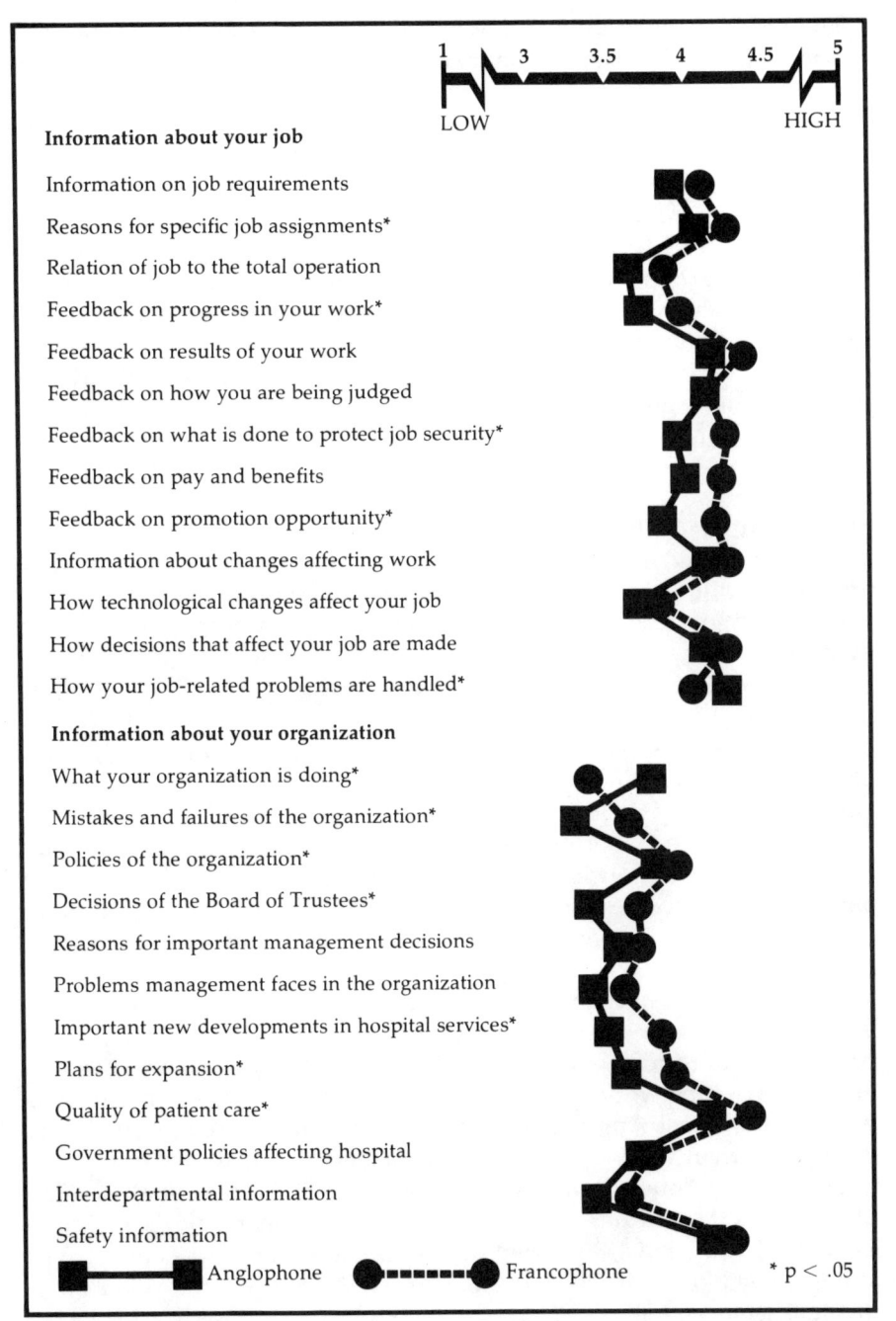

Figure 17: *Mean Importance of Information Received*

The results with respect to downward communication reveal that both Anglophone and Francophone employees experienced higher levels of satisfaction with job-related information they received from management than with organization-related information. Both groups also attached greater importance to receiving job-related information than to receiving organization-related information. Taking the twenty-five mean satisfaction scores (Figure 16) and calculating the median of these scores for each group, gives median values of 2.99 and 3.31 for the Anglophone and the Francophone groups respectively. When the means are compared against the median values, we find that for each group, in nine out of thirteen job-related information items the means fall above the median values. On the other hand, in only two out of twelve organizational items (in the case of the Anglophone group) and three out of twelve such items (in the case of the Francophone group) are the means above the median values. Very similar trends can be seen in Figure 17, where the mean perceived importance scores are plotted. The median values in this case are 3.75 for the Anglophone group and 3.94 for the Francophone group. For both groups, there are ten job-related information items and only two organization-related information items where the means are above the median value. The results suggest that job related information from management may have greater personal relevance for the employees, and in fact such information may satisfy personal needs to a greater extent than does organization-related information.

When the relative levels of satisfaction experienced by the two groups of employees are compared with one another for downward communication items (Figure 16), it is clear that both groups felt more or less equally satisfied with the organization-related information they received from management. Only in two (policies of the organization and quality of patient care) out of twelve such cases did the Anglophone employees show significantly lower levels of satisfaction. However, with regard to the job-related information received by the employees, the Anglophone employees showed lower levels of satisfaction on several items. They were less satisfied with the information available from management on job requirements, work progress, work results, work appraisal, job security, pay and benefits, how decisions affecting work are made, and how job-related problems are handled. It seems that Anglophone employees wanted more information on these items than was available from management. Greater need for more information on job-related matters may be an indication of the Anglophone need for greater feedback on the job. The results reported in Chapters 4 and 5 have suggested that Anglophone employees may have a stronger need for feedback on the job due to the emphasis they place on individual achievement.

Francophone employees placed greater value on six out of seven organization-related items where statistically significant differences were seen

(Figure 17). Similarly, on four out of five job-related information items where significant differences were seen, Francophone employees attached greater value than did the Anglophones. These results suggest that the information received from the management was valued more highly by Francophones, but that Francophone needs for receiving such information seem to be more easily satisfied than Anglophone needs. This pattern may reflect a more positive Francophone attitude toward management as shown by Nightingale and Toulouse (1977).

Attitudes Toward Upward Communication

Three kinds of information sent by the employees to the management (upward communication items) were classified: personal information, work-related information, and evaluative information on others. Employees were asked to indicate how satisfied they were with the opportunity they had to send information to management in each category, and how important they felt such opportunities were. The mean levels of satisfaction and the perceived importance of items in the three categories are shown in Figures 18 and 19 respectively.

The results show that Anglophone employees were less satisfied with the effectiveness of work-related and evaluative information sent by employees to the management. However, Francophone employees attached relatively greater importance to communicating with management. Thus, sending information and suggestions to the management and asking for clarifications of job instructions were valued more by Francophones, but the Francophone expectations of influencing management behavior through upward communication were perhaps more easily met than were Anglophone expectations.

Figure 19 also shows that both groups of employees considered sending personal information to the management to be of much less importance than sending work-related information.

Attitudes Towards Communication Channels

Employees were asked to indicate how satisfied they were with various communication channels and how important they felt each channel was as a means of receiving information. The mean levels of satisfaction with and the importance attached to the various communication channels used for receiving information are presented in Figures 20 and 21 respectively. Two kinds of channels were identified: those used for direct person-to-person communication and those used to reach group targets or more than one person. The mean scores reveal that both Anglophone and Francophone employees exhibited higher levels of satisfaction with and attached greater

92 BICULTURALISM AND MANAGEMENT

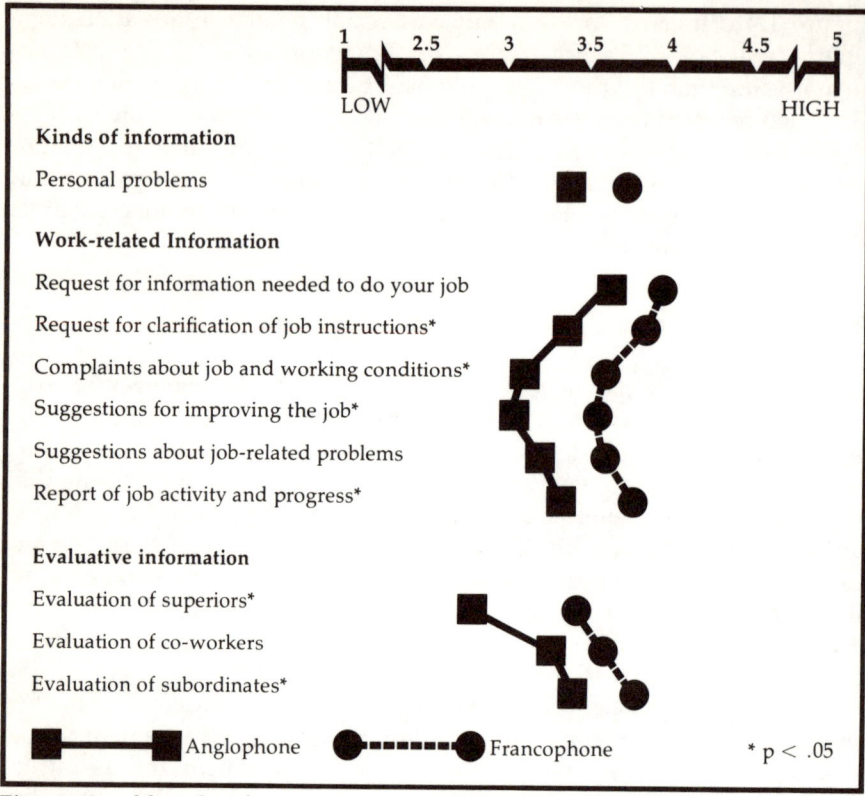

Figure 18: *Mean Satisfaction with Information Sent*

importance to the person-to-person channels than the channels used to reach group targets. Channels that provide opportunity for direct personal communication were probably better able to meet the specific needs of individual employees. Hence, they were valued more highly and perceived to be more satisfactory. Although no significant differences in the levels of satisfaction experienced by the two groups were observed with respect to direct communication channels, the Francophone employees experienced greater satisfaction with the use of channels aimed at reaching group targets. It appears that the Anglophone employees tended to rely mostly on direct communication channels, whereas both types of channels were considered useful by the Francophone group. The Francophones attached greater importance not only to direct channels (such as written memos and letters), but also to computer printouts and closed circuit television (Figure 21).

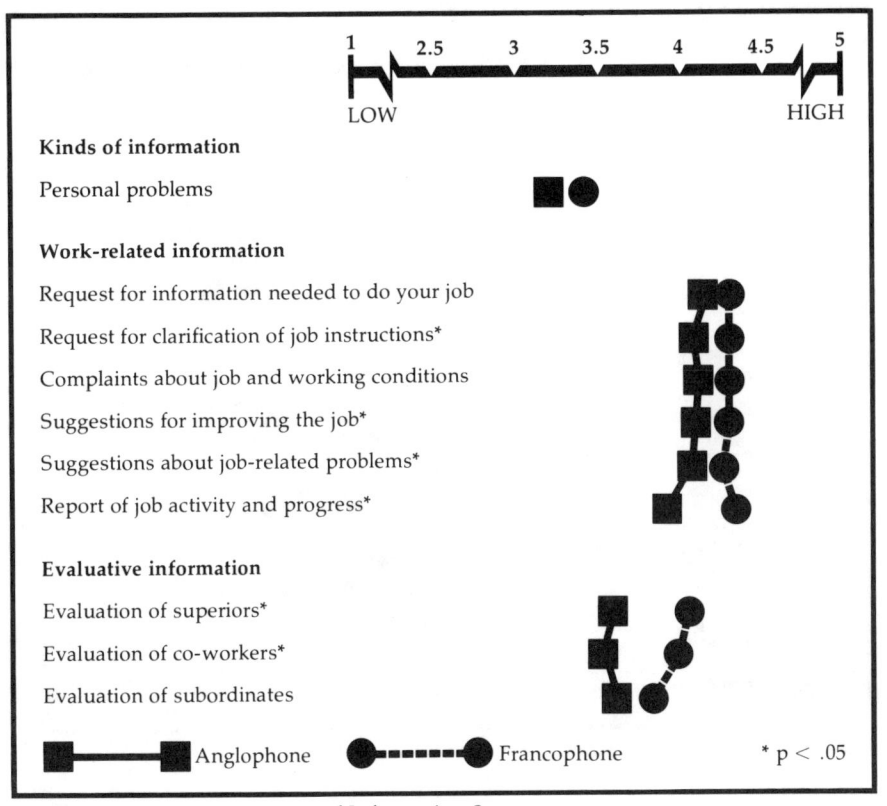

Figure 19: Mean Importance of Information Sent

	1	2.5	3	3.5	4	4.5	5
	LOW						HIGH

Kinds of information

Personal problems

Work-related information

Request for information needed to do your job

Request for clarification of job instructions*

Complaints about job and working conditions

Suggestions for improving the job*

Suggestions about job-related problems*

Report of job activity and progress*

Evaluative information

Evaluation of superiors*

Evaluation of co-workers*

Evaluation of subordinates

■——■ Anglophone   ●----● Francophone   * $p < .05$

Attitudes Toward Organizational Outcomes and Overall Communication Effort

Employees were asked to indicate their levels of satisfaction with three sets of organizational outcomes: intrinsic, extrinsic, and interpersonal. Intrinsic outcomes such as "interesting nature of one's work" tend to be inherent in the job itself. Extrinsic outcomes such as "pay" and "promotion" are rewards that are administered by higher levels of management and are therefore not inherent in the job. Interpersonal outcomes are those that are affected by the nature of the relationship of employees with other people in the organization. The three-way categorization of organizational outcome is similar to the grouping of job factors described in Chapters 4 and 5 (see, for example, Figures 1 and 5). Employees were also asked to indicate their level of satisfaction with the overall communication effort within the organization.

94 BICULTURALISM AND MANAGEMENT

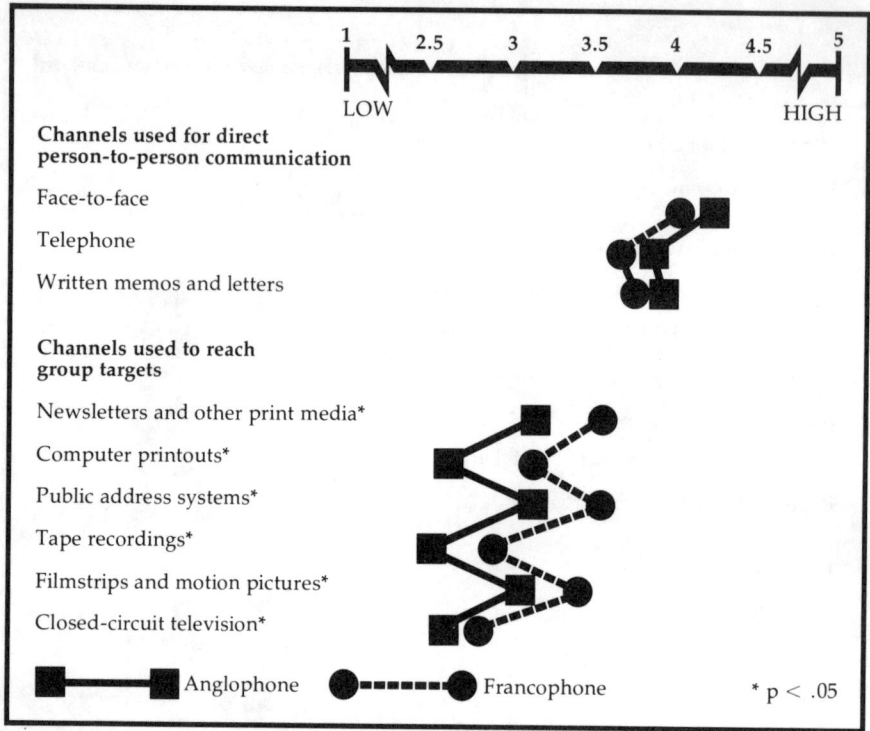

```
                            1    2.5    3    3.5    4    4.5    5
                           LOW                                 HIGH
Channels used for direct
person-to-person communication

Face-to-face
Telephone
Written memos and letters

Channels used to reach
group targets

Newsletters and other print media*
Computer printouts*
Public address systems*
Tape recordings*
Filmstrips and motion pictures*
Closed-circuit television*

    ■——■ Anglophone      ●-----● Francophone         * p < .05
```

Figure 20: *Mean Satisfaction with Communication Channels*

The mean levels of satisfaction experienced by the two groups of employees with organizational outcomes and overall communication efforts are presented in Figure 22. The Anglophone employees were less satisfied than were the Francophone employees not only with intrinsic job outcomes, but also with their relationships with superiors. These results are consistent with the earlier observation that, relative to the Francophone employees, the Anglophones wanted more job-related feedback from management. Perhaps for this reason, they were also less satisfied with the overall communication efforts in the organization.

This pattern shows some degree of internal consistency. For instance, Anglophone employees consistently showed lower levels of satisfaction over several communication scales used in this study. Francophone employees, on the other hand, consistently attached greater value to various aspects of the communication system. Such consistency perhaps stems from the differing cultural values of the two groups of employees. Francophones, being more affiliative, may find organizational communication more important than do Anglophones. The Anglophone emphasis on individuality and personal achievement may have created expectations that are

Channels used for direct person-to-person communication

Face-to-face

Telephone

Written memos and letters*

Channels used to reach group targets

Newsletters and other print media

Computer printouts*

Tape recordings

Filmstrips and motion pictures

Closed-circuit television*

■——■ Anglophone   ●------● Francophone   * $p < .05$

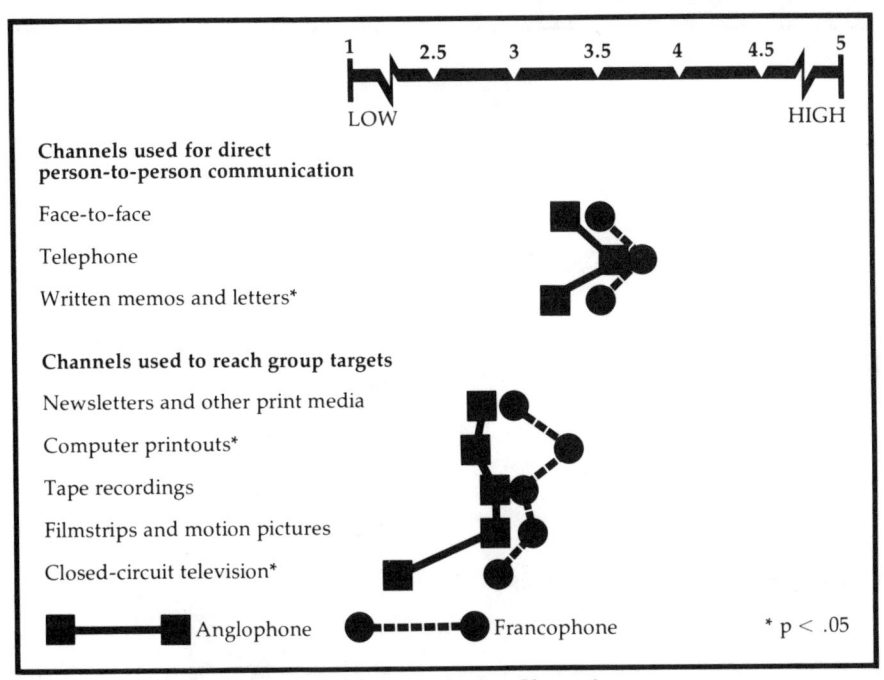

Figure 21: *Mean Importance of Communication Channels*

more difficult to satisfy. In this respect, the results of this study are consistent with findings reported in previous chapters.

Relationship Between Satisfaction and Importance

In both groups, the satisfaction scores on most of the items correlated positively with the perceived importance scores. For the twenty-five downward communication items, the average correlations were .33 (with a range of .09 to .53) in the Francophone group and .29 (with a range of .06 to .53) in the Anglophone group. For the ten upward communication items, the average correlations were .35 (with a range of .17 to .74) in the Francophone group and .28 (with a range of .04 to .67) in the Anglophone group. For the nine items on communication channels, the average correlations were .61 (with a range of .48 to .71) in the Francophone group and .52 (with a range of .47 to .58) in the Anglophone group. The consistency of the direction and the degree of correlations may be the result of the questionnaire format used. The satisfaction and the importance scales were presented side by side for each item. The employees were required to respond to each item by first responding on the satisfaction scale, and then re-

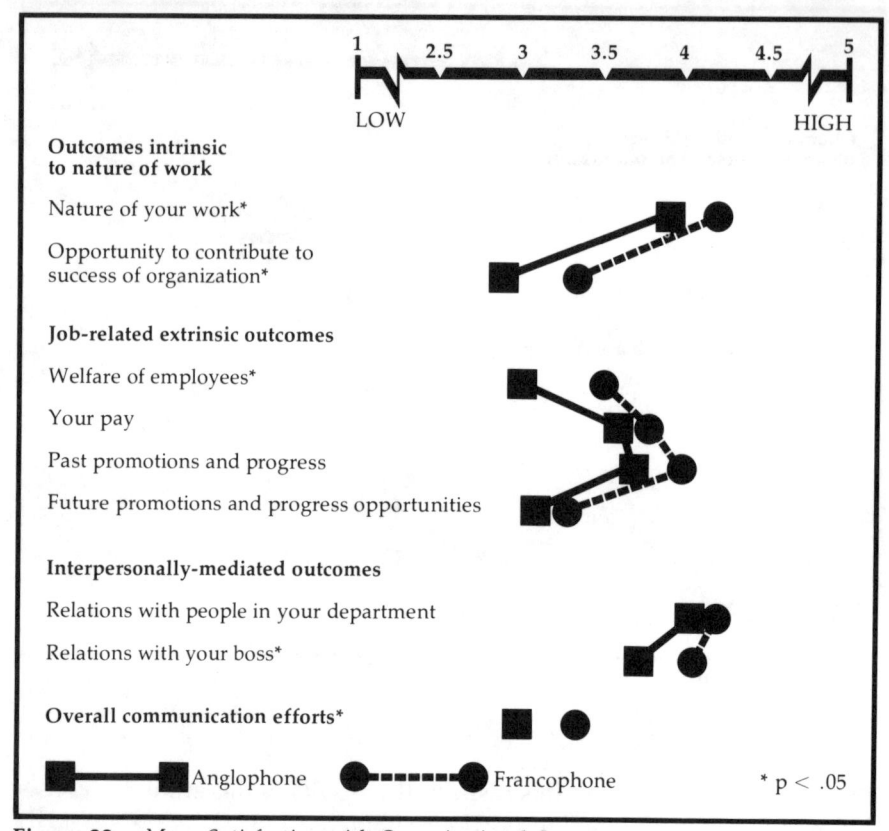

Figure 22: Mean Satisfaction with Organizational Outcomes

Outcomes intrinsic to nature of work
- Nature of your work*
- Opportunity to contribute to success of organization*

Job-related extrinsic outcomes
- Welfare of employees*
- Your pay
- Past promotions and progress
- Future promotions and progress opportunities

Interpersonally-mediated outcomes
- Relations with people in your department
- Relations with your boss*

Overall communication efforts*

Anglophone ■——■   Francophone ●----●   * $p < .05$

---

sponding immediately afterwards on the importance scale. Such a procedure may have caused a "halo" effect, resulting in the increased correspondence between the two ratings (positive correlations) in both groups. The results suggest that future studies on the relationship between satisfaction and importance scores should use separate sections in a questionnaire. Although the present format makes it difficult to draw any conclusions about the satisfaction-importance relationship, it does not invalidate separate intergroup comparisons (Figure 16 and 22) of satisfaction and importance scores. Both groups used the same format; hence any differences between them must be due to the characteristics of the group rather than the characteristics of the questionnaire.

The reactions of Anglophone and Francophone employees to organizational communication systems as discussed in this chapter are sufficiently different to deserve management attention and appropriate policy action. Effectiveness in downward communications can better be achieved by a careful analysis of the information needs of both groups of employees. For instance, management needs to impart more information more often in a continual effort to communicate with Anglophone employees in order to raise their level of satisfaction. Anglophones tend to demonstrate a greater need for feedback, and only increased communication can meet their need. Increased communication can also improve Anglophone satisfaction with organizational outcomes as well as attitudes toward the organization itself. Muchinsky (1977) found that an employee's satisfaction with communication was related to perceptions of other organizational properties or practices, such as an organization's psychological environment, management practice and the way the employees identified with the organization. Thus, satisfaction with organizational outcomes may well depend on satisfaction of employees with the communication system within the organization.

To improve upward communication, management must also learn to monitor feedback, that is, to listen and watch for employee responses and adjust its communication behavior accordingly. Relative dissatisfaction of Anglophone employees with upward communication calls for greater management attention to the reasons for dissatisfaction and possible remedies.

Communication effectiveness can also be increased by using a combination of media and methods (Dahle 1954, Hsia 1968) to suit the communication needs of the two groups of employees. It has been suggested that opinion change is greater in face-to-face situations, (Porter & Roberts, 1976) and employees prefer oral and personal communication to written or impersonal methods (Level 1959, Sanborn 1961, Tompkins 1962). Such methods could be used more often with both groups of employees. Finally, it is necessary for organizations to perform periodic formal appraisals of the general communication system in order to maintain and develop its effectiveness (Jain 1977, Greenbaum 1974) for both groups of employees.

CHAPTER 9

Attitudes Toward Supervision and In-House Training Programs

EVERY ORGANIZATION, WHETHER an industrial firm, a governmental agency, a hospital, or a university has a primary objective of producing and/or distributing goods or services for its customers. This is generally accomplished by employees of the organization. The employees enter the organization with different types and levels of abilities, training, cultural backgrounds, and personal needs. The human elements within the organization are varied and heterogeneous, and need to be coordinated and regularized so that employees can behave dependably, predictably and according to acceptable performance standards in spite of the diversity of their needs and abilities. They need to share the organizational objectives and to coordinate their own job activities with those of others in order to achieve the common organizational purpose. If these goals are to be realized, it is necessary that the organization provide proper supervision and training programs. However, the effectiveness of supervision and training programs in regulating employee behavior rests to a large extent on the employees' attitudes. For clarity, employees' attitudes toward supervision and toward training are treated separately in the following sections.

Attitudes Toward Supervisory Practice

Every organization is concerned with the effectiveness of its supervisors in influencing and controlling subordinates' behavior. How does a supervisor exert influence and control over his subordinates? A review of the theories of social influence (Cartright, 1965) suggests that the effectiveness of a supervisor stems from his subordinates' perception that he possesses and controls the resources valued by them. According to Dahl (1957), possession of such resources forms the basis of a supervisor's power over subordinates. French and Raven (1960) have distinguished five bases of power—

the means which a supervisor is perceived to be using in order to influence or elicit compliance behavior. Job attitudes can be analyzed on the basis of these bases of power.

Reward Power of a Supervisor   A supervisor may be seen as having the ability to bring in rewards such as higher pay or promotion for subordinates. Subordinates' perception that a supervisor can mediate rewards for them provides the supervisor with greater power over them. However, it must be emphasized that supervisory influence through reward power increases only when the subordinates value the rewards that the supervisor can mediate and when they believe that by conforming to the supervisor's directives they can in fact obtain these rewards.

Coercive Power of a Supervisor   The "coercive power" of a supervisor stems from the subordinates' perception that the supervisor can punish them if they do not comply with his directives. The manifestation of coercive power can be seen in situations where the supervisor threatens the subordinates with negative consequences such as demotion, loss of job, etc., for non-compliance behavior, and where the subordinates accept the supervisor's influence in order to avoid these unpleasant consequences.

Referent power of a supervisor   A supervisor is perceived to have referent power over his subordinates when the subordinates feel a strong sense of identification with or a liking for the supervisor as a person. The pleasant personal characteristics and interpersonal sensitivity of the supervisor may induce in the subordinates a feeling of "oneness" or "identity" with him. This kind of identification will result in greater liking for the supervisor. In order to maintain the close association with the supervisor, the subordinates will try to please him by their compliant behavior.

Expert Power of a Supervisor   The expert power of a supervisor stems from the subordinates' perception that he possesses advanced knowledge or expertise to handle job-related problems. When subordinates believe that the supervisor can assist them in solving their problems at work because he has greater job skills, experience, and training, they are more inclined to follow supervisory directives on the job.

Legitimate power of a supervisor   A supervisor assumes legitimate power over his subordinates when the subordinates perceive that the supervisor, by virtue of his authority position within the organization, has a right to influence them and that they as subordinates have an obligation to accept this influence. Recently, two forms of legitimate power bases have been identified (Tannenbaum, Kavcic, Rosner, Vianello and Wieser, 1974). One form of legitimate power is based on the subordinates' belief in the "law of the situation"; that supervisory influence is necessary to increase the efficiency of the organization. The other form of legitimate power is based on the subordinate's perception of his compliance with supervisory influence as an expression of his personal sense of duty, regardless of whether it increases organizational efficiency.

During the past decade, several studies (for example, Burke and Wilcox, 1971; Student, 1968) dealt with the relative effectiveness of the five bases of supervisory power within organizations. The study reported in this chapter was designed as an extension of this line of investigation and deals with several major issues in the Canadian bicultural context.

The first and perhaps the most significant issue is understanding the nature of perceived supervisory power and its relation to compliance behavior in a bicultural context. Earlier studies have not dealt with the general question of cultural differences among the respondents and how such differences may affect the perceptions of the supervisory power base. In the present study, however, two groups of culturally identifiable employees (Francophone and Anglophone) were studied to reveal the effects of the cultural variable. Since the results reported in the previous chapters have revealed significant differences in job perceptions among the two groups, it is quite reasonable to assume that significant differences exist with respect to their perceptions of bases of supervisory power at work and their reasons for acceding to supervisory control. The issue can be stated as follows: which of the five power bases is perceived to produce greater frequency of compliance behavior among the subordinates? How do the Anglophone employees differ from the Francophone employees in this regard?

This chapter also examines another issue closely related to the issue of subordinates' compliance with supervisory control. Employees need varying degrees of supervision for better handling of their jobs. An employee with a strong need for job autonomy may not prefer close supervision, whereas an employee who thinks supervisory help is necessary for better performance may prefer close supervision. How do Anglophone and Francophone employees view close supervision on the job? Do they differ from each other with regard to their preference for closer supervision?

Besides the cultural variables, the differential effects of the five bases of power may depend partly on the type of organizational and occupational setting in which the employees work. For example, in an educational organization, expert power of the supervisor may be perceived by faculty members to be a more important base of subordinate compliance than legitimate power, while in an industrial organization, the workers may perceive the reverse to be true (Backman, 1968; Burke and Wilcox, 1971). This study explored this third issue within an industrial organization, using three groups of employees with distinct job functions. It seems reasonable to assume that even within a given organization, the nature of job functions (such as sales, administration etc.) will enhance the subordinate's perception of one supervisory power base rather than another. Due to different norms of supervision existing in different departments, subordinates will differ from each other in their perception of which power-base creates greater frequency of compliance behavior.

Another major issue is the relationship between the perceived supervisory power-base and satisfaction with various job outcomes. For example, Burke and Wilcox (1971) suggest that referent power of a supervisor should be positively related to subordinates' satisfaction with considerate supervision and the presence of a helping relationship between supervisor and subordinates. Expert power, on the other hand, should be positively related to satisfaction with the job, the way it is handled, and the company as a whole. In this chapter, the relationship of the perceived supervisory power-base to satisfaction with job outcomes and to the overall job satisfaction of subordinates is explored.

Finally, there is the theoretical issue of the degree of independence among the perceived bases of supervisory power. Earlier studies (Burke and Wilcox, 1971, Student, 1968) have suggested that although the bases of power as defined by French and Raven (1960) seem to be conceptually independent dimensions, in actual organizational settings they seem to be related. Quite frequently, any instance of compliance behavior of subordinates in an organizational context seems to stem from more than one perceived supervisory power base. In the present study, an attempt has been made to reveal the nature of the relationship among the various bases of supervisory power and to compare the results with those of the earlier studies.

In order to deal with these issues an employee survey was conducted in several Canadian branches of an international organization. The sample and the procedure used in the survey have been described in detail in Chapter 4. Briefly, the questionnaire used in the survey was prepared after several pretesting sessions. It was written both in English and in French, following a translation-retranslation procedure for its use in Québec. The sample consisted of 379 Francophone and 210 Anglophone employees belonging to the sales, service, and administration divisions. (The questionnaire appears in Appendix F, p. 173.)

In order to measure subordinates' need for close supervision, the questionnaire included one item on the employee's preference for close supervision on the job: "I like a job where my boss supervises my work very closely." The employees were asked to indicate their responses to the item on a five-point scale ranging from "all the time" (ordinal weight 5) to "never" (ordinal weight 1).

In addition, six other items assessed subordinates' perceptions of the bases of supervisory power: coercive, expert, reward, referent, and two kinds of legitimate powers (duty- and efficiency-based). All six items contained the statement "Whenever my boss asks me to do something on the job, I do it because . . . " followed by specific reasons. The specific reasons represented the six bases of power:

(a) my boss causes trouble for me if I do not comply (coercive);
(b) I respect the superior knowledge and the technical competence of my boss (expert);
(c) my boss can give special help and benefits to me (reward);
(d) my boss is a very friendly person whom I like (referent);
(e) I consider it my duty to obey my boss (legitimate-duty);
(f) obeying my boss is necessary for organizational efficiency (legitimate-efficiency).

For each of the items, the employees were asked to respond on a five-point scale.

To assess the levels of satisfaction with various job outcomes, the questionnaire included items similar to those described in Chapter 5. The employees were asked to indicate their overall job satisfaction and satisfaction with fifteen different job factors on six-point scales ranging from "extremely satisfied" (ordinal weight 6) to "extremely dissatisfied" (ordinal weight 1).

Perceived Nature of Supervisory Influence   The mean scores with respect to the need for close supervision and each of the six bases of supervisory power are shown in Figure 23 (for employees in each of three departments) and Figure 24 (Francophone and Anglophone employees). Both reveal that legitimate power of supervisors is perceived to produce greater frequency of compliance behavior. Coercive power, on the other hand, is perceived to produce compliance behavior least frequently. Expert, reward and referent power bases fall in the middle. This pattern is consistent with the results of earlier studies in industrial contexts (Tannenbaum *et al.*, 1974). It seems that in most industrial organizations, the members are guided by the norms that emphasize the formal aspects of organizations, such as hierarchical structure, rules and regulations, etc. This is reflected in the greater effectiveness of legitimate supervisory power. The figures also show that employees in general want only occasional close supervision, and that coercive power does not produce much subordinate compliance.

104 BICULTURALISM AND MANAGEMENT

These trends are to be expected in a democratic society where people abhor fear-based authority and value individual freedom and responsibility.

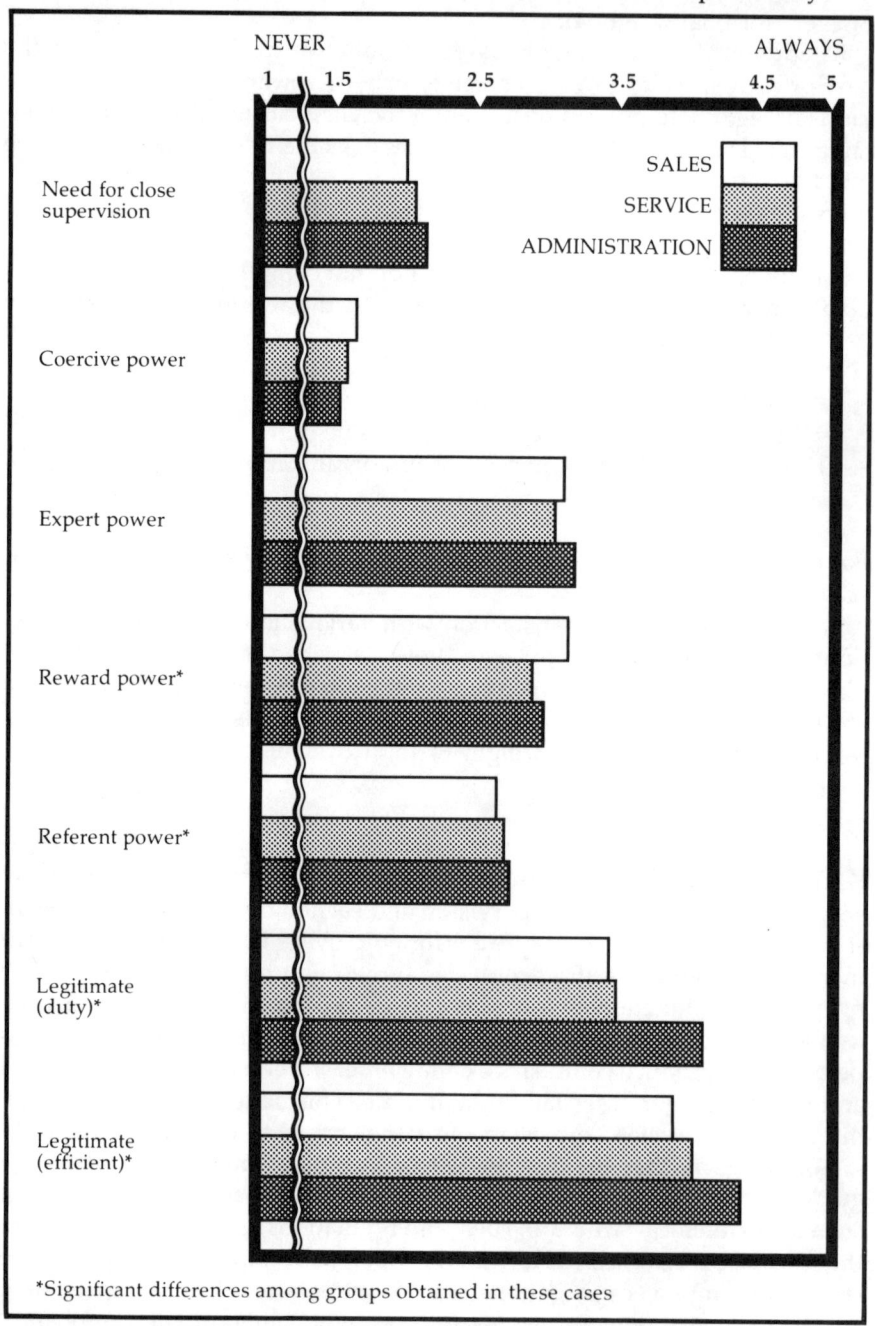

Figure 23: *Basis of Supervisory Power in Three Departments*

*Significant differences among groups obtained in these cases

More interesting aspects of the data shown in Figure 23 are revealed when the differences among the job functions are analyzed. After eliminating the effects of the covariants (cultural background and salary), we find that employees from each of the three departments differ in their perception of reward and legitimate power bases. Sales employees (N = 173) saw reward power of their superior as producing greater compliance behavior (mean=3.31) as compared to either service (N−223, mean = 2.89, $t = 3.31$, $p < .001$) or administrative employees (N = 89, mean = 2.95,

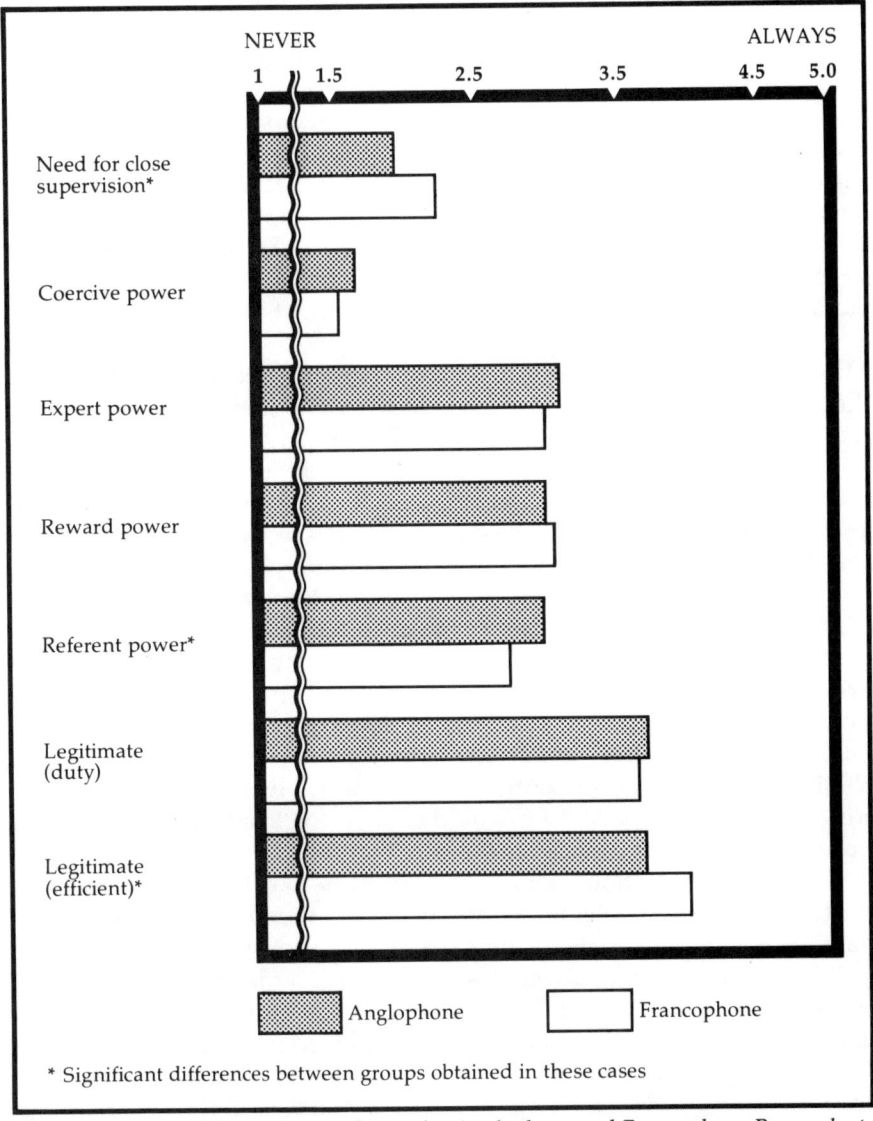

Figure 24: *Basis of Supervisory Power for Anglophone and Francophone Respondents*

$t = 2.65$, $p < .01$). On the other hand, administrative employees saw the two forms of legitimate power bases as being more effective in producing compliance behavior (mean for duty = 4.41; mean for efficiency = 4.19) than did sales (mean for duty = 3.83, mean for efficiency = 3.76, $t = 2.19$, $p < .05$, and $t = 3.32$, $p < .001$ respectively) or service employees (mean for duty = 3.86, mean for efficiency = 3.96, $t = 2.08$, $p < .05$, and $t = 1.90$, $p < .06$ respectively). These results can be explained in terms of the dominant departmental norms that govern the behavior of members. For instance, sales employees are motivated to a greater extent than other employees by concrete feedback on their job in terms of money, recognition, etc. (McClelland (1961) has suggested that high-need achievers who have a strong need for concrete feedback are attracted to sales because the profession offers feedback opportunities). Administrative employees are more concerned with maintaining rules, regulations, and the formal structure within the organization. Thus, it is natural that while governing their own behavior, they will focus more on legitimate authority of the supervisor than will either sales or service employees. Different departmental norms will influence a subordinate's perception of a supervisor's power, and it may be appropriate for a supervisor to adjust his influence attempts accordingly.

Some interesting cultural differences were also noticed among Anglophone and Francophone employees with respect to their perceptions of the nature of supervisory influence. Figure 24 reveals that Francophone employees showed a relatively greater need for close supervision (Anglophone mean = 1.91, Francophone mean = 2.23, $t = 5.34$, $p < .001$). Francophone employees also perceived efficiency-based legitimate power to be more effective (mean = 4.01) than did Anglophones (mean = 3.78, $t = 2.62$, $p < .01$). Anglophone employees, on the other hand, saw reference power as being more effective (mean = 3.03) than did Francophones (mean = 2.69, $t = 3.19$, $p < .01$). These differences can be explained in terms of the profiles of Anglophone and Francophone managers documented in previous chapters. Empirical data suggests that Francophones tend to be role-bound while Anglophones tend to be person-bound. Within the organizational context, Francophones tend to emphasize role prescriptions on their job. They would be expected to attach greater importance to closer supervision (to make sure that they are in fact behaving according to role definitions) and to the legitimate power of the supervisor. Anglophones tend to look for greater personal autonomy on the job. They want fewer supervisory restrictions placed on their own ways of handling their jobs. They place relatively less importance on legitimate power, but respond favorably to the referent power of the supervisor who understands their personal needs for autonomy and responsibility. Anglophones like and identify with such supervisors, and feel that they can work better under them.

Relationship Between Supervisory Influence and Job Satisfaction Measures In order to see how employee need for close supervision and perceived bases of supervisory power are related to satisfaction with job outcomes, correlation coefficients were calculated separately for Francophone and Anglophone employees. The results are presented in Table 3. Several interesting trends can be observed. First, it may be noticed that one's need for close supervision seems to have very little relation to the job satisfaction measures. For example, out of a total of sixteen correlation coefficients, one was significant in the case of Francophone employees, and six were significant in the case of Anglophone employees. Second, perceived coercive supervisory power tends to appear with lower levels of satisfaction (evidenced by the negative correlations shown in Table 3). Thirteen correlations (Anglophones) and twelve correlations (Francophones) were found to be significant. It is clear that utilization of coercive power by the supervisors will decrease employee job satisfaction. Third, perceived expert, reward, and referent powers of the supervisor seem to appear with higher levels of job satisfaction in the case of Anglophone employees. This trend is not as strong in Francophone employees. In the case of expert power, eleven (Anglophone) and six (Francophone) correlations were significant. The corresponding numbers for reward power are eleven and seven, and for referent power fifteen and seven. This might indicate that referent, expert, and reward powers may contribute more towards job satisfaction in Anglophone employees than they do in Francophone employees. Fourth, with regard to the two kinds of legitimate supervisory powers, a greater number of significant correlations were seen in the case of Francophone employees (fourteen and sixteen) than in the case of Anglophone employees (two and three). This suggests that legitimate power contributes significantly toward job satisfaction for Francophone employees, but very little for Anglophones.

Relationship of Supervisory Influence Measures Intercorrelations among the measures of perceived supervisory influence and the need for close supervision were calculated separately for Anglophones and Francophones. The results are presented in Table 4. For Francophone employees, the need for close supervision is positively related to each of the two kinds of legitimate power, but for the Anglophones, it is related (a low but significant correlation) only to efficiency-based legitimate power. As expected, for both groups of employees, the two kinds of legitimate powers are positively related. Employees who comply with a supervisor's directives because they consider it their duty also feel that such compliance increases organizational efficiency. Both of these beliefs derive from the perceived legitimacy of the supervisor's position within the organization. For both Anglophone and Francophone employees, expert, reward, and referent

108 BICULTURALISM AND MANAGEMENT

TABLE 3
Relationship Between Measures of Supervisory Influence and Job Satisfaction for Anglophone and Francophone Employees

Job outcome items	Close supervision Anglo-phone	Close supervision Franco-phone	Coercive Anglo-phone	Coercive Franco-phone	Expert Anglo-phone	Expert Franco-phone	Reward Anglo-phone	Reward Franco-phone	Referent Anglo-phone	Referent Franco-phone	Legal duty Anglo-phone	Legal duty Franco-phone	Legal efficiency Anglo-phone	Legal efficiency Franco-phone
Security	−.05	.06	−.18*	−.08	.09	.02	−.01	.00	.12*	.09	.01	.13*	.03	.10*
Company policy	.05	.09	−.22*	−.13*	.27*	.07	.08	.01	.23*	.19*	.08	.22*	.05	.20*
Salary	.11	.09	−.29*	−.08	.14*	.07	.19*	.07	.17*	.01	.17*	.17*	.29*	.12*
Benefits	.13*	.03	−.20*	−.04	.16*	.06	.20*	.00	.10	−.04	.10	.17*	.15*	.11*
Chance of promotion	.05	.03	−.06	.11*	.24*	.17*	.19*	.16*	.21*	.18*	−.06	.07	.04	.10*
Working counditions	.03	.07	.02	−.17*	.00	.09	.10	.10*	.16*	.04	.01	.10*	.00	.15*
Interesting work	.12*	.05	−.15*	−.11*	.14*	.09	.18*	.04	.18*	−.04	.00	.10*	.10	.10*
Recognition	.01	.04	−.23*	−.14*	.22*	.22*	.22*	.12*	.33*	.18*	.06	.21*	.04	.19*
Peer relation	.12*	.07	.00	−.13*	.04	.13*	.10	.09	.16*	.17*	.04	.13*	.05	.12*
Technical supervision	.17*	.06	−.36*	−.15*	.59*	.47*	.39*	.19*	.44*	.32*	.15*	.13*	.11	.12*
Achievement	.00	.09	−.12*	−.18*	.20*	.15*	.26*	.10*	.20*	.06	.06	.16*	.10	.16*
Sympathetic supervision	.11*	−.01	−.41*	−.18*	.47*	.35*	.35*	.16*	.55*	.34*	.07	.11*	.07	.13*
Responsible individual	.14*	.10*	−.29*	−.12*	.09	.02	.07	.05	.26*	.06	.08	.11*	.07	.11*
Opportunity for skill	.10	.00	−.17*	−.09	.14*	.09	.19*	.10*	.20*	.09	−.06	.09	.00	.13*
Fair pay	.08	.09	−.31*	−.11*	.11	.09	.19*	.09	.16*	.10*	.08	.20*	.19*	.20*
Overall	.08	.05	−.26*	−.21*	.28*	.08	.25*	.06	.25*	.06	.02	.14*	.01	.20*

* p<.05

TABLE 4

Intercorrelation Among Supervisory Influence Variables for Anglophone and Francophone Employees

	Coercive		Expert		Reward		Referent		Legitimate duty		Legitimate efficiency	
	Anglo-phone	Franco-phone	Anglo-phone	Franco-phone	Anglo-phone	Franco-phone	Anglo-phone	Franco-phone	Anglo-phone	Franco-phone	Anglo-phone	Franco-phone
Need for close supervision	−.07	−.06	−.14*	.15*	.09	.00	.19*	.14*	.06	.27*	.12*	.25*
Coercive power			−.15*	−.13*	−.06	.07	−.23*	−.04	.01	−.19*	−.09	−.27*
Expert power					.54*	.31*	.56*	.41*	.21*	.16*	.10	.14*
Reward power							.52*	.33*	.19*	.03	.20*	.12*
Referent power									.17*	.12*	.16*	.15*
Legitimate (duty)											.54*	.56*

* $p < .05$

powers are positively related to one another. Supervisors may be perceived to be utilizing these power bases together more often than any other combination. Similar relationships have been reported by Student (1968) in his study on supervisory power in an industrial context.

In summary, the results of the study reveal that prevailing group norms, whether organizational (relative importance of legitimate and expert power in industry and university), departmental (relative importance of reward and legitimate power in sales, service and administration departments), or cultural (relative importance of referent and legitimate power for Francophones and Anglophones), tend to influence the perceived effectiveness of different bases of supervisory power. Such norms also determine in part the degree to which different bases of supervisory power influence job satisfaction. In order to be effective, a supervisor should exhibit influence behavior consistent with his subordinates' perceptions of what constitutes effective bases of supervisory power. By doing so, a supervisor may also contribute toward the subordinate's job satisfaction.

Attitudes Toward In-House Training Programs

Large corporations often have in-house training programs of their own that help employees develop necessary skills. In smaller organizations, supervisors often train employees on the job. Sometimes, employees are sent to training programs operated by an outside agency. Whatever the mode of training, its importance to both new and old employees cannot be overemphasized.

Training new employees to develop appropriate job skills and old employees to keep up-to-date with new technology and changing work methods should be viewed as an investment in the human resources of the organization. In order to realize an adequate return on this investment, it is necessary not only to design and institute sound training programs based on the needs of the organization, but also to evaluate the effectiveness of such training programs by assessing employee attitude toward the various components of the programs. A training program is successful when the trainees feel that it helps them to learn new skills. However, if the trainees feel that the program causes them considerable difficulty in achieving their learning goals, it is time for program revision. Feedback from trainees on various aspects of the program such as materials, location, instructor, etc. provides vital information which can help managers to evaluate and revise training programs.

Evaluation of training programs becomes even more important in a bicultural context. For instance, Québec training programs should meet the needs of both Francophone and Anglophone employees. If the language of materials is English and the trainer is a unilingual Anglophone, the program might cause problems of comprehension for Francophone trainees.

Similarly, if the training materials are presented only in French and the trainer is a unilingual Francophone, the Anglophone trainees might derive little benefit from the program. In order to maximize the benefits to all employees, a manager in a bicultural organization should gather employee feedback on a regular basis and assess the training needs of both groups of employees from time to time. On the basis of such information, the manager will be better able to redesign the program. One such attempt at evaluating the training programs of a bicultural organization is described below.

A survey of employee attitude toward various aspects of orientation and training programs was conducted in the same organization referred to in the section on supervision. The organization had training programs at six different levels. The first level orientation (and pre-school) training for new Canadian recruits to the organization took place in Canada. The second level training took place at the basic school located in the United States. The employees were sent there for one to two months. The third level, or post-school training took place on the return of employees to branch offices in Canada. There were three other levels of training in Canada: advanced training, day-to-day job training, and pre-management training. At each level, different materials and instructors were used. All materials and instructions were in English.

The questionnaire used to assess employee attitude toward the programs included two sets of items. The first set was designed to indicate whether the employees faced any difficulty at each of the six levels. Specifically, the employees were asked whether they faced difficulty due to (a) use of English in training materials, (b) use of an Anglophone trainer, and (c) the presence of Anglophone co-trainees. The second set was designed to determine employee preference for (a) use of French in training materials, (b) use of unilingual or bilingual trainers, (c) use of culturally homogeneous co-trainee groups, and (d) suitable location of the basic school training. The responses of the employees to each item in the questionnaire were recorded on five-point scales. (The questionnaire is presented in Appendix G, p. 175.)

Training Difficulty due to English Materials   Employees were asked to indicate on a five-point agree-disagree scale (with ordinal weights of 1 to 5 respectively) whether they had difficulty in comprehending and assimilating information presented to them in English in each of the six training situations. The mean scores of Anglophone and Francophone employees calculated separately are presented in Figure 25. Comparison of the two groups reveals that both manage adequately with English materials. Their mean scores fall on the "disagreement" side of the scale. However, the mean scores also indicate that, relative to Anglophone employees, Francophone employees face significantly greater difficulty in comprehension and assimilation because of the use of English materials. Furthermore, for Anglophone employees, different training situations made no difference with respect to the ease of handling materials. For Francophone employees, however, the basic school training in the United States caused relatively greater difficulty in comprehension of materials. Difficulties in comprehension during training increase as Francophones move out from their local branch office in Québec. While they are in the branch office, the Francophone employees are able to seek assistance in matters of comprehension and assimilation from their more experienced bilingual peers. Such benefits from peer consultation are substantially reduced during training in the United States.

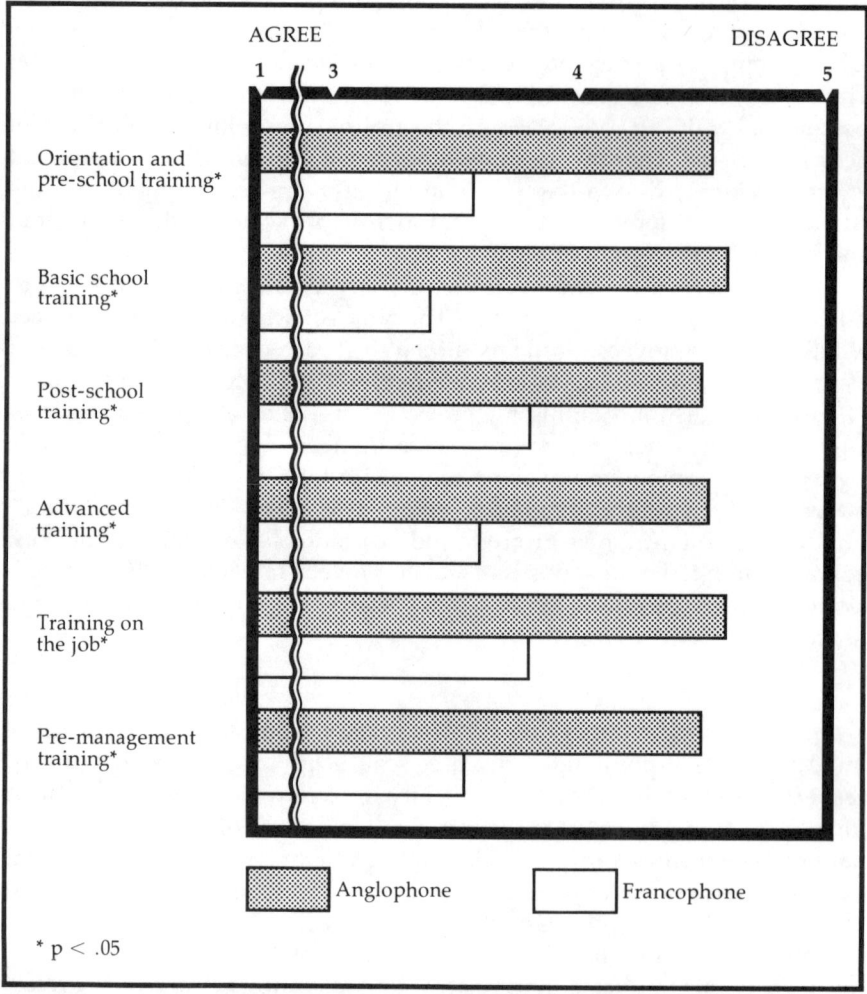

*$p < .05$

Figure 25: *Training Difficulty Due to English Materials*

Training Difficulty due to Anglophone Trainer   When employees were asked to indicate (on a five-point agree-disagree scale) whether trainers who spoke only in English caused difficulties for them, the two groups responded much as they did with respect to English training materials. The mean score comparisons are presented in Figure 26. Both groups found the Anglophone trainer acceptable, but the Francophone trainees faced greater difficulty in understanding and communicating with the trainer than the Anglophone trainees. The difficulty was greater for the Francophone trainees at the basic school in the United States than it was at the local branch office.

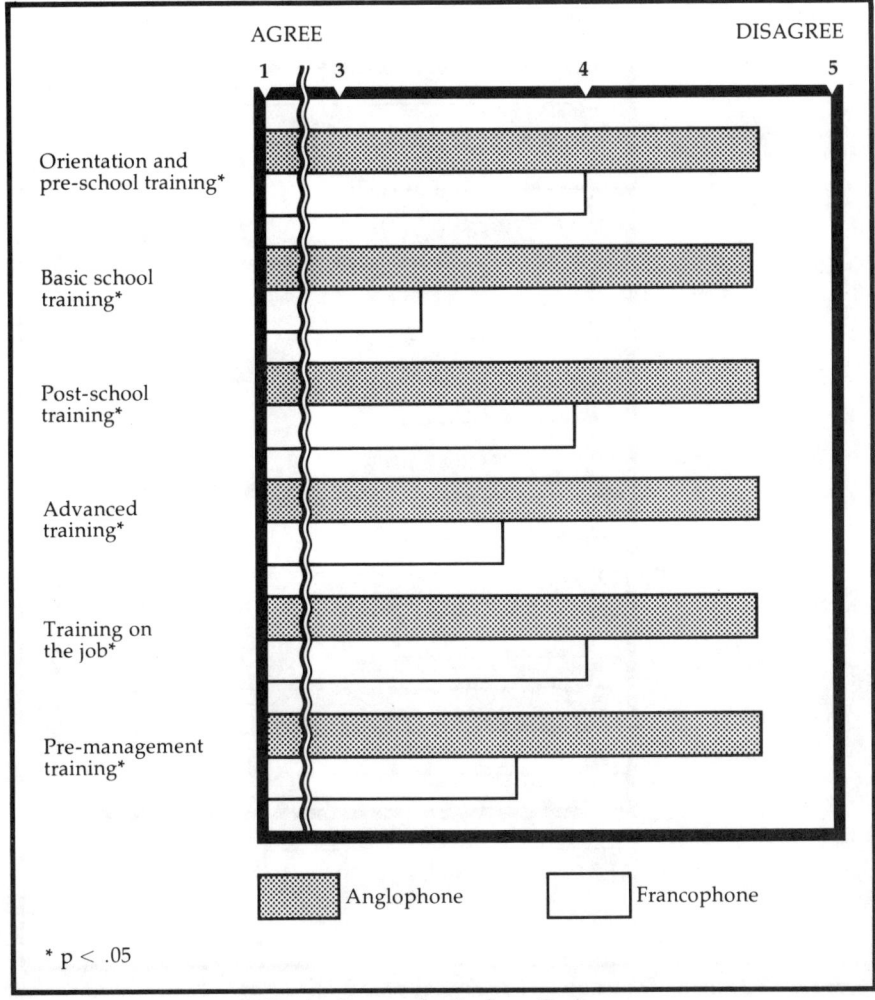

Figure 26: *Training Difficulty Due to Anglophone Trainer*

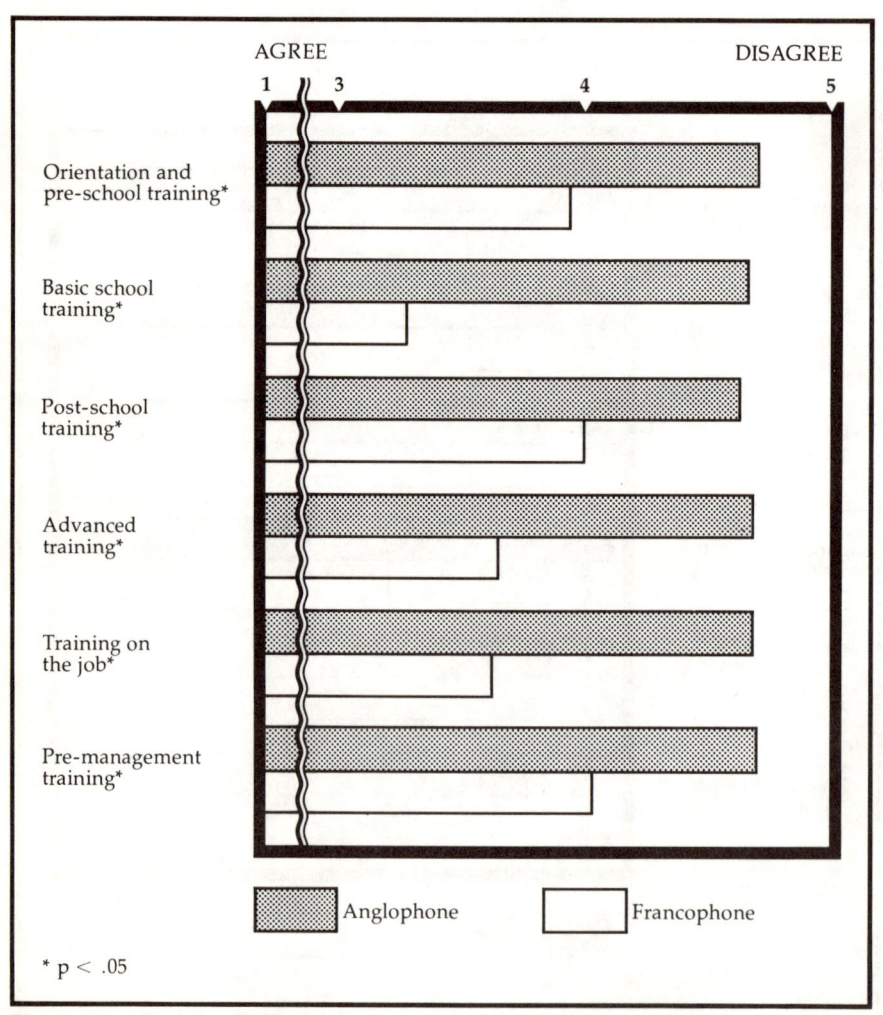

Training Difficulty due to Anglophone Co-Trainees Because of the international character of the company's operations, very often the training situations involve large numbers of Anglophone co-trainees. Their presence may cause some difficulties for Francophone trainees. Since English is not the first language of the Francophone trainees, they may feel reluctant to express themselves freely in English, particularly when Anglophone co-trainees are present. To avoid embarrassment in front of their colleagues, they may prefer to take the passive role of a listener rather than to actively participate during the sessions. In order to explore this possibility, employees were asked to indicate (on a five-point agree-disagree scale) whether they felt uncertain and uneasy interacting with Anglophone co-trainees

Figure 27: *Training Difficulty Due to Anglophone Co-Trainees*

during training sessions. Comparison of the mean scores of the two groups is presented in Figure 27. Here again, the pattern of results is similar to those described in the preceding sections. Francophone employees faced more difficulty than did Anglophone employees in expressing themselves and interacting freely with others during training (classroom interactions, role-playing situations, etc). Furthermore, these difficulties were manifested to a greater extent during basic school training in the United States than in other training situations at local branch offices.

Employee Preference for French Training Material   The employees were asked to show their agreement or disagreement on a five-point scale to the item which read "The company should make all the training material available in French." The mean scores of Francophone and Anglophone employees are presented in Figure 28. It is clear that the Francophone employees considered the availability of French materials more desirable than did the Anglophone employees.

Employee Preference for Unilingual or Bilingual Trainer   The trainee's attitude towards the trainer or instructor will influence how well and how

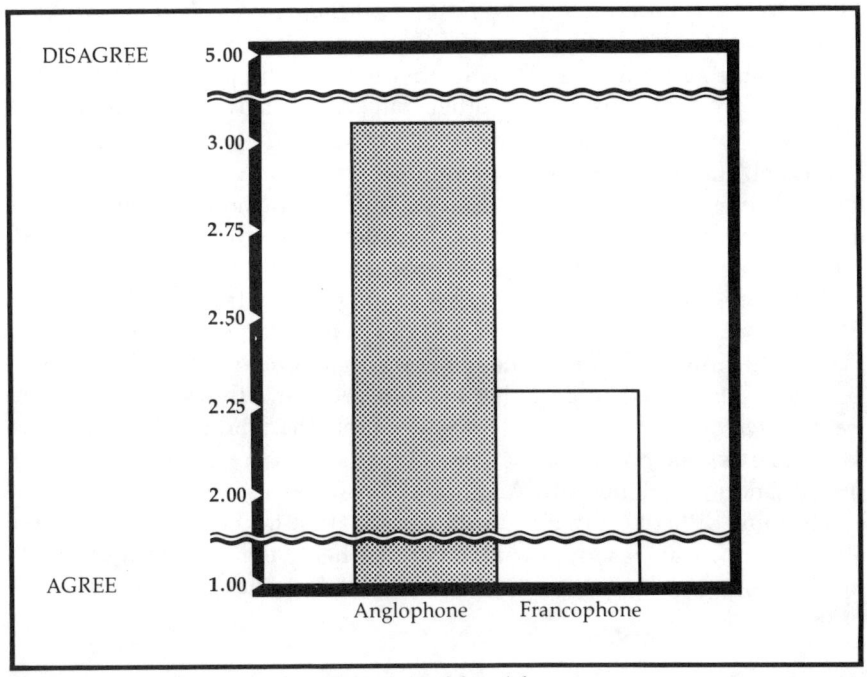

Figure 28:   *Preference for French Training Materials*

much he learns. If the attitude is favorable, the trainee will probably benefit more from the program than he will if the attitude is unfavorable. In a bicultural context, the attitudes of trainees may be largely determined by the perceived similarity or difference in the cultural and linguistic backgrounds of themselves and the trainers.

In the context of the present study it was expected that the employees would prefer trainers belonging to a cultural background similar to their own. The questionnaire probed the preference of employees on a five-point desirable-undesirable scale. Employees were asked to indicate the desirability of four types of trainers (unilingual Anglophone, bilingual Anglophone, unilingual Francophone, and bilingual Francophone) in two locations (basic school and branch office). The mean scores of Anglophone and Francophone employees are presented in Figure 29. In general, employees did not consider it desirable to have a unilingual Anglophone trainer. A unilingual Francophone trainer, on the other hand, was favored by Francophone employees, but was considered undesirable by Anglophone trainees; bilingual trainers were favored by both groups. Within each group, however, Francophone bilingual trainers were considered most desirable by Francophone employees and Anglophone bilingual trainers were considered most desirable by Anglophone employees.

Employee Preference for Homogeneous Francophone Co-Trainee Group at Basic School The composition of the trainee groups may affect the degree to which a trainee can benefit from the training program. Very often trainees learn a great deal from other trainees through mutual interaction, discussion and clarification sessions both inside and outside the classroom. In organizations with both Anglophone and Francophone employees, training programs can be offered either to mixed or homogeneous groups of Francophones and Anglophones. In order to determine employee preference, respondents to this study were asked to indicate on a five-point scale the desirability of mixed versus homogeneous trainee groups at the basic school training in the United States. The mean scores presented in Figure 30 show that homogeneous Francophone co-trainee groups were generally considered undesirable by both groups, although Francophone trainees felt such groups were less undesirable than did the Anglophones. This indicates the possibility of some benefits from the mixed-group training situation. Working with Anglophone co-trainees during training may create some difficulties in classroom participation for Francophones, but it also helps the trainees to understand each other better and to acquire ways of anticipating and adapting to difficulties arising out of similar situations in their jobs.

CHAPTER NINE—ATTITUDES TOWARD SUPERVISION

[Chart showing preferences on a Desirable (1) to Undesirable (5) scale]

Basic training
- Unilingual Anglophone
- Unilingual Francophone*
- Bilingual Francophone*
- Bilingual Anglophone

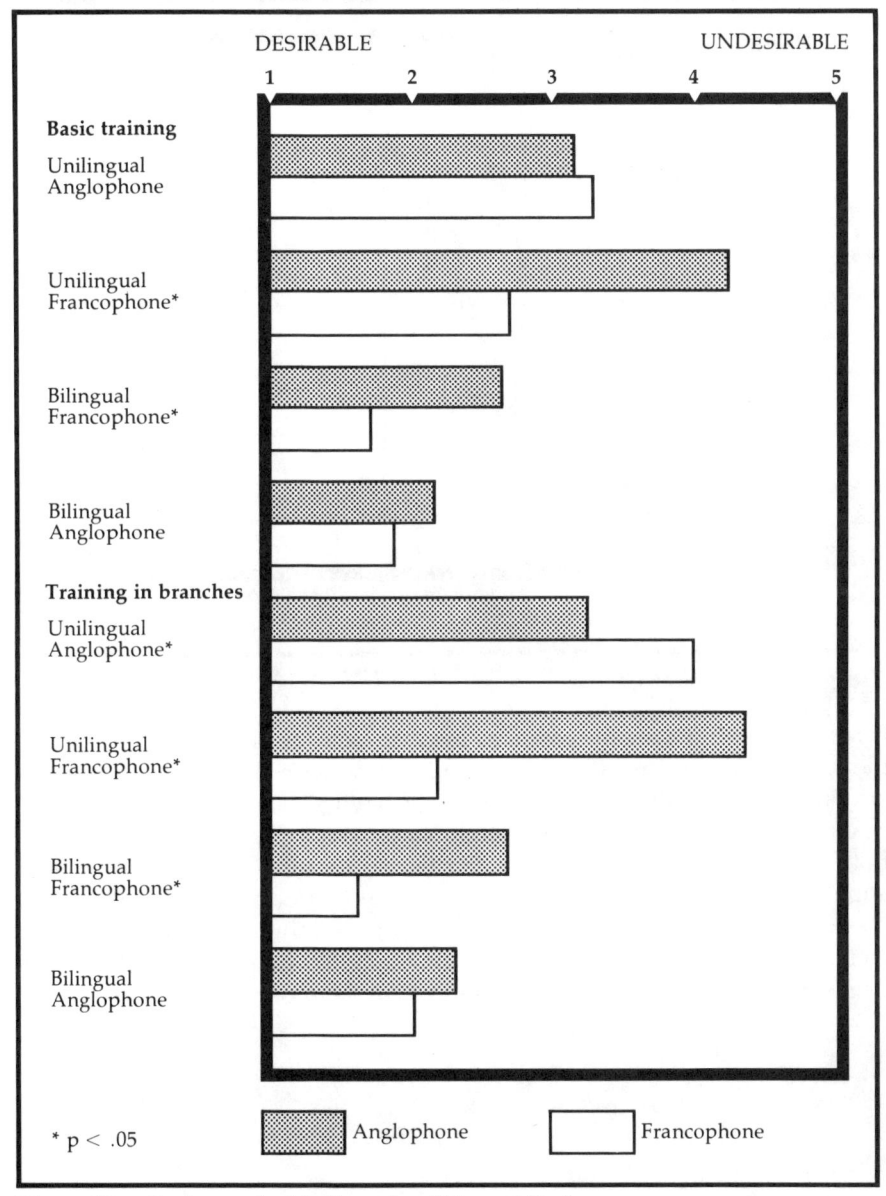

Training in branches
- Unilingual Anglophone*
- Unilingual Francophone*
- Bilingual Francophone*
- Bilingual Anglophone

* $p < .05$

Legend: Anglophone (shaded), Francophone (white)

Figure 29: *Preference for Unilingual or Bilingual Trainer*

Employee Preference for Location of Basic School Training Where should a large corporation with Anglophone and Francophone employees and branches all over the country locate its basic training school? Employees were asked to indicate their preference (on a five-point agree-disagree scale) for having the training school in (a) the province of Québec and

118 BICULTURALISM AND MANAGEMENT

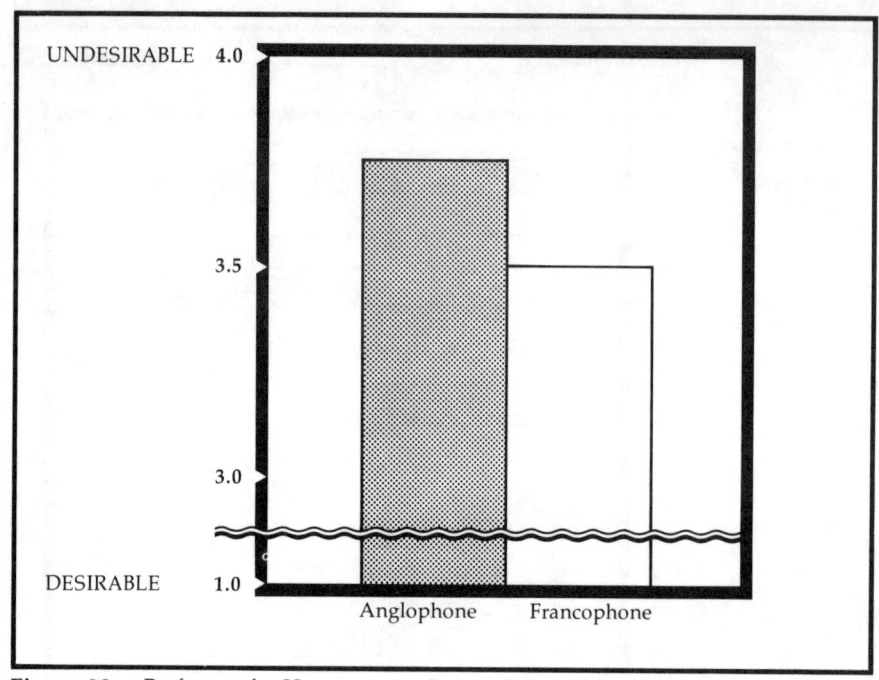

```
UNDESIRABLE  4.0

              3.5

              3.0

DESIRABLE     1.0
              Anglophone   Francophone
```

Figure 30: *Preference for Homogeneous Francophone Co-Trainee Group*

(b) in Canada. The mean scores for the Anglophone and Francophone employees are shown in Figure 31. It may be noticed that the Francophone employees were very much in favour of having basic school training located in Québec. However, the Anglophone employees opposed this idea. Both groups were in agreement with the idea that the basic training school should be located in Canada and not in the United States. It seems that home-based training schools are preferred to training schools abroad. In a bicultural context, perhaps two training schools catering to the cultural needs of the two groups of employees would be more appropriate.

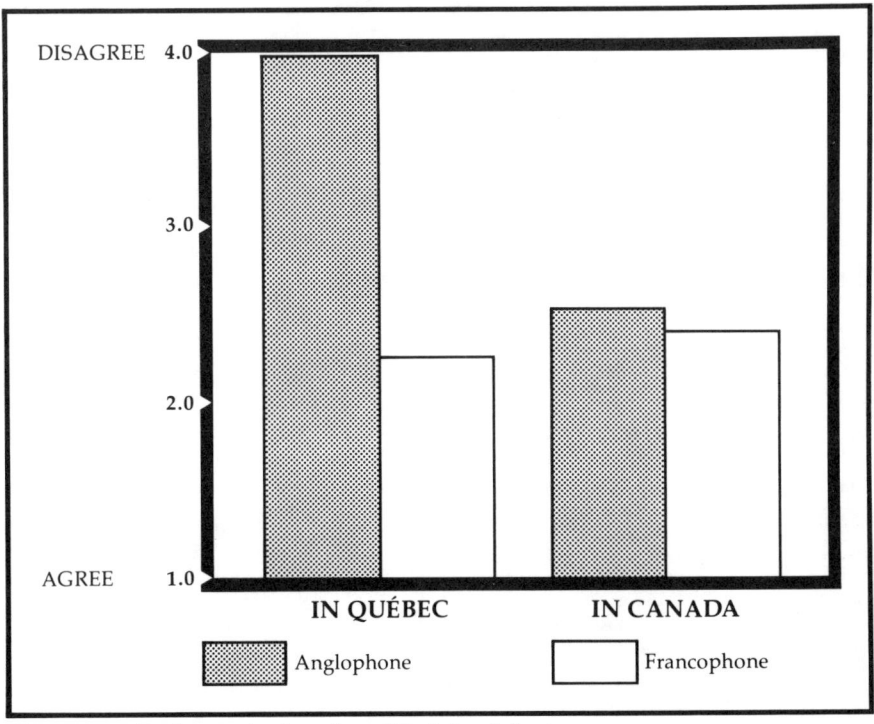

Figure 31: *Preference for Location of Training School*

CHAPTER 10

Summary and Conclusions: *Implications for Management*

THIS BOOK REPRESENTS an exploration into the nature of management in a bicultural context. The study of large Canadian organizations provides a unique opportunity for such exploration. Many organizations in Canada face the problem of effectively managing two culturally-distinct groups of employees—Anglophones and Francophones. These two groups constitute the major manpower resources of many Canadian organizations. In order to operate successfully, managers need to create and provide environmental conditions which will maximize the work motivation of the two groups of employees. To accomplish this objective, managers must first understand the job-related needs, expectations and attitudes of both their Francophone and Anglophone employees, and then they must establish management policies that are sensitive to these employee needs, expectations and attitudes.

A commonplace managerial practice is to develop a single set of policies based on bureaucratic principles (and sometimes managerial intuition), and apply these policies uniformly to all employees. The needs and expectations of culturally-distinct groups of employees are hardly taken into consideration. This phenomenon of "mirror management" or a single uniform management policy for every employee (discussed in Chapter 4) may seem equitable and fair in an organization where employees share similar job needs and expectations. But such a practice may not be beneficial for employees in an organization that contains two culturally distinct groups with different sets of job attitudes. Different job attitudes may require different management policies designed to motivate and satisfy the needs of the two groups of employees. Thus, in a bicultural context, application of the motto "business is business and therefore one set of management policies is best for everybody" may not be a prudent practice.

North American management practice has consistently promoted the idea that managers should follow a single set of personnel policies believed to be most effective in maintaining high motivation and morale among all employees. Organization theorists in the United States from Fredrick Taylor (1911) to Rensis Likert (1967) have consistently advocated use of a single set of management techniques for all employees. For example, Taylor's scientific management principles (such as the use of monetary incentives, work specialization etc.) have been indiscriminately used in organizations to increase worker productivity without the realization that for a sizable number of employees, use of such principles may be demotivating. Consider, for instance, the indiscriminate use of monetary incentives. In many organizations, failure of monetary incentives results from the fact that employees differ with respect to the strength of their need for financial incentives. While some employees find financial incentives motivating, others find them to have either no effect or a detrimental effect on their performance. In the recent wake of the humanistic approach to management, techniques like participative management, job enrichment, etc., advocated by Likert (1967), McGregor (1960), Herzberg (1966) and others have turned into organizational fads. Here again management gives no consideration to the possibility that these techniques may not be appropriate for all employees. For instance, workers in many developing countries prefer dependent rather than participative behavior at the work place. Likert (1961) has suggested that employees coming from authoritarian backgrounds respond less favorably to participative styles of management. Blake and Mouton (1964) indicate that many employees want direction and control of their on-the-job efforts because they feel threatened by the prospect of independently handling the technically complex work situation. In a recent study, Champagne and Tausky (1978) observed that while some workers reacted positively to a job enrichment program, many other workers quickly rejected the program when they found no financial gain from their participation in the program. These observations suggest that greater participation or enriched jobs with greater responsibility may be motivating only for those employees who place a high value on participation and autonomy. In spite of these observations, most managers consider it wrong for organizations to develop different policies for different groups of employees based on recognizable differences in employee needs, values and expectations.

Very often managers believe that, like American society, organizations should be seen as "melting pots." In such organizations, individual employees are viewed as "hired hands" paid to follow organizational policies and to provide their services as required by the organization. Their personal needs and expectations as determined by their own cultural norms are no business of the organization. Employees are viewed as passive creatures who should be socialized through organizational policies and practices and should leave their culture at home. This attitude is fairly common among North American managers and is often reflected in management practice, but it contradicts a body of recent literature on contingency theories of management. Of late, an increasing number of behavioral scientists are questioning the universal applicability of single management techniques such as participation, incentive system, job enrichment, etc. (see, for example, Lupton, 1971). Their number is small but is growing. These behavioral scientists suggest that organizations should individualize their management policies (Lawler, 1971). The policies should reflect managerial awareness of the culture-based needs and expectations of various groups of employees. The policies should be formulated with a view to motivating and increasing the job performance of all categories of employees through satisfaction of their needs. Organizational goals can be best accomplished when individual employees find adequate satisfaction of their salient needs through job performance. Since the cultural environment of the employees plays a major role in determining their needs, management cannot simply ignore the effects of cultural variables. Disregard of the cultural environment and culture-based needs and values of specific groups of employees may result in organizational failure, such as that experienced by managers trying to implement North American corporate policies in Afro-Asian and Latin American countries (Davis, 1969).

It is important for a manager in a bicultural setting in Canada to appreciate and understand the culture-based characteristics of Anglophone and Francophone employees. On the basis of such understanding the manager should develop appropriate management policies and adopt management practices suited to the needs and values of the two groups of employees.

In Chapter 4, consideration of occupational values of both groups of employees (the importance attached to job outcomes) suggests that the primary source of intrinsic motivation of both groups stems from engaging in interesting work. Both groups considered "interesting nature of work" to be the most desired job outcome. How can a manager make the job more interesting for the employees? Available research literature on work behavior (Lawler, 1971) suggests that a job becomes interesting for the employee when (a) it requires full utilization of employee's abilities, and (b) it provides feedback on employee performance in a meaningful task. Thus, in order to make work more interesting for employees, there should first be an attempt at assessing the specific abilities of employees, particularly those that the employees value most. Second, there should be an attempt to assess the extent to which various jobs within the organization demand the use of specific abilities. This will help the management to determine the best "fit" between an employee and a job. Very often, mismatching of employee ability and job demand results in boredom and monotony (in the case of under-utilization of abilities) or anxiety and exhaustion (in the case of over-utilization of abilities). Third, management policy should be formulated to provide meaningful performance feedback to employees on a regular basis. Work becomes interesting when employees are aware of a clear goal and a work method that leads them to such a goal. By establishing appropriate goal-setting procedures and performance feedback mechanisms, a manager can provide the employees with a constant sense of progress and of worthwhile accomplishment.

Besides being sensitive to the common desire of both groups of employees for more interesting work, the manager must also take into account the differing emphasis placed by the two groups on other intrinsic needs. For instance, Francophone employees put greater value on training opportunities to increase their skill level than do Anglophone employees, while Anglophones value individual autonomy and responsibility on the job more than do Francophones. This implies that organizations and jobs with training opportunities that can advance the skill levels of the employees will have greater attraction for Francophones than for Anglophones, while organizations and jobs that offer a greater degree of personal autonomy at work will have greater attraction for Anglophones than for Francophones.

The major source of extrinsic motivation for both groups stems from the adequacy of salaries and wages they receive to maintain a reasonably good standard of living. Many organization theorists advocating the humanistic approach to management (for example, Herzberg, 1966) have understated the importance of salaries and wages in job motivation. However, the results reported in this book suggest that salaries and wages are considered by the employees as relatively high in importance. In this respect, the results support the view expressed by Lawler (1971) "Pay should, in most instances, be rated high in importance because of its assumed ability to satisfy a large variety of needs [p. 39]"

Comparison of Anglophone and Francophone employees with respect to the importance they attach to various extrinsic job factors reveal some interesting differences. Anglophones attach greater importance to earnings, sound company policy and recognition for their work. On the other hand, job security, benefits, good working conditions and fair pay are more valued by Francophones. The presence or absence of these extrinsic job factors will influence the work motivation of both groups.

Comparative data on importance of job factors suggests that the nature of interpersonal relationships and supervision at work are of little importance to either group. These interpersonally-mediated job outcomes are least valued and therefore have the least potential for motivating employees. When employees find that their social (belonging) needs and their needs for supervisory assistance on the job are adequately met, they consider these job outcomes as relatively unimportant. Living in urban centres reduces the employee need for closer interpersonal relations at work. Constant availability of the supervisor in relatively safe jobs reduces the need for supervision. It is quite conceivable that the nature of supervision and good peer relations at work can become very important when the jobs create unsafe conditions and social isolation for employees (such as among mine workers in northern Canada).

Differences between Francophone and Anglophone employees with respect to perceived levels of commitment and participation have several implications for management practice. The results presented in Chapter 4 reveal that relative to Anglophone employees, Francophone employees exhibit lower levels of personal commitment to their job, department, and organization. They also participate less, but desire more participation at work. It is important that management policies be formulated to encourage a greater degree of participation and commitment among Francophone employees. At the job and departmental levels, Francophone employees must be given greater opportunity for participation in the decision-making process. Deliberate and systematic attempts should be made to constantly seek their opinions and suggestions in arriving at decisions that affect them. They should be provided with specific feedback with respect to how they perform on their jobs and how their performance influences departmental success. Commitment of Francophone employees can be enhanced only when they realize that the organization needs their job skills and their effort. At the organizational level, increased commitment and participation among Francophone employees can only be achieved through explicit policies that emphasize the non-regional (or national) character of the organization and reject the ideas of Anglophone domination and ownership. Such policies should aim at removing discriminating practices in hiring and promotions, and in language use in day-to-day communication. Visibility of Francophones at various levels within an organization and a corporate policy of bilingualism will help Francophone employees to participate and identify more with the organization.

In Chapter 5, the job satisfaction profiles and turnover potential of the Francophone and Anglophone employees are discussed. The data on the levels of satisfaction with various job outcomes suggest that both groups show a lower level of satisfaction with earnings, fairness of pay, and opportunity for promotion. These findings are not uncommon. Employees generally tend to show less satisfaction with salary and promotion than with other job outcomes. The basic reason for such feelings among employees lies in faulty management practice. Very often management does not clearly formulate salary and promotion policies. Even where sound policies do exist, they are not explicitly communicated to employees. Without adequate information on salary and promotion policies, employees tend to underestimate their earnings and chances of promotion. This contributes toward lower levels of satisfaction and job motivation. In order to overcome this problem, management must establish equitable salary and promotion policies and periodically provide information on these policies to employees at all levels within the organization.

The data presented in Chapter 5 also reveal that Francophone employees show a higher level of job satisfaction and a lower level of turnover potential than do Anglophone employees. It is quite natural to expect lower turnover potential among more satisfied employees. But the turnover potential is lower among Francophones not only because they are most satisfied in their jobs, but also because their work place is located in Québec. If potential turnover and employee dissatisfaction are viewed as human resource risks (involving greater cost) for organizations, unilingual Anglophone employees represent a greater risk (particularly in Québec) than do Francophone employees. In order to minimize such risk and its associated cost, organizations will be better off engaging in active recruiting of Francophones (preferably bilingual) for their Québec operations.

There is yet another reason why hiring and retaining Francophone employees may be beneficial for organizations in Québec. Data on employees' involvement in their jobs presented in Chapter 6, reveal that in general, Francophones show greater job involvement than do Anglophones. However, it must be emphasized that the sources of job involvement in the two groups are different. For Anglophone employees, if a job provides personal autonomy, responsibility, and recognition, the likelihood of their involvement is greater. Francophone employees are more likely to become involved if a job provides a training opportunity to acquire new skills, in addition to good working conditions, job security, benefits etc. In most organizations, the job outcomes do not meet salient autonomy and achievement needs of Anglophones to the same extent that they meet salient social and security needs of Francophones. It is relatively more difficult to restructure or redesign a job to provide greater autonomy than it is to create secure working conditions.

National and international organizations with Québec operations may find it more to their advantage to post in Québec Francophone employees (who show greater job satisfaction and job involvement and lower turnover potential) than Anglophone employees. However, data on readiness to accept transfers presented in Chapter 7 show that Francophone employees are less willing to accept transfers; they are reluctant because they feel more insecure and socially isolated when they are transferred to a location outside Québec. Consequently, Francophone employees want to stay in Québec even if they find that this may limit their career progress to a certain extent. This state of affairs causes some concern both to Francophone employees and to their employers. Advancement opportunities are lost for the employees, and the organization fails to properly utilize its manpower potential. An organization needs to take some active steps to assist Francophone employees in their career progress and encourage them to accept transfers wherever necessary. This can be achieved in several ways. The organization may transfer Francophone employees on a trial basis for a short period of time. They may be given the assurance of returning to the home office in Québec after the specified period. When the employees arrive on the new job location outside Québec, they may be given a "buddy" system of orientation to familiarize them with the new environment. Such orientation should be given by other experienced bilingual Francophone employees in the new location. The organization should also provide similar orientation programs to the families of newly-arrived Francophone employees. All these measures should be directed at meeting the social and security needs of transferred employees. In addition to making the unfamiliar job environment more attractive for the employees, the organization should provide other sought-after inducements such as a raise in salary or a promotion, or requiring the employee to master some novel skill in the job.

With respect to designing an effective communication system within an organization, as discussed in Chapter 8, it may be emphasized that both Francophone and Anglophone employees find job-related feedback from management to be of greater importance than organization-related feedback. While it is necessary that from time to time management should provide information about the objectives and long-term goals of the organization to employees, it is of even greater necessity that management provide, on a regular basis, information about the day-to-day work the employees perform. Since the need for job-related feedback is stronger among Anglophone employees, management needs to communicate with them more often to raise their level of satisfaction. Furthermore, effectiveness of organizational communication can improve if management can rely more heavily on direct and personal rather than indirect and impersonal channels of communication. Finally, it is of vital importance to any organization to monitor its communication system at regular intervals by conducting appropriate communication audits.

Chapter 9 deals with perceptions of Anglophone and Francophone employees with respect to the nature of supervisory influence and in-house training programs. Francophone employees find position power of the supervisor (legitimate power or authority vested in a supervisor) to be more effective, while Anglophone employees find personal or referent power of the supervisor to be more effective. The results suggest that Francophone employees will derive greater satisfaction from working under a supervisor who structures the task for them and provides them with clear-cut prescribed roles and expectations. Anglophone employees, on the other hand, will find greater satisfaction working under a supervisor who tends to leave them alone and who gives them maximum personal autonomy at work. This implies that in order to increase employees' work motivation, management should first try to assess the job expectations of subordinates with regard to supervisory behavior and then try to meet such expectations by forming compatible supervisor-subordinate teams.

Employee attitudes toward training programs, discussed in Chapter 9, show that Francophone employees face difficulty during training due to English materials and Anglophone instructors. In view of this it is desirable that training materials be made available also in French. It is also desirable that trainers be bilingual. There is much less resistance among employees to bilingual Anglophone trainers. However, Francophone bilingual trainers will be more appreciated by Francophone employees in Québec. The data also suggest that it is not desirable to form exclusive Francophone trainee groups during basic school training. A mixed group of trainees with bilingual trainers seems to be more useful. Finally, in a bicultural context, parallel training programs in two languages meeting the training needs of the two groups of employees would be more effective than a single program offered in one language. Such training programs should preferably be located close to home office.

As a final comment, it might be emphasized that modern management policies and practices must reflect a concern for needs and expectations of employees belonging to different cultural groups. In a bicultural or multicultural society where people come from different cultural backgrounds, organizations face a complex social environment. In these societies, organizations have to find their human resources in different cultural groups representing different values, attitudes, and expectations. If maximum utilization of human potential is desired by these organizations, then it is essential that the values and interests of distinct cultural groups be incorporated in corporate objectives.

APPENDIX A

Employee Survey Questionnaire

I. Questionnaire on Demographic Variables
II. Questionnaire on Perceived Importance of Job Outcomes.
III. Questionnaire on Personal Responsibility and Commitment.
IV. Questionnaire on Perceived and Desired Levels of Participation.
V. Questionnaire on Job Enrichment Potential.

I. Questionnaire on Demographic Variables

Please indicate your response to each item in appropriate spaces or boxes provided.

1. Your present work function (department or division)
2. Your present job category (with job title if necessary)
3. Do you supervise others? Yes ☐ 1   No ☐ 2
4. Your branch location (city and province) _____.
5. Indicate the highest educational qualification you have attained:
   Grade school   ☐ 1
   High school   ☐ 2
   University (3 or 4 years)   ☐ 3
   Graduate studies   ☐ 4
   Other   ☐ 5
6. Sex:
   Male   ☐ 1
   Female   ☐ 2
7. Marital status:
   Married   ☐ 1
   Single   ☐ 2
8. Your age: _____ years

9. Indicate your gross average annual earnings (including all sources).
    $ 5,001-$10,000 ☐ 1
    $10,001-$15,000 ☐ 2
    $15,001-$20,000 ☐ 3
    $20,001-$25,000 ☐ 4
    Over $25,001 ☐ 5
10. Indicate your mother tongue (Language mainly spoken by you from early childhood)
    French ☐ 1
    English ☐ 2
    Both ☐ 3
    Other _____ ☐ 4
11. How long have you been employed by your present employer?
    _____ years/months
12. How long have you been in your present job?
    _____ years/months
13. How many other organizations have you worked for before joining this organization?
    _____
14. How many years were you working before joining this organization?
    _____ years/months
15. How many years have you lived in:
    Québec _____
    Ontario _____
    Canada _____

II. Questionnaire on Importance of Job Outcomes

Below is a list of things people look for in their job career. Please read all the items from top to bottom before making any choice. First decide which one you think is the most important to you in your present job and then place 1 in the blank provided for the item. Do the same for your choice 2, 3, 4, 5, etc. Since there are 15 items in the list given below, your choice 15 would represent the thing that is least important to you in your present job. Please be sure you have placed a number opposite each item.

    _____ Security (permanent job, steady work)
    _____ Adequate earning (for a better standard of living)
    _____ Benefits (vacations, bonus, pension, insurance, profit sharing, medical benefits, disability, dental benefits etc.)
    _____ Opportunity for future promotion
    _____ Comfortable working conditions (pleasant surrounding, good lighting, air-conditioning, good office space, etc.)

_____ Interesting nature of work (a job that you very much enjoy)
_____ Sound company policies and practices (reasonable and non-discriminatory)
_____ Respect and recognition (from superiors and co-workers for your work)
_____ Responsibility and independence (a job that gives you responsibility to work in your own way)
_____ Achievement (opportunity to achieve excellence in your work)
_____ Good interpersonal relations (a job that gives you the opportunity to work with others whom you like)
_____ Considerate and sympathetic superior
_____ Technically competent superior
_____ Opportunity for professional growth (to become more skilled and competent on the job)
_____ Fair pay for the work you do

III. Questionnaire on Personal Responsibility and Commitment

To what extent do you feel really responsible and committed in achieving success

1. in your own job:
   - To a great extent ☐ 4
   - To a moderate extent ☐ 3
   - To a very limited extent ☐ 2
   - Not at all ☐ 1
2. in your own department:
   - To a great extent ☐ 4
   - To a moderate extent ☐ 3
   - To a very limited extent ☐ 2
   - Not at all ☐ 1
3. in the whole company:
   - To a great extent ☐ 4
   - To a moderate extent ☐ 3
   - To a very limited extent ☐ 2
   - Not at all ☐ 1

IV. Questionnaire on Perceived and Desired Levels of Participation

1. When decisions are being made, should the people affected by such decisions be asked for their opinions and suggestions?
    - They should almost never be asked □ 1
    - They should be asked sometimes □ 2
    - They should be asked most of the time □ 3
    - They should be asked always □ 4
2. When decisions are being made that affect you and your job, how often are your opinions and suggestions solicited?
    - Almost always □ 4
    - Very frequently □ 3
    - Occasionally □ 2
    - Never □ 1

V. Questionnaire on Job Enrichment Potential

1. Do you think you have more ability than your job demands?
    Yes □ 0   No □ 1
2. If yes, would you say you have:
    - A great deal more ability than your job demands □ 4
    - A little more ability than your job demands □ 3
    - Just enough to do the job □ 2

La Version Française

Spécifiez clairement à l'endroit indiqué
1. Indiquez votre genre de travail (département ou division)
2. Indiquez votre catégorie de travail (avec votre titre, si nécessaire)
3. Est-ce que vous supervisez quelqu'un dans votre travail?
    - Oui □ 1
    - Non □ 2
4. Nommez l'endroit de votre succursale. Ville et Province _____
5. Indiquez le plus haut degré d'études obtenu:
    - études élémentaires □ 1
    - études secondaires □ 2
    - études universitaires □ 3
    - études post-universitaires □ 4
    - autres □ 5
6. Votre sexe:
    - Masculin □ 1
    - Féminin □ 2

7. Etat civil:
   Marié ☐ 1
   Célibataire ☐ 2
8. Votre âge: _____
9. Indiquez votre revenu annuel brut (de toutes les sources de votre revenu).
   $ 5,001-$10,000 ☐ 1
   $10,000-$15,000 ☐ 2
   $15,001-$20,000 ☐ 3
   $20,001-$25,000 ☐ 4
   de $25,001 ☐ 5
10. Indiquez votre langue maternelle (la langue que vous parlez depuis votre enfance).
    Français ☐ 1
    Anglais ☐ 2
    Français-Anglais ☐ 3
    Autres ☐ 4
11. Depuis combien de temps êtes-vous à l'emploi de votre employeur actuel?
    _____ années/mois
12. Depuis combien de temps détenez-vous votre poste actuel?
    _____ années/mois
13. A combien d'autres endroits avez-vous travaillé avant de travailler dans cette organisation?
    _____
14. Pendant combien d'années avez-vous travaillé avant de joindre cette organisation?
    _____ années
15. Combien de temps avez-vous demeuré au:
    Québec _____
    Ontario _____
    Canada _____

Voici une liste d'éléments recherchés dans le choix d'une carrière. Lisez attentivement tous les éléments avant de faire un choix. Choisissez d'abord le facteur que vous croyez être le plus important et inscrivez 1 à l'endroit indiqué (à gauche). Faites de même pour vos choix 2-3-4-5 etc. Puisqu'il y a quinze éléments dans cette liste, votre quinzième choix doit représenter l'élément qui vous semble le moins important dans la poursuite de votre future carrière. Assurez-vous d'inscrire un numéro à gauche de chaque facteur.

_____ Sécurité (travail constant et permanent)
_____ Salaire adéquat (pour un meilleur niveau de vie)
_____ Avantages sociaux (vacances, bonis pensions, assurances, bénéfices médicaux, et participation aux bénéfices)
_____ Possibilité d'une future promotion
_____ Conditions de travail adéquates (environnement plaisant)
_____ Travail intéressant (un travail qui vous plait beaucoup)
_____ Des politiques et pratiques bien adaptées
_____ Du respect et de la reconnaissance (de vos supérieurs, co-travailleurs)
_____ Responsabilité et indépendance (un travail qui vous offre la possibilité de travailler à votre façon)
_____ Accomplissement (possibilité d'exceller dans votre travail)
_____ Bonnes relations inter-personnelles (un travail qui vous offre la possibilité de travailler avec des gens que vous aimez)
_____ Un supérieur attentionné et sympathique
_____ Un supérieur techniquement compétent
_____ Possibilité d'avancement (acquérir de l'habileté et de la compétence)
_____ Salaire adéquat et juste pour le travail que vous faites.

1. Dans quelle mesure vous sentez-vous vraiment responsable et engagé dans la poursuite du succès?
   Dans votre travail:
   Dans une grande mesure □ 4
   Dans une mesure moyenne □ 3
   Dans une petite mesure □ 2
   Pas du tout □ 1
2. Dans votre département:
   Dans une grande mesure □ 4
   Dans une mesure moyenne □ 3
   Dans une petite mesure □ 2
   Pas du tout □ 1
3. Dans la compagnie:
   Dans une grande mesure □ 4
   Dans une mesure moyenne □ 3
   Dans une petite mesure □ 2
   Pas du tout □ 1

1. Dans les prises de décisions, devrait-on demander les opinions et les suggestions des personnes concernées?
   - On ne devrait presque jamais le faire ☐ 1
   - On devrait le faire parfois ☐ 2
   - On devrait le faire la plupart du temps ☐ 3
   - On devrait toujours le faire ☐ 4
2. Dans les prises de décisions, demande-t-on vos suggestions et opinions:
   - Presque toujours ☐ 4
   - Très fréquemment ☐ 3
   - A l'occasion ☐ 2
   - Jamais ☐ 1

Dans votre travail, croyez-vous posséder plus d'habileté qu'il n'est requis?
   Oui ☐ 0   Non ☐ 1
Si oui, croyez-vous avoir:
   - Beaucoup plus d'habileté qu'il n'est requis ☐ 4
   - Un peu plus d'habileté qu'il n'est requis ☐ 3
   - Juste assez d'habileté ☐ 2

APPENDIX B

Employee Survey Questionnaire

I. Job Satisfaction Questionnaire
II. Questionnaire on Turnover Potential

I. Job Satisfaction Questionnaire

In this part are listed some job characteristics or qualities that people look for in their jobs. We would like to know the degree of your satisfaction or dissatisfaction with each of the job qualities as they relate to your job. For each job quality listed below, you will find six answer categories. Please indicate your feeling by putting a cross (X) mark in the appropriate space representing your answer. Make sure that you indicate your feelings for each item.

	6 Extremely satisfied	5 Moderately satisfied	4 Mildly satisfied	3 Mildly dissatisfied	2 Moderately dissatisfied	1 Extremely dissatisfied
1. With the *amount of security* I have on my job, I feel	___	___	___	___	___	___
2. With the *kind of company policies and practices* that govern my job, I feel	___	___	___	___	___	___
3. With the *amount of compensation* that I receive to maintain a reasonably good living, I feel	___	___	___	___	___	___
4. With the *kind of benefits plans* (vacation, retirement, medical, etc.) that goes with my job, I feel	___	___	___	___	___	___
5. With the *chance of future promotion* that I have in my job, I feel	___	___	___	___	___	___
6. With the *kind of working conditions* (lighting, noise, office space, etc.) surrounding my job, I feel	___	___	___	___	___	___
7. With the *interesting or enjoyable nature of the work* in my job, I feel	___	___	___	___	___	___

	6 Extremely satisfied	5 Moderately satisfied	4 Mildly satisfied	3 Mildly dissatisfied	2 Moderately dissatisfied	1 Extremely dissatisfied
8. With the *amount of recognition and respect* that I receive for my work, I feel						
9. With the *opportunity I have in my job to work with people I like*, I feel						
10. With the *technical competence of my immediate superior*, I feel						
11. With the *opportunity that I have in my job to achieve excellence in my work*, I feel						
12. With the *considerate and sympathetic nature of my immediate superior*, I feel						
13. With the *kind of responsibility and independence* that I have in my job, I feel						
14. With the *opportunity for acquiring higher skill*, I feel						
15. With *the amount of compensation I receive for the work I do*, I feel						
16. From an *overall consideration, with respect to my job*, I feel						

II. Questionnaire on Turnover Potential

What are the chances of your leaving the company?
- Extremely good ☐ 4
- Possible ☐ 3
- Not very likely ☐ 2
- Impossible ☐ 1

APPENDIX B   141

Vous trouverez dans cette section quelques caractéristiques que les gens recherchent dans leur travail. On aimerait savoir jusqu'à quel point, vous êtes satisfait, *ou pas*, de chacune de ces caractéristiques. Vous trouverez, pour chaque caractéristique six catégories de réponses. Indiquez par une croix (X) dans l'espace approprié, la catégorie de réponse qui représente le mieux vos sentiments pour chacune des caractéristiques. Indiquez vos sentiments pour chaque poste.

	6 Extrêmement satisfait	5 Modérément satisfait	4 Plus ou moins satisfait	3 Indifférent	2 Modérément mécontent	1 Extrêmement mécontent
1. Par rapport *au degré de sécurité* que j'éprouve dans mon travail, je me sens	___	___	___	___	___	___
2. Par rapport *au genre et au nombre de règlements* que la compagnie m'impose, je me sens	___	___	___	___	___	___
3. Par rapport à mon *revenu* pour maintenir un niveau de vie raisonable, je me sens	___	___	___	___	___	___
4. Par rapport aux *avantages sociaux* (vacances pension, etc) que je reçois au travail, je me sens	___	___	___	___	___	___
5. Par rapport aux *chances de recevoir une promotion dans l'avenir*, je me sens	___	___	___	___	___	___
6. Quant aux *conditions de travail actuelles*, je me sens	___	___	___	___	___	___

142 BICULTURALISM AND MANAGEMENT

	6 Extrêmement satisfait	5 Modérément satisfait	4 Plus ou moins satisfait	3 Indifférent	2 Modérément mécontent	1 Extrêmement mécontent
7. Quant à la *nature de mon travail*, je me sens						
8. Par rapport *au respect et à l'appréciation que je reçois au travail*, je me sens						
9. Par rapport aux *occasions que j'ai de travailler avec des gens que j'aime*, je me sens						
10. Par rapport à la *compétence technique de mon supérieur immédiat*, je me sens						
11. Par rapport aux *occasions que j'ai d'améliorer mon travail*, je me sens						
12. Par rapport à la *nature tolérante et sympathique de mon supérieur immédiat*, je me sens						
13. Par rapport à l'*initiative que je peux montrer au travail*, je me sens						
14. Par rapport à l'*occasion d'acquérir une meilleur compétence*, je me sens						

	6 Extrêmement satisfait	5 Modérément satisfait	4 Plus ou moins satisfait	3 Indifférent	2 Modérément mécontent	1 Extrêmement mécontent
15. Par rapport *au revenu que j'obtiens pour le travail accompli*, je me sens	——	——	——	——	——	——
16. En considérant *l'ensemble de mon travail*, je me sens	——	——	——	——	——	——

Quelle est la certitude que vous laissiez cette organisation?

Très bonnes changes ☐ 4
Possiblement ☐ 3
Pas probable ☐ 2
Impossible ☐ 1

APPENDIX C

Employee Survey Questionnaire

I. Lodahl and Kejner (1965) Job Involvement Questionnaire

Given below are a number of statements with each of which you may agree or disagree depending on your own personal experience with your job. Please indicate the degree of your agreement or disagreement with each statement by putting a cross (X) mark in one of the four blanks representing the answer categories (strongly agree; agree; disagree; strongly disagree) that appear against the statement.

Statements	Strongly agree	Agree	Disagree	Strongly disagree
1. I'll stay overtime to finish a job, even if I'm not paid for it.	___	___	___	___
2. You can measure a person pretty well by how good a job he does.	___	___	___	___
3. The major satisfaction in my life comes from my job.	___	___	___	___
4. For me, hours at work really fly by.	___	___	___	___
5. I usually show up for work a little early, to get things ready.	___	___	___	___
6. The most important things that happen to me involve my work.	___	___	___	___

		Strongly agree	**Agree**	**Disagree**	**Strongly disagree**
7.	Sometimes I lie awake at night thinking ahead to the next day's work.	_____	_____	_____	_____
8.	I'm really a perfectionist about my work.	_____	_____	_____	_____
9.	I feel depressed when I fail at something connected with my job.	_____	_____	_____	_____
10.	I have other activities more important than my work.	_____	_____	_____	_____
11.	I live, eat, and breathe my job.	_____	_____	_____	_____
12.	I would probably keep working even if I didn't need the money.	_____	_____	_____	_____
13.	Quite often I feel like staying home from work instead of coming in.	_____	_____	_____	_____
14.	To me, my work is only a small part of who I am.	_____	_____	_____	_____
15.	I am very much involved personally in my work.	_____	_____	_____	_____
16.	I avoid taking on extra duties and responsibilities in my work.	_____	_____	_____	_____
17.	I used to be more ambitious about my work than I am now.	_____	_____	_____	_____
18.	Most things in life are more important than work.	_____	_____	_____	_____
19.	I used to care more about my work, but now other things are more important to me.	_____	_____	_____	_____
20.	Sometimes I'd like to kick myself for the mistakes I make in my work.	_____	_____	_____	_____

La Version Française

Vous trouverez ci-dessous quelques faits pouvant se rapporter à votre travail. Selon votre expérience personnelle, vous pouvez être d'accord ou non avec ces faits. Marquez d'une croix à la réponse qui vous convient.

Faits	Catégories de réponses			
	Fortement d'accord	D'accord	Pas d'accord	Fortement en désaccord
1. Je ferais du temps supplémentaire pour finir un travail même si je n'étais pas payé.	_____	_____	_____	_____
2. On peut évaluer une personne assez bien par son travail.	_____	_____	_____	_____
3. Les plus grandes satisfactions de ma vie proviennent de mon travail.	_____	_____	_____	_____
4. Pour moi, les heures au travail passent très vite.	_____	_____	_____	_____
5. J'arrive normalement tôt au travail pour préparer ma journée.	_____	_____	_____	_____
6. Les choses les plus importantes qui m'arrivent concernent mon travail.	_____	_____	_____	_____
7. Le soir en me couchant, je pense souvent au travail du lendemain.	_____	_____	_____	_____

Faits	Catégories de réponses			
	Fortement d'accord	D'accord	Pas d'accord	Fortement en désaccord
8. Je suis un véritable perfectionniste au travail.	_____	_____	_____	_____
9. Je suis déprimé quand j'ai un échec au travail.	_____	_____	_____	_____
10. J'ai d'autres activités plus importantes que mon travail.	_____	_____	_____	_____
11. Je ne vis que pour mon travail.	_____	_____	_____	_____
12. Je continuerais de travailler même si je n'avais pas besoin d'argent.	_____	_____	_____	_____
13. Je préfèrerais souvent rester à la maison au lieu d'aller travailler.	_____	_____	_____	_____
14. Mon travail n'est pour moi, qu'une petite partie de ma vie.	_____	_____	_____	_____
15. Je suis personnellement très absorbé par mon travail	_____	_____	_____	_____
16. J'évite de prendre des tâches et des responsabilités additionnelles à mon travail.	_____	_____	_____	_____

Faits	Catégories de réponses			
	Fortement d'accord	D'accord	Pas d'accord	Fortement en désaccord
17. J'étais auparavant plus ambitieux au travail que je ne le suis maintenant.	___	___	___	___
18. La plupart des choses dans la vie sont plus importantes que le travail.	___	___	___	___
19. J'aimais mieux mon travail auparavant, mais maintenant il y a des choses plus importantes pour moi.	___	___	___	___
20. Souvent je voulais cogner ma tête au mur pour des erreurs que j'avais commises.	___	___	___	___

APPENDIX D

Employee Survey Questionnaire

I. Questionnaire on Readiness to Accept Transfer
II. Questionnaire on Reasons for Reluctance to Accept Transfer
III. Questionnaire on Reasons for Accepting Transfer
IV. Questionnaire on Location Preference

I. Questionnaire on Readiness to Accept Transfer

1. For the sake of your career progress, would you be prepared to accept transfer from your present location and be relocated in a different location?
    Yes ☐ 0   No ☐ 1
2. If yes, indicate your degree of willingness.
    Very much willing   ☐ 4
    Willing   ☐ 3
    Willing with some reservation   ☐ 2

II. Questionnaire on Reasons for Reluctance to Accept Transfer

1. The following statements describe some of the reasons why you may feel reluctant to accept a transfer to a different location. Read the statements carefully and indicate your agreement or disagreement with each of them as they apply to you.

	Completely agree			**Completely disagree**	
a) If a transfer means moving to a strange environment, I would feel very uneasy and uncertain about my future.	☐ 1	☐ 2	☐ 3	☐ 4	☐ 5

	Completely agree				Completely disagree
b) My family would feel socially isolated in a new location because of language and cultural differences.	☐ 1	☐ 2	☐ 3	☐ 4	☐ 5
c) A transfer would mean a financial loss to me.	☐ 1	☐ 2	☐ 3	☐ 4	☐ 5
d) A transfer would mean additional responsibility on the job and I do not want it.	☐ 1	☐ 2	☐ 3	☐ 4	☐ 5
e) If I like my job and am satisfied with it, I should not be pushed for a promotion to another location.	☐ 1	☐ 2	☐ 3	☐ 4	☐ 5

2. Specify any other reason you may have for your reluctance to accept a transfer.

_____
_____
_____
_____
_____

III. Questionnaire on Reasons for Accepting Transfer

1. If the company wants to transfer or relocate you outside your own home province, you may be willing to accept the move for several reasons. Listed below are a number of reasons that make people accept their transfers. Indicate for each of the items, how important it is for you in accepting your transfer.

	Not at all important				Very important
a) Get an adequate raise in salary	☐ 1	☐ 2	☐ 3	☐ 4	☐ 5
b) Get a promotion to a higher level job	☐ 1	☐ 2	☐ 3	☐ 4	☐ 5
c) Get a job that involves very different activities as compared to what you are doing now	☐ 1	☐ 2	☐ 3	☐ 4	☐ 5

	Not at all important				Very important
d) Get a job that involves same activities as you are doing now	☐ 1	☐ 2	☐ 3	☐ 4	☐ 5
e) Get opportunity for working with people of your own linguistic and cultural background	☐ 1	☐ 2	☐ 3	☐ 4	☐ 5
f) Get opportunity for working with people of different linguistic and cultural background	☐ 1	☐ 2	☐ 3	☐ 4	☐ 5
g) Get to a bigger city environment	☐ 1	☐ 2	☐ 3	☐ 4	☐ 5
h) Get to a smaller city environment	☐ 1	☐ 2	☐ 3	☐ 4	☐ 5
i) Get the assurance that I shall return to home province after a specified period	☐ 1	☐ 2	☐ 3	☐ 4	☐ 5

2. Specify other reasons that you consider important while accepting a transfer.

	Not at all important				Very important
_____	☐ 1	☐ 2	☐ 3	☐ 4	☐ 5
_____	☐ 1	☐ 2	☐ 3	☐ 4	☐ 5

IV. Questionnaire on Location Preference

For your own career progress, the company may transfer you from your present location to any of the following locations. Indicate your preference for those locations by assigning 1 to the location you prefer most, 2 to the next preferred location and so on.

- _____ Québec City
- _____ Montréal
- _____ Other locations in Québec province
- _____ Small cities outside Québec province but within Canada
- _____ Large cities outside Québec province but within Canada (Toronto, Vancouver, etc.)
- _____ Locations in U.S.A.

_____ Locations in England
_____ Locations in France
_____ Locations in other European cities

La Version Française

1. Pour améliorer votre situation, seriez-vous prêt à déménager?
   Oui ☐ 0   Non ☐ 1
2. Si oui, indiquez votre degré de consentement.
   Bien consentant   ☐ 4
   Consentant   ☐ 3
   Consentant avec réserve   ☐ 2

1. Les énoncés qui suivent expliquent pourquoi vous seriez hésitant à accepter une mutation dans un nouvel endroit. Lisez attentivement les énoncés et indiquez votre accord ou désaccord avec ceux-ci.

	Entièrement d'accord				Entièrement en désaccord
a) Si le fait d'accepter une mutation signifié déménager dans un endroit inconnu, je me sens mal à l'aise et incertain au sujet de mon avenir.	☐ 1	☐ 2	☐ 3	☐ 4	☐ 5
b) Ma famille se sentirait isolée dans un nouvel endroit à cause des différences linguistiques et culturelles du milieu.	☐ 1	☐ 2	☐ 3	☐ 4	☐ 5
c) Une mutation signifie une perte financière pour moi.	☐ 1	☐ 2	☐ 3	☐ 4	☐ 5
d) Une mutation signifie des responsabilités additionnelles pour moi et je n'en veux pas.	☐ 1	☐ 2	☐ 3	☐ 4	☐ 5

	Entièrement d'accord				Entièrement en désaccord

e) Si j'aime mon travail et en suis satisfait, on ne devrait pas me pousser à accepter une promotion dans un nouvel endroit.   ☐ 1   ☐ 2   ☐ 3   ☐ 4   ☐ 5

2. Spécifiez toutes autres raisons qui expliqueraient votre hésitation à accepter une mutation.

_____
_____
_____
_____

1. Si votre compagnie désirait vous transférer à l'extérieur de votre province, vous seriez peut-être d'accord avec ce changement pour plusieurs raisons. Les énoncés qui suivent expliquent pourquoi les gens acceptent ces mutations. Indiquez le degré d'importance pour chaque raison.

	Pas importante				Très importante

a) Avoir une augmentation de salaire adéquate.   ☐ 1   ☐ 2   ☐ 3   ☐ 4   ☐ 5

b) Obtenir une promotion à un niveau de travail plus élèvé.   ☐ 1   ☐ 2   ☐ 3   ☐ 4   ☐ 5

c) Faire un travail qui comporte des responsabilités différentes de ce que vous faites présentement.   ☐ 1   ☐ 2   ☐ 3   ☐ 4   ☐ 5

d) Faire un travail qui comporte des responsabilités semblables à ce que vous faites présentement.   ☐ 1   ☐ 2   ☐ 3   ☐ 4   ☐ 5

	Pas importante			Très importante	
e) Avoir la possibilité de travailler avec des gens qui ont les mêmes antécédents linguistiques et culturels que vous.	☐ 1	☐ 2	☐ 3	☐ 4	☐ 5
f) Avoir la possibilité de travailler avec des gens qui ont des antécédents linguistiques et culturels différents des vôtres.	☐ 1	☐ 2	☐ 3	☐ 4	☐ 5
g) Travailler dans une ville plus grande.	☐ 1	☐ 2	☐ 3	☐ 4	☐ 5
h) Travailler dans une ville plus petite.	☐ 1	☐ 2	☐ 3	☐ 4	☐ 5
i) Être certain de retourner dans ma province après une période determinée.	☐ 1	☐ 2	☐ 3	☐ 4	☐ 5

2. Indiquez d'autres raisons que vous croyez importantes dans l'acceptation d'une mutation.

	Pas importante			Très importante	
_____	☐ 1	☐ 2	☐ 3	☐ 4	☐ 5
_____	☐ 1	☐ 2	☐ 3	☐ 4	☐ 5

En vous offrant une promotion, votre compagnie pourra aussi vous faire déménager dans une des villes ci-dessous. Indiquez votre choix par ordre de préférence. (1 premier choix, 2 deuxième choix et ainsi de suite).

_____ Ville De Québec
_____ Montréal
_____ D'autres villes au Québec
_____ Petites villes à l'extérieur du Québec mais au Canada
_____ Grandes villes à l'extérieur du Québec mais au Canada (Toronto, Vancouver etc. . .)
_____ Aux Etats Unis
_____ En Angleterre
_____ En France
_____ Dans d'autres villes européennes.

APPENDIX E

Employee Survey Questionnaire

I. Questionnaire on Downward Communication
II. Questionnaire on Upward Communication
III. Questionnaire on Communication Channels
IV. Questionnaire on Communication About Organizational outcomes

I. Questionnaire on Downward Communication

There are many topics of information that can be communicated from management to you. For each topic listed on the following pages, indicate: (1) how SATISFIED you are with the information you receive on that topic, and (2) how IMPORTANT you feel it is to receive information on that topic.

Kinds of information

Topic area	How satisfied are you with information received on this topic? Very dissatisfied / Somewhat dissatisfied / Neither satisfied nor dissatisfied / Fairly satisfied / Very satisfied	How important to you is receiving information on this topic? Not at all important / Somewhat important / Fairly important / Very important / Extremely important
Progress in your work	1 2 3 4 5	1 2 3 4 5
Your work requirements	1 2 3 4 5	1 2 3 4 5
Hospital policies	1 2 3 4 5	1 2 3 4 5
Pay and benefits	1 2 3 4 5	1 2 3 4 5
Advance notice about changes affecting your work	1 2 3 4 5	1 2 3 4 5
How technological changes affect your work	1 2 3 4 5	1 2 3 4 5
News and reports from other units (or departments) in the hospital	1 2 3 4 5	1 2 3 4 5
Mistakes and failures of the hospital	1 2 3 4 5	1 2 3 4 5
How you are being judged	1 2 3 4 5	1 2 3 4 5
Safety information	1 2 3 4 5	1 2 3 4 5

APPENDIX E 159

Kinds of information Topic area	How satisfied are you with information received on this topic? Very dissatisfied / Somewhat dissatisfied / Neither satisfied nor dissatisfied / Fairly satisfied / Very satisfied	How important to you is receiving information on this topic? Not at all important / Somewhat important / Fairly important / Very important / Extremely important
What the hospital is doing to protect your job security	1 2 3 4 5	1 2 3 4 5
How your work-related problems are being handled	1 2 3 4 5	1 2 3 4 5
How hospital decisions are made that affect your work	1 2 3 4 5	1 2 3 4 5
How government policies affect the hospital	1 2 3 4 5	1 2 3 4 5
What your hospital is doing	1 2 3 4 5	1 2 3 4 5
The "results" of your work	1 2 3 4 5	1 2 3 4 5
Promotion and advancement opportunities in the hospital	1 2 3 4 5	1 2 3 4 5

BICULTURALISM AND MANAGEMENT

Kinds of information Topic area	How satisfied are you with information received on this topic? Very dissatisfied / Somewhat dissatisfied / Neither satisfied nor dissatisfied / Fairly satisfied / Very satisfied	How important to you is receiving information on this topic? Not at all important / Somewhat important / Fairly important / Very important / Extremely important
Quality of patient care in the hospital	1 2 3 4 5	1 2 3 4 5
Plans for expansion	1 2 3 4 5	1 2 3 4 5
Important new developments in hospital services	1 2 3 4 5	1 2 3 4 5
How your work relates to the total operation of the hospital	1 2 3 4 5	1 2 3 4 5
Specific problems management faces in the hospital	1 2 3 4 5	1 2 3 4 5
Reasons for important management decisions	1 2 3 4 5	1 2 3 4 5
Decisions made by the Board of Trustees	1 2 3 4 5	1 2 3 4 5
Reasons for specific tasks you are given	1 2 3 4 5	1 2 3 4 5

II. Questionnaire on Upward Communication

In addition to information received, there are different kinds of information that you can *send* to management. For each information topic listed on the following pages, indicate: (1) how SATISFIED you are with the opportunity you have to send information on that topic to management, and (2) how IMPORTANT it is for you to have the opportunity to send information on that topic to management.

	How satisfied are you with your opportunity to send information to management on this topic area?					How important to you is having the opportunity to send information to management on this topic area?				
	Very dissatisfied	Somewhat dissatisfied	Neither satisfied nor dissatisfied	Fairly satisfied	Very satisfied	Not at all important	Somewhat important	Fairly important	Very important	Extremely important
Kinds of information											
Topic area											
Suggestions for improving your job	1	2	3	4	5	1	2	3	4	5
Reports of your work activity and progress	1	2	3	4	5	1	2	3	4	5
Complaints about your job and/or working conditions	1	2	3	4	5	1	2	3	4	5
Your suggestions about work-related problems	1	2	3	4	5	1	2	3	4	5
"Personal" problems	1	2	3	4	5	1	2	3	4	5
Requests for information you need to do your work	1	2	3	4	5	1	2	3	4	5
Your evaluation(s) of the performance of superiors	1	2	3	4	5	1	2	3	4	5
Your evaluation(s) of the performance of co-workers	1	2	3	4	5	1	2	3	4	5

Kinds of information
Topic area

	How satisfied are you with your opportunity to send information to management on this topic area?					How important to you is having the opportunity to send information to management on this topic area?				
	Very dissatisfied	Somewhat dissatisfied	Neither satisfied nor dissatisfied	Fairly satisfied	Very satisfied	Not at all important	Somewhat important	Fairly important	Very important	Extremely important
Your evaluation(s) of the performance of those who work for you	1	2	3	4	5	1	2	3	4	5
Requests for clarification of confusing work instructions	1	2	3	4	5	1	2	3	4	5

III. Questionnaire on Communication Channels

There are a variety of channels or ways through which information is communicated to employees. Listed on the following page are a number of such channels. For each one listed, please indicate: (1) how SATISFIED you are with that channel as a means to receive information and (2) how IMPORTANT you feel that channel is as a means of receiving information.

APPENDIX E 163

Means of information Channel/mode	How satisfied are you with this channel (way) as a means of receiving information? Very dissatisfied / Somewhat dissatisfied / Neither satisfied nor dissatisfied / Fairly satisfied / Very satisfied	How important to you is this channel (way) as a means of receiving information? Not at all important / Somewhat important / Fairly important / Very important / Extremely important
Face-to-face	1 2 3 4 5	1 2 3 4 5
Telephone	1 2 3 4 5	1 2 3 4 5
Written (memos, letters notices)	1 2 3 4 5	1 2 3 4 5
Newsletter and other internal printed media	1 2 3 4 5	1 2 3 4 5
Tape recordings, cassettes	1 2 3 4 5	1 2 3 4 5
Films, motion pictures	1 2 3 4 5	1 2 3 4 5
Computer printouts	1 2 3 4 5	1 2 3 4 5
Public address system(s)	1 2 3 4 5	1 2 3 4 5
Closed-circuit television	1 2 3 4 5	1 2 3 4 5

IV. Questionnaire on Communication About Organizational Outcomes

One of the most important "outcomes" of working in an organization is the satisfaction one receives or fails to receive through working there. Such "satisfaction" can relate to the job, one's co-workers, supervisor, or the organization as a whole. Please mark your response which best indicates your *satisfaction* with:

	Very dissatisfied	Somewhat dissatisfied	Neither satisfied nor dissatisfied	Fairly satisfied	Very satisfied
Your relationship(s) with people in your department or unit	1	2	3	4	5
Your relationship with your boss	1	2	3	4	5
Your work	1	2	3	4	5
Your pay	1	2	3	4	5
Your progress in the organization up to this point	1	2	3	4	5
Your chances or opportunities for getting ahead in the organization	1	2	3	4	5
The organization's overall communication efforts	1	2	3	4	5
Your opportunity to "make a difference"—to contribute to the overall success of the organization	1	2	3	4	5
The organization's concern for the welfare of its employees	1	2	3	4	5

APPENDIX E 165

Types d'information Sujets	Jusqu'à quel point êtes-vous satisfait(e) de l'information que vous recevez à ce sujet? Très Insatisfait(e) / Quelque Peu Insatisfait(e) / Ni Satisfait(e) Ni Insatisfait(e) / Quelque Peu Satisfait(e) / Très Satisfait(e)	Jusqu'à quel point est-il important pour vous d'être informé(e) à ce sujet? Aucune Importance / Peu D'Importance / Une Certaine Importance / Très Important / Extrêmement Important
Progrès dans votre Travail	1 2 3 4 5	1 2 3 4 5
Exigences de votre Poste	1 2 3 4 5	1 2 3 4 5
Règlements de l'Hôpital	1 2 3 4 5	1 2 3 4 5
Salaires et Avantages Sociaux	1 2 3 4 5	1 2 3 4 5
Avis Préalable de Changements Touchant votre Poste	1 2 3 4 5	1 2 3 4 5
Comment les Changements Technologiques Touchent votre Travail	1 2 3 4 5	1 2 3 4 5
Nouvelles et Comptes Rendus d'Autres Unités (ou Départements) de l'Hôpital	1 2 3 4 5	1 2 3 4 5
Erreurs et Défauts de l'Hôpital	1 2 3 4 5	1 2 3 4 5
Comment vous êtes jugé(e)	1 2 3 4 5	1 2 3 4 5
Renseignements sur la Sécurité	1 2 3 4 5	1 2 3 4 5
Ce que Fait l'Hôpital pour Protéger votre Sécurité	1 2 3 4 5	1 2 3 4 5

BICULTURALISME ET GESTION

Types d'information Sujets	Jusqu'à quel point êtes-vous satisfait(e) de l'information que vous recevez à ce sujet? Très Insatisfait(e) / Quelque Peu Insatisfait(e) / Ni Satisfait(e) Ni Insatisfait(e) / Quelque Peu Satisfait(e) / Très Satisfait(e)	Jusqu'à quel point est-il important pour vous d'être informé(e) à ce sujet? Aucune Importance / Peu D'Importance / Une Certaine Importance / Très Important / Extrêmement Important
Comment sont Traités vos Problèmes ayant Rapport à votre Hôpital	1 2 3 4 5	1 2 3 4 5
Comment sont Prises les Décisions de l'Hôpital Touchant votre Travail	1 2 3 4 5	1 2 3 4 5
Comment les Politiques du Gouvernement Affectent l'Hôpital	1 2 3 4 5	1 2 3 4 5
Ce que Font les Autres Hôpitaux	1 2 3 4 5	1 2 3 4 5
Les "Résultats" de votre Travail	1 2 3 4 5	1 2 3 4 5
Possibilités de Promotion et d'Avancement dans l'Hôpital	1 2 3 4 5	1 2 3 4 5
La Qualité des Soins aux Malades à l'Hôpital	1 2 3 4 5	1 2 3 4 5
Les Plans pour Expansion	1 2 3 4 5	1 2 3 4 5

APPENDIX E 167

Types d'information Sujets	Jusqu'à quel point êtes-vous satisfait(e) de l'information que vous recevez à ce sujet? Très Insatisfait(e) / Quelque Peu Insatisfait(e) / Ni Satisfait(e) Ni Insatisfait(e) / Quelque Peu Satisfaite(e) / Très Satisfait(e)	Jusqu'à quel point est-il important pour vous d'être informé(e) à ce sujet? Aucune Importance / Peu D'Importance / Une Certaine Importance / Très Important / Extrêmement Important
Les Evènements Importants Concernant les Services de l'Hôpital	1 2 3 4 5	1 2 3 4 5
Quelle est la Relation Entre votre Poste et l'Ensemble des Activités de l'Hôpital	1 2 3 4 5	1 2 3 4 5
Des Problèmes Auxquels l'Administration fait Face	1 2 3 4 5	1 2 3 4 5
Les Raisons qui Motivent les Décisions Administratives Importantes	1 2 3 4 5	1 2 3 4 5
Les Décisions Prises par le Conseil d'Administration	1 2 3 4 5	1 2 3 4 5
Les Raisons pour Lesquelles on vous Donne Certaines Tâches à Accomplir	1 2 3 4 5	1 2 3 4 5

168 BICULTURALISM AND MANAGEMENT

Types d'information Sujets	Jusqu'à quel point êtes-vous satisfait(e) de la possibilité que vous avez d'informer vos supérieurs à ce sujet?					Jusqu'à quel point est-il important que vous ayiez la possibilité d'informer vos supérieurs à ce sujet?				
	Très Insatisfait(e)	Quelque Peu Insatisfait(e)	Ni Satisfait(e) Ni Insatisfait(e)	Quelque Peu Satisfait(e)	Très Satisfait(e)	Aucune Importance	Peu D'Importance	Une Certaine Importance	Très Important	Extrêmement Important
Suggestions pour Améliorer votre Travail	1	2	3	4	5	1	2	3	4	5
Rapports sur votre Travail et votre Progrès	1	2	3	4	5	1	2	3	4	5
Plaintes au sujet de votre Travail et/ou de vos Conditions de Travail	1	2	3	4	5	1	2	3	4	5
Vos Suggestions au Sujet de Problèmes Ayant Trait à votre Travail	1	2	3	4	5	1	2	3	4	5
Problèmes "Personnels"	1	2	3	4	5	1	2	3	4	5
Demandes de Renseignements Nécessaires à votre Travail	1	2	3	4	5	1	2	3	4	5
Votre(vos) Evaluation(s) du Rendement de vos Supérieurs	1	2	3	4	5	1	2	3	4	5
Votre(vos) Evaluation(s) du Rendement de vos Compagnons de Travail	1	2	3	4	5	1	2	3	4	5

APPENDIX E 169

Types d'information *Sujets*	Jusqu'à quel point êtes-vous satisfait(e) de la possibilité que vous avez d'informer vos supérieurs à ce sujet?					Jusqu'à quel point est-il important que vous ayiez la possibilité d'informer vos supérieurs à ce sujet?				
	Très Insatisfait(e)	Quelque Peu Insatisfait(e)	Ni Satisfait(e) Ni Insatisfait(e)	Quelque Peu Satisfait(e)	Très Satisfait(e)	Aucune Importance	Peu D'Importance	Une Certaine Importance	Très Important	Extrêmement Important
Votre(Vos) Evaluation(s) du Rendement de Ceux qui Travaillent pour Vous	1	2	3	4	5	1	2	3	4	5
Questions afin D'Eclaircir des Instructions Confuses Concernant votre Travail	1	2	3	4	5	1	2	3	4	5

170 BICULTURALISM AND MANAGEMENT

Moyens d'information *Modes*	Jusqu'à quel point êtes-vous satisfait(e) de ce mode en tant que moyen de recevoir l'information					Jusqu'à quel point ce mode de recevoir l'information est-il important en tant que moyen d'information				
	Très Insatisfait(e)	Quelque Peu Insatisfait(e)	Ni Satisfait(e) Ni Insatisfait(e)	Quelque Peu Satisfait(e)	Très Satisfait(e)	Aucune Importance	Peu D'Importance	Une Certaine Importance	Très Important	Extrêmement Important
Face-à-Face	1	2	3	4	5	1	2	3	4	5
Téléphone	1	2	3	4	5	1	2	3	4	5
Ecrit (Mémos, Lettres, Avis)	1	2	3	4	5	1	2	3	4	5
Bulletin de Nouvelles et autre Média Imprimés Internes	1	2	3	4	5	1	2	3	4	5
Enregistrements sur Magnétophone, cassettes	1	2	3	4	5	1	2	3	4	5
Films, Vues animées	1	2	3	4	5	1	2	3	4	5
Rapports Produits par Ordinateur	1	2	3	4	5	1	2	3	4	5
Systèmes de Hauts-parleurs	1	2	3	4	5	1	2	3	4	5
Télévision en Circuit-fermé	1	2	3	4	5	1	2	3	4	5

	Très Insatisfait(e)	Quelque Peu Insatisfait(e)	Ni Satisfait(e) Ni Insatisfait(e)	Quelque Peu Satisfait(e)	Très Satisfait(e)
Votre(vos) relation(s) avec les personnes de votre département ou unité	1	2	3	4	5
Votre relation avec votre patron	1	2	3	4	5
Votre travail	1	2	3	4	5
Votre salaire	1	2	3	4	5
Votre progrès à l'intérieur de l'organisation jusqu'à maintenant	1	2	3	4	5
Vos possibilités ou chances d'avancement dans l'organisation	1	2	3	4	5
Les efforts d'ensemble que fait l'organisation pour communiquer	1	2	3	4	5
La possibilité que vous avez de "jouer un rôle" contribuer au succès général de l'organisation	1	2	3	4	5
L'intérèt que l'organisation porte au bien-être de ses employés	1	2	3	4	5

APPENDIX F

Employee Survey Questionnaire

I. Questionnaire on Supervision

1. I like a job where my boss supervises my work very closely.
    All the time ☐ 5
    Very frequently ☐ 4
    Frequently ☐ 3
    Occasionally ☐ 2
    Never ☐ 1

2. Whenever my boss asks me to do something on the job, I do it because (check one box on each line across):

	Never	Occasionally	Frequently	Very frequently	All the time
a) He/she causes trouble for me if I do not comply	☐ 1	☐ 2	☐ 3	☐ 4	☐ 5
b) I respect his/her technical competence	☐ 1	☐ 2	☐ 3	☐ 4	☐ 5
c) He/she can give special help and benefits to me	☐ 1	☐ 2	☐ 3	☐ 4	☐ 5
d) He/she is a very friendly person whom I like	☐ 1	☐ 2	☐ 3	☐ 4	☐ 5
e) I consider it my duty	☐ 1	☐ 2	☐ 3	☐ 4	☐ 5
f) It is necessary for organizational efficiency	☐ 1	☐ 2	☐ 3	☐ 4	☐ 5

La Version Française

1. J'aime un emploi où le patron surveille le travail de très près.
   - _____ Tout le temps ☐ 5
   - _____ Très fréquemment ☐ 4
   - _____ Fréquemment ☐ 3
   - _____ Occasionnellement ☐ 2
   - _____ Jamais ☐ 1
2. Quand mon patron me demande de faire quelque chose, je le fais parce que:

	Jamais	Occasionnellement	Fréquemment	Très fréquemment	Toute Le temps
a) On peut me causer des difficultés.	☐ 1	☐ 2	☐ 3	☐ 4	☐ 5
b) Je respecte sa compétence technique.	☐ 1	☐ 2	☐ 3	☐ 4	☐ 5
c) On peut m'apporter de l'aide et des bénéfices.	☐ 1	☐ 2	☐ 3	☐ 4	☐ 5
d) C'est une personne très aimable et je l'aime bien.	☐ 1	☐ 2	☐ 3	☐ 4	☐ 5
e) Je considère cela mon devoir.	☐ 1	☐ 2	☐ 3	☐ 4	☐ 5
f) Cela est nécessaire pour une organisation efficace	☐ 1	☐ 2	☐ 3	☐ 4	☐ 5

APPENDIX G

Employee Survey Questionnaire

I. Questionnaire on In-House Training Programs

Following are a few statements that describe employee opinion towards various orientation, training, and recruitment programs within the company. Please read each statement carefully and if it applies in your case, indicate your agreement or disagreement.

1. Since most of the training materials are in English, I had considerable difficulty in assimilating the training materials during:

	Completely agree			Completely disagree	
a) Orientation and pre-school training program in the branch	□ 1	□ 2	□ 3	□ 4	□ 5
b) Basic school training program in the U.S.A.	□ 1	□ 2	□ 3	□ 4	□ 5
c) Post-school training program in the branch	□ 1	□ 2	□ 3	□ 4	□ 5
d) Advanced training program	□ 1	□ 2	□ 3	□ 4	□ 5
e) Day-to-day job activities	□ 1	□ 2	□ 3	□ 4	□ 5
f) Pre-management training	□ 1	□ 2	□ 3	□ 4	□ 5

176   BICULTURALISM AND MANAGEMENT

2. Since the trainer under whom I was being trained spoke only English, I faced considerable difficulty understanding him, communicating with him, seeking his help etc. during:

	Completely agree			Completely disagree	
a) Orientation and pre-school training program in the branch	□ 1	□ 2	□ 3	□ 4	□ 5
b) Basic school training program in the U.S.A.	□ 1	□ 2	□ 3	□ 4	□ 5
c) Post-school training program	□ 1	□ 2	□ 3	□ 4	□ 5
d) Advance training program	□ 1	□ 2	□ 3	□ 4	□ 5
e) Day-to-day job activities	□ 1	□ 2	□ 3	□ 4	□ 5
f) Pre-management training program	□ 1	□ 2	□ 3	□ 4	□ 5

3. Since many of my co-trainees spoke only English, I felt very uncertain and uneasy with them (role-playing situations, classroom interactions, etc.) during

	Completely agree			Completely disagree	
a) Orientation and preschool training program in the branch	□ 1	□ 2	□ 3	□ 4	□ 5
b) Basic school training program in U.S.A.	□ 1	□ 2	□ 3	□ 4	□ 5
c) Post-school training program	□ 1	□ 2	□ 3	□ 4	□ 5
d) Advanced training program	□ 1	□ 2	□ 3	□ 4	□ 5
e) Pre-management training program	□ 1	□ 2	□ 3	□ 4	□ 5

4. Since many of my co-workers speak only English, I feel uneasy dealing with them in my day-to-day job activities.   □ 1   □ 2   □ 3   □ 4   □ 5

5. The company should make all the training materials available in French.   □ 1   □ 2   □ 3   □ 4   □ 5

6. In my opinion, it is desirable to have trainers in basic school training programs who:

	Very desirable			Very undesirable	
Speak English only	☐ 1	☐ 2	☐ 3	☐ 4	☐ 5
Speak French only	☐ 1	☐ 2	☐ 3	☐ 4	☐ 5
Are Francophones but speak both French and English	☐ 1	☐ 2	☐ 3	☐ 4	☐ 5
Are Anglophones but speak both English and French	☐ 1	☐ 2	☐ 3	☐ 4	☐ 5

7. In my opinion, it is desirable to have trainers in the branch who:

	Very desirable			Very undesirable	
Speak English only	☐ 1	☐ 2	☐ 3	☐ 4	☐ 5
Speak French only	☐ 1	☐ 2	☐ 3	☐ 4	☐ 5
Are Francophones but speak both French and English	☐ 1	☐ 2	☐ 3	☐ 4	☐ 5
Are Anglophones but speak both English and French	☐ 1	☐ 2	☐ 3	☐ 4	☐ 5

8. During the training period at the basic school, it is desirable to put all the Francophone trainees together into one group, so that they may not have to interact with other Anglophone trainees.

Very desirable   Very undesirable
☐ 1   ☐ 2   ☐ 3   ☐ 4   ☐ 5

9. I would prefer basic training program to be located in Québec Province.
☐ 1   ☐ 2   ☐ 3   ☐ 4   ☐ 5

10. I would prefer basic school training program to be located in Canada.
☐ 1   ☐ 2   ☐ 3   ☐ 4   ☐ 5

11. If you agree with the previous item, in which province would you prefer to locate the basic school training program? _____

La Version Française

Vous trouverez ci-dessous des énoncés décrivant des opinions d'employés vis-à-vis les programmes de recrutement et de formation de la compagnie. Lisez chaque énoncé attentivement et *s'il s'applique à votre cas, indiquez votre accord ou désaccord.*

1. Puisque la plus grande partie du matériel des cours de formation est en anglais, j'ai eu beaucoup de difficulté à assimiler ce matériel pendant:

	Entièrement d'accord			Entièrement en désaccord	
a) Le programme d'orientation et de formation pré-scolaire à la succursale	☐ 1	☐ 2	☐ 3	☐ 4	☐ 5
b) Le programme de formation de base au Etats-Unis	☐ 1	☐ 2	☐ 3	☐ 4	☐ 5
c) Le programme de formation post-scolaire à la succursale	☐ 1	☐ 2	☐ 3	☐ 4	☐ 5
d) Le programme de formation avancé	☐ 1	☐ 2	☐ 3	☐ 4	☐ 5
e) Les activités quotidiennes	☐ 1	☐ 2	☐ 3	☐ 4	☐ 5
f) Le programme de formation pre-administrateur	☐ 1	☐ 2	☐ 3	☐ 4	☐ 5

2. Puisque notre instructeur ne parlait que l'anglais, j'ai éprouvé beaucoup de difficulté à le comprendre, à communiquer avec lui etc. .... Pendant:

	Entièrement d'accord			Entièrement en désaccord	
a) Le programme d'orientation et de formation pré-scolaire à la succursale	☐ 1	☐ 2	☐ 3	☐ 4	☐ 5
b) Le programme de formation de base au Etats-Unis	☐ 1	☐ 2	☐ 3	☐ 4	☐ 5

c) Le programme de
formation post-scolaire
à la succursale □ 1 □ 2 □ 3 □ 4 □ 5
d) Le programme de
formation avancé □ 1 □ 2 □ 3 □ 4 □ 5
e) Les activités
quotidiennes □ 1 □ 2 □ 3 □ 4 □ 5
f) Le programme de
formation
pre-administrateur □ 1 □ 2 □ 3 □ 4 □ 5

3. Puisque la plupart de mes collègues dans les cours de formation étaient anglophones je me suis sente mal à l'aise et incertain dans mes rapports avec eux (participer dans des rôles et activités en classe) pendant:

                                          D'accord   Pas D'accord

a) Le programme
d'orientation et de
formation pré-scolaire
à la succursale □ 1 □ 2 □ 3 □ 4 □ 5
b) Le programme de
formation de base au
Etats-Unis □ 1 □ 2 □ 3 □ 4 □ 5
c) Le programme de
formation post-scolaire
à la succursale □ 1 □ 2 □ 3 □ 4 □ 5
d) Le programme de
formation avancé □ 1 □ 2 □ 3 □ 4 □ 5
e) Le programme de
formation
pre-administrateur □ 1 □ 2 □ 3 □ 4 □ 5

4. Je me sens mal à l'aise
dans les travaux
quotidiens parce que mes
collègues parlent
seulement anglais. □ 1 □ 2 □ 3 □ 4 □ 5

5. La compagnie devrait
rendre tout le matériel de
programme de formation
disponible en français. □ 1 □ 2 □ 3 □ 4 □ 5

6. Je crois qu'il est préférable d'avoir à Leesburg des instructeurs dans les cours de formation de base qui soient:

	Très désirable				Indésirable
Anglais	☐ 1	☐ 2	☐ 3	☐ 4	☐ 5
Français	☐ 1	☐ 2	☐ 3	☐ 4	☐ 5
Français & Anglais	☐ 1	☐ 2	☐ 3	☐ 4	☐ 5
Anglais & Français	☐ 1	☐ 2	☐ 3	☐ 4	☐ 5

7. Je crois qu'il est préférable d'avoir des instructeurs dans les succursales qui soient:

	Très désirable				Indésirable
Anglais	☐ 1	☐ 2	☐ 3	☐ 4	☐ 5
Français	☐ 1	☐ 2	☐ 3	☐ 4	☐ 5
Français & Anglais	☐ 1	☐ 2	☐ 3	☐ 4	☐ 5
Anglais & Français	☐ 1	☐ 2	☐ 3	☐ 4	☐ 5

8. Pendant la période de formation de base il serait souhaitable de placer tous les stagiaires Francophones dans un groupe et ainsi on éviter des intéractions avec les stagiaires anglophones.

Très désirable				Indésirable
☐ 1	☐ 2	☐ 3	☐ 4	☐ 5

9. Je préfèrerais que le programme de formation de base soit donné dans la province de Québec.   ☐ 1   ☐ 2   ☐ 3   ☐ 4   ☐ 5

10. Je préfèrerais que le programme de formation de base soit donné au Canada.   ☐ 1   ☐ 2   ☐ 3   ☐ 4   ☐ 5

11. Si vous êtes d'accord à la question 10, dans quelle province préferez-vous que le cours de formation de base soit donné?   _____

References

Chapter 1

Barnouw, V. *Culture and Personality.* Homewood, Illinois: The Dorsey Press, 1963.
Basu, K. S. "Job Involvement: An Analysis in a Bicultural Context." Master's thesis, McGill University, 1976.
Graves, D. "Cultural Determinism and Management Behaviour." *Organizational Dynamics,* 1 (1972): 46-49.
Graves, D., ed. *Management Research: A Cross-Cultural Perspective.* San Francisco: Jossey-Bass, 1973.
Kanungo, R. N., Misra, S., and Dayal, I. "Relationship of Job Involvement to Perceived Importance and Satisfaction of Employee Needs." *International Review of Applied Psychology* 24 (1975): 49-59.
Khandwalla, P. N. *The Design of Organizations.* New York: Harcourt Brace Jovanovich, 1977.
Likert, R. *New Patterns of Management.* New York: McGraw-Hill, 1961.
Likert, R. *The Human Organization.* New York: McGraw-Hill, 1967.
Linton, R. *The Cultural Background of Personality.* New York: Appleton-Century, 1945.
McClelland, D. C. *The Achieving Society.* New York: Norstrand, 1961.
McClelland, D. C. and Winter, D. G. *Motivating Economic Achievement.* New York: Free Press, 1969.
Thompson, J. D. *Organizations in Action.* New York: McGraw-Hill, 1967.
Tylor, E. B. *Primitive Culture: Researches into the Development of Mythology, Philosophy, Religion, Language, Art, and Customs.* Vol. 1. New York: Henry Holt, 1877.
Webber, R. A., ed. *Culture and Management: Text and Readings in Comparative Management.* Homewood, Illinois: Irwin-Dorsey, 1969.
Whyte, W. F. *Men at Work,* Homewood, Illinois: Irwin-Dorsey, 1961.
Woodward, Joan. *Industrial Organization: Theory and Practice.* London: Oxford University Press, 1965.
Zaleznik, A. "Managerial Behaviour and Interpersonal Competence." *Behavioral Science* 9 (1964): 156-66.

Chapter 2

Brazeau, J. "Quebec's Emerging Middle Class." In *Marketing: Canada*, edited by I. Litvak and B. Mallen. Toronto: McGraw-Hill, 1964.
Henripin, J. "From Acceptance of Nature to Control: The Demography of the French Canadians since the Seventeenth Century." *Canadian Journal of Economics and Political Science* 23 (1957):10-19.
Hughes, E. C. "Industry and the Rural System in Quebec" (1938), In *French-Canadian Society*, Vol. 1, edited by M. Roux and Y. Martin. Toronto: McClelland and Stewart, 1964.
Jamieson, S. M. "French and English in the Institutional Structure of Montreal: A Study of the Social and Economic Division of Labour." Master's thesis, McGill University, 1938.
Parenteau, K. "The Impact of Industrialization in Quebec" (1954). In *Marketing: Canada*, edited by I. Litvak and B. Mallen. Toronto: McGraw-Hill, 1964.
Royal Commission on Bilingualism and Biculturalism. *The New World III*. Ottawa: The Queen's Printer, 1969.
Sandwell, B. K. Quoted in "Social Class in French Canada" (1962), by J. Dofny and M. Rioux in *French Canadian Society*, Vol. 1, edited by M. Rioux and Y. Martin. Toronto: McClelland and Stewart, 1964.
Sauvy, M. Quoted in "Planned Migration: The Social Determinants of the Dutch-Canadian Movement" by William Paterson in *The Vertical Mosaic*, by J. Porter. Toronto: University of Toronto Press, 1965.
Scott, F., and Oliver, M. *Quebec States Her Case*. Toronto: Macmillan of Canada, 1964.

Chapter 4

Alderfer, C. P. *Existence, Relatedness, Growth: Human Needs in Organizational Settings*. New York: The Free Press, 1972.
Auclair, G. A., and Read, W. H. "A Cross-Cultural Study of Industrial Leadership." In Report of the *Royal Commission on Bilingualism and Biculturalism*. Vol. 2. Ottawa: Government of Canada, 1966.
Cuthill, R. "Are you a Victim of Mirror Management?" *Quest*, December 1977, pp. 25-31.
Graves, D. "Cultural Determinism and Management Behavior." *Organizational Dynamics* 1 (1972): 46-59.
Herzberg, F. *Work and the Nature of Man*. Cleveland: World Publishing, 1966.
Jamieson, S. M. "French and English in the Institutional Structure of Montreal: A Study of the Social and Economic Division of Labor." Master's thesis, McGill University, 1938.
Kanungo, R. N., Gorn, G. J., and Dauderis, H. J. "Motivational Orientation of Canadian Anglophone and Francophone Managers." *Canadian Journal of Behavioural Science* 8 (1976): 107-21.
Korman, A. R. *Industrial and Organizational Psychology*. Englewood Cliffs, N.J.: Prentice-Hall, 1971.
Jain, H. C., Normand, J., and Kanungo R. N. "Job Motivation of Canadian Anglophone and Francophone Hospital Employees." *Canadian Journal of Behavioural Science* 11 (1979): 160-63.
Lambert, W. E., Yackley, A., and Hein, R. N. "Child Training Values of English Canadian and French Canadian Parents." *Canadian Journal of Behavioural Science* 3 (1971): 217-36.

Lawler, E. E. *Motivation in Work Organizations.* Belmont, California: Wadsworth, 1973.
Maslow, A. H. *Motivation and Personality.* New York: Harper, 1954.
McClelland, D. C. *The Achieving Society,* New York: Norstrand, 1961.
Parenteau, K. The Impact of Industrialization in Quebec. In *Marketing: Canada,* edited by I. Litvak and B. Mallen. Toronto: McGraw-Hill, 1964.
Rosen, B. C., and D'Andrade, R. G. "The Psychological Origins of Achievement Motivation." *Sociometry* 22 (1959): 185-218.
Rowe, P. "Choosing the Most Satisfied [sic] Job, or the Evaluation of Own Needs and of Opportunities for Need Satisfaction." Paper presented at Canadian Psychological Association Convention, Victoria, B.C., 1973.
Taylor, N. W. "The French-Canadian Industrial Entrepreneur and his Social Environment." In *French Canadian Society,* Vol. 1, edited by M. Rioux and Y. Martin. Toronto: McClelland and Stewart, 1964.
Tremblay, M. "Orientations de la pensée sociale." In Essais sur le Québec Contemperain, edited by J. C. Falardeau. Laval, Québec: Les Presses Universitaires, 1953.
Vroom, V. H. *Work and Motivation.* New York: Wiley, 1964.
Yackley, A., and Lambert, W. E. "Interethnic Group Competition and Levels of Aspiration." *Canadian Journal of Behavioural Science* 3 (1971): 135-47.

Chapter 5

Festinger, L. A Theory of Social Comparison Processes. *Human Relations* 7 (1954): 117-40.
Jain, H. C., Normand, J., and Kanungo, R. N. "Job Motivation of Canadian Anglophone and Francophone Hospital Employees." *Canadian Journal of Behavioural Science* 11 (1979): 160-63.
Kanungo, R. N. "Managerial Job Satisfaction: A Comparison Between Anglophones and Francophones." In *Canadian Industrial Relations,* edited by S. M. A. Hameed. Toronto: Butterworths, 1975.
Korman, A. R. *Industrial and Organizational Psychology.* Englewood Cliffs, N.J.: Prentice-Hall, 1971.
Lawler, E. E. *Pay and Organizational Effectiveness: A Psychological View.* New York: McGraw-Hill, 1971.
McClelland, D. C. *The Achieving Society,* New York: Norstrand, 1961.
Porter, L. W. "A Study of Perceived Need Satisfactions in Bottom and Middle Management Jobs." *Journal of Applied Psychology,* 45 (1961): 1-10.
Spector, A. J. "Expectations, Fulfillments and Morale." *Journal of Abnormal and Social Psychology* 52 (1956): 51-56.

Chapter 6

Alderfer, C. P. *Existence, Relatedness, Growth: Human Needs in Organizational Settings.* New York: Free Press, 1972.
Allport, G. W. *Pattern and Growth in Personality.* New York: Holt, Rinehart and Winston, 1961.
Argyris, C. *Integrating the Individual and the Organization.* New York: Wiley, 1964.
Bass, B. M. *Organizational Psychology.* Boston: Allyn and Bacon, 1965.
Blauner, R. *Alienation and Freedom: The Factory Worker and his Industry.* Chicago: University of Chicago Press, 1964.

Blood, M. R., and Hulin, C. L. "Alienation, Environmental Characteristics, and Worker Responses." *Journal of Applied Psychology* 51 (1967): 284-90.

Clark, J. P. "Measuring Alienation within a Social System." *American Sociological Review* 24 (1959): 849-52.

Dubin, R. "Industrial Workers' Worlds: A Study of the Central Life Interests of Industrial workers." *Social Problems* 3 (1956): 131-42.

Dubin, R., Champoux, J. E., and Porter, L. W. "Central Life Interests and Organizational Commitment of Blue Collar and Clerical Workers." *Administrative Science Quarterly* 20 (1975): 411-21.

Durkheim, E. *De la division du travail social*. Paris: F. Alcan, 1893.

Faunce, W. "Occupational Involvement and Selective Testing of Self-Esteem." Paper presented at the meeting of the American Socialogical Association, Chicago, 1959.

Festinger, L. "A Theory of Social Comparison Processes." *Human Relations* 7 (1954): 117-40.

Gerth, H. H., and Mills, C. W. *From Max Weber: Essays in Sociology*. New York: Oxford University Press, 1946.

Hall, D. T., and Schneider, B. "Correlates of Organizational Identification as a Function of Career Pattern and Organizational Type." *Administrative Science Quarterly* 17 (1972): 340-50.

Hall, D. T., Schneider, B., and Nygren, H. T. "Personal Factors in Organizational Identification." *Administrative Science Quarterly* 15 (1970): 176-90.

Herzberg, F. *Work and the Nature of Man*. Cleveland, Ohio: World Publishing, 1966.

Hulin, C. L., & Blood, M. R. "Job Enlargement, Individual Differences, and Worker Responses." *Psychological Bulletin* 69 (1968): 41-65.

Johnson, F., ed. *Alienation: Concept, Term, and Meanings*. New York: Seminar Press, 1973.

Jones, E. E., and Gerard, H. B. *Foundations of Social Psychology*. New York: Wiley, 1967.

Josephson, E., and Josephson, M. R. "Alienation: Contemporary Sociological Approaches." In *Alienation: Concept, Term, and Meanings* edited by F. Johnson. New York: Seminar Press, 1973.

Lawler, E. E. *Motivation in Work Organizations*. Belmont, Calif.: Wadsworth, 1973.

Lawler, E. E., and Hackman, J. R. "Corporate Profits and Employee Satisfaction: Must They be in Conflict?" *California Management Review* 14 (1971): 46-55.

Lawler, E. E., and Hall, D. T. "Relationship of Job Characteristics to Job Involvement, Satisfaction, and Intrinsic Motivation." *Journal of Applied Psychology* 54 (1970): 305-12.

Lodahl, T. M. "Patterns of Job Attitudes in Two Assembly Technologies." *Administrative Science Quarterly* 8 (1964): 482-519.

Lodahl, T. M., and Kejner, M. "The Definition and Measurement of Job Involvement." *Journal of Applied Psychology* 49 (1965): 24-33.

Marx, K. [Economic and philosophical manuscripts.] *Marx-Engels Gesamtausgabe* (Vol. 3). Berlin: Marx-Engels Institute, 1932.

Maslow, A. H. *Motivation and Personality*. New York: Harper, 1954.

McGregor, D. *The Human Side of Enterprise*. McGraw-Hill, 1960.

Mills, C. W. *White Collar*. New York: Oxford University Press, 1951.

Normand J. and Kanungo, R. N. "Job Motivation and Involvement: A Comparison of Francophone and Anglophone Hospital Employees." Unpublished working paper, Faculty of Management, McGill University, 1978.

Patchen, M. *Participation, Achievement, and Involvement on the Job.* Englewood Cliffs, N.J.: Prentice-Hall, 1970.
Rabinowitz, S., and Hall, D. T. "Organizational Research on Job Involvement." *Psychological Bulletin* 84 (1977): 265-88.
Saal, F. E. "Job Involvement: A Multivariate Approach." *Journal of Applied Psychology* 63 (1978): 53-61.
Salch, S. D., and Hosek, J. "Job Involvement: Concepts and Measurements." *Academy of Management Journal* 19 (1976): 213-24.
Seeman, M. "On the Meaning of Alienation." *American Sociological Review* 24 (1959): 783-91.
Seeman, M. "The Urban Alienations: Some Dubious Theses from Marx to Marcuse." *Journal of Personality and Social Psychology* 19 (1971): 135-43.
Shepard, J. M. *Automation and Alienation: A Study of Office and Factory Workers.* Cambridge: MIT Press, 1971.
Siegel, L. *Industrial Psychology.* Homewood, Ill.: Irwin, 1969.
Taylor, F. W. *Principles of Scientific Management.* New York: Harper, 1911.
Vroom, V. "Ego Involvement, Job Satisfaction, and Job Performance." *Personnel Psychology* 15 (1962): 159-77.
Vroom, V. *Work and Motivation.* New York: Wiley, 1964.
Weissenberg, P., and Gruenfeld, L. W. "Relationship Between Job Satisfaction and Job Involvement." *Journal of Applied Psychology* 52 (1968): 469-73.

Chapter 8

Auclair, G. A. and Read, W. H. "A Cross-Cultural Study of Industrial Leadership." *Royal Commission on Bilingualism and Biculturalism Report.* Vol. 2. Ottawa: Government of Canada, 1966.
Dahle, Thomas L. "An Objective and Comparative Study of Five Methods of Transmitting Information to Business and Industrial Employees." *Speech Monographs* 21 (1954): 21-28.
Georgopolous, B. S., and Mann, F. C. *The Community General Hospital.* New York: Macmillan, 1962.
Goldhaber, G. M. "The ICA Communication Audit: Rationale and Development." Paper presented at the Academy of Management Conference, Kansas City, 1976.
Greenbaum, Howard H. "The Audit of Organizational Communication." *Academy of Management Journal* 17 (1974): 739-54.
Hsia, Hower J. "Output, Error, Equivocation, and Recalled Information in Auditory, Visual, and Audiovisual Information Processing with Constraint and Noise." *Journal of Communication* 18 (1968): 325-45.
Jain, H. C. "Organizational Communication: A Case Study of a Large Urban Hospital." *Relations Industrielles* 31 (1977): 588-608.
Jain, H. C. "Supervisory Communication and Performance in Urban Hospitals." *Journal of Communication* 23 (1973): 103-17.
Jain, H. C., and Kanungo, R. N., eds. *Behavioral Issues in Management: The Canadian Context.* Toronto: McGraw-Hill Ryerson, 1977.
Level, Dale A., Jr. "A Case Study of Human Communications in an Urban Bank." Ph.D. dissertation; Purdue University, 1959.
Muchinsky, Paul A. "Organizational Communication: Relationships to Organizational Climate and Job Satisfaction." *Academy of Management Journal* 20 (1977): 592-607.

Nightingale, D. V., and Toulouse, J. M. "Values, Structure, Process, and Reactions/Adjustments: A Comparison of French and English Canadian Industrial Organizations." *Canadian Journal of Behavioural Science* 9 (1977): 37-48.

Porter, Lyman W. and Roberts, Karlene H. "Communication in Organizations." In *Handbook of Industrial and Organizational Psychology*, edited by Marvin D. Dunnette. Chicago: Rand McNally, 1976.

Redding, G. W. *Communication within the Organization*, New York: Industrial Communication Council and Lafayette: Purdue University, 1972.

Revans, R. W. *Standards for Morale: Cause and Effect in Hospitals*, London: Oxford University Press, 1964.

Sanborn, George A. "An Analytical Study of Oral Communication Practices in a Nationwide Retail Sales Organization." Ph.D. dissertation, Purdue University, 1961.

Sigband, N. B. *Communication for Management*. Glenview, Ill.: Scott, Foresman, 1969.

Tompkins, Phillip K. "An Analysis of Communication Between Headquarters and Selected Units of a National Labour Union." Ph.D. dissertation, Purdue University, 1962.

Chapter 9

Backman, J. G. "Faculty Satisfaction and the Dean's Influence: An Organizational Study of Twelve Liberal Arts Colleges." *Journal of Applied Psychology* 52 (1968): 55-61

Burke, R. J., & Wilcox, D. S. "Bases of Supervisory Power and Subordinate Job Satisfaction." *Canadian Journal of Behavioural Science* 3 (1971): 183-93.

Cartwright, D. "Influence, Leadership, Control." In *Handbook of Organizations*, edited by J. G. March. Chicago: Rand McNally, 1965.

Dahl, R. A. "The Concept of Power." *Behavioral Science* 2 (1957): 210-18.

French, J. R. P., Jr., and Raven, B. "The Bases of Social Power." In *Group Dynamics*, edited by D. Cartwright and A. Zander. Evanston, Ill.: Row Peterson and Company, 1960.

McClelland, D. C. *The Achieving Society*. New York: Van Nostrand, 1961.

Student, K. R. "Supervisory Influence and Work Group Performance." *Journal of Applied Organizations* 52 (1968): 188-94.

Tannenbaum, A. S., Kavcic, B., Rosner, M., Vianello, M. and Wieser, G. *Hierarchy in Organizations*. San Francisco: Jossey-Bass, 1974.

Chapter 10

Blake, R. R. and Mouton, J. S. *The Managerial Grid*, Houston: Gulf Publishing Co., 1964.

Champagne, P. J. and Tausky, C. When Job enrichment doesn't work. *Personnel* January-February 1978, pp. 30-40.

Davis, S. M. "U.S. versus Latin America: business and culture." *Harvard Business Review*, November-December 1969, pp. 88-98.

Herzberg, F. *Work and the Nature of Man*. Cleveland: World Publishing, 1966.

Lawler, E. E. *Pay and Organizational Effectiveness: A Psychological View*. New York: McGraw-Hill, 1971.

Likert, R. *New pattern of management*, New York: McGraw-Hill, 1961.

Likert, R. *The Human Organization.* New York: McGraw-Hill, 1967.
Lupton, T. *Management and the Social Sciences.* Middlesex, U.K.: Penguin Books, 1971.
McGregor, D. *The Human Side of Enterprise.* New York: McGraw-Hill, 1960.
Taylor, F. W. *Principles of Scientific Management,* New York: Harper, 1911.

Subject Index

Commitment and responsibility
    Department   30-32
    Job   30-32
    Organization   30-32
    Relation to management practice   125

Communication
    Attitudes towards   19
    Audit   82, 127
    Channels   91-92, 127
    Downward communication   82, 87-91, 127
    Effort   93-95
    Hierarchy of ranks   81
    Upward communication   81-82, 91

Culture
    Definition   2-3
    Influence on employee behavior   3-6
    Influence on job-related attitudes   6-7
    Influence on management policy   5-6
    Influence on motivation at work   6

Environment of organization
    External   17
    Internal   2

History of English and French Canadians in industry
    Educational systems   12
    Francophone perception of job opportunities   15
    Gendron Commission Report   15

Rural-agricultural traditions　　　　　　　　10
　　　Urban-industrial traditions　　　　　　　　11
　　　Working language　　　　　　　　　　　　13

In-house training program
　　　Co-trainees　　　　　　　　　　　　　　114-115, 116, 128
　　　Employee attitudes towards　　　　　　　19, 110-111
　　　Location　　　　　　　　　　　　　　　117-118
　　　Trainer　　　　　　　　　　　　　　　113, 115, 127-128
　　　Training materials　　　　　　　　　　111-112, 115, 127-128

Job alienation
　　　Anomie　　　　　　　　　　　　　　　48, 50, 57
　　　Central life interest　　　　　　　　　49
　　　Definition　　　　　　　　　　　　　60
　　　Meaninglessness　　　　　　　　　　49-50, 57, 63
　　　Normlessness and isolation　　　　　　50, 57, 62
　　　Powerlessness　　　　　　　　　　　49, 57, 63
　　　Psychological approaches　　　　　　52-56
　　　Self-estrangement　　　　　　　　　51
　　　Sociological approach　　　　　　　　46-52

Job enrichment potential　　　　　　　　　34-35

Job factors
　　　Extrinsic　　　　　　　　　　　　　　22, 23, 124
　　　Internally-mediated outcome　　　　　38
　　　Interpersonally-mediated outcome　　　38, 124
　　　Intrinsic　　　　　　　　　　　　　　22, 23, 123
　　　Organizationally-mediated outcomes　　38
　　　Value to Anglophones vs. Francophones　25

Job involvement
　　　Conceptual confusion　　　　　　　　56-59
　　　Definition　　　　　　　　　　　　　18, 60
　　　Employee attitudes　　　　　　　　　64-68
　　　Employee needs　　　　　　　　　　126-127
　　　Job design　　　　　　　　　　　　　64
　　　Motivational theory　　　　　　　　　59-64
　　　Psychological approach　　　　　　　53

Job perception　　　　　　　　　　　　　18, 21

Job satisfaction

Definition	18, 37-38
In relation to job involvement	53
In relation to job outcomes	38-41, 125
In relation to supervisory practices	102, 107, 127
Turnover potential	43-44, 125-126

Management policy — 121-124

Individualized management policy	123
Scientific management	122

Mirror management — 21, 121

Mobility and transfer potential

Definition	18, 71-72
Manpower planning	71
Reluctance to transfer	72-74, 126
Transfer inducement	74-77
Transfer location	77-79, 126

Participation — 32-34, 125

Supervision

Attitudes towards	19
Compliance with	101
In relation to job satisfaction	102, 107, 127
Power bases	99-101, 103-107, 127

Work Ethic

Catholic	11, 23, 28, 42
Protestant	12, 23, 28, 41